WHY YOU THINK

THE WAY YOU DO

WHY YOU THINK

THE WAY YOU DO

THE STORY OF
WESTERN WORLDVIEWS
FROM ROME TO HOME

GLENN S. SUNSHINE

ZONDERVAN

ZONDERVAN.com/
AUTHORTRACKER
follow your favorite authors

We want to hear from you. Please send your comments about this book to us in care of zreview@zondervan.com. Thank you.

ZONDERVAN

Why You Think the Way You Do
Copyright © 2009 by Glenn S. Sunshine

This title is also available as a Zondervan ebook.
Visit www.zondervan.com/ebooks.

Requests for information should be addressed to:

Zondervan, *Grand Rapids, Michigan 49530*

Library of Congress Cataloging-in-Publication Data

Sunshine, Glenn S., 1958-
    Why you think the way you do : the story of western worldviews from Rome to home / Glenn S. Sunshine.
        p. cm.
    Includes bibliographical references.
    ISBN 978-0-310-29230-2 (softcover)
    1. Philosophy — History. 2. Christianity — Influence. 3. Christianity — Philosophy. I. Title.
    B72.S86 2009
    190 — dc22
                                     2009005601

Interior design by Ben Fetterley

Printed in the United States of America

---

09 10 11 12 13 14 • 23 22 21 20 19 18 17 16 15 14 13 12 11 10 9 8 7 6 5 4 3 2 1

This book is dedicated with love to my children, Elizabeth and Brendan Sunshine, who have attended worldview conferences with me for several years now and have put up with more discussions of worldview over dinner and in car rides with far better humor than I had any right to expect. Thanks for your patience!

CONTENTS

Foreword by Charles W. Colson   9
Acknowledgments   11

1. What Is a Worldview and Why Should I Care?   13
2. The Worldview of Ancient Rome   19
3. Christianity and the Transformation of the Pagan World   35
4. The Emergence of the Medieval Worldview   55
5. Medieval Economics and Politics   75
6. The Breakdown of the Medieval Model   95
7. A New Paradigm of Knowledge   115
8. Enlightenment and Revolutions   135
9. Modernity and Its Discontents   163
10. The Decay of Modernity   183
11. Trajectories   203

Notes   217
Name Index   223
Subject Index   227

FOREWORD

BY CHARLES W. COLSON

American culture is at a crossroads. The Judeo-Christian foundations of the society are facing an unprecedented assault from within, both through the crisis of truth in postmodernism and the assault on religion of the "new atheists," and from without, with the rise of Islamofascism and the growing demographic power of Muslim immigrant communities in Europe. Each of these is a clash of worldviews, a conflict over the fundamental ideas we have about the world and how we fit in it, and all of them are aimed squarely at the biblical worldview that helped frame Western culture. Unfortunately, much of the church has been slow to recognize the nature of the threat, instead ignoring the challenges or at best offering piecemeal rebuttals of individual points without dealing with the underlying worldview issues at stake. Much of my work over the past decade has been focused on alerting the church to the nature of the dangers that we face, to the threats not only to our way of life but to the gospel itself, and I have been working to raise up a new generation of worldview thinkers and scholars to help the church answer the challenges we are facing.

Dr. Glenn Sunshine is one such scholar who has become an active partner in this work. After hearing one of his lectures, I invited Dr. Sunshine to join the faculty for the Centurions, a worldview training program we established through the Wilberforce Forum of Prison Fellowship. It was a good call. He proved to be a remarkable teacher and thinker, bringing not only his knowledge of history but also the ability to synthesize and communicate that knowledge clearly and winsomely. He has consistently been one of the most popular teachers in the program, and the Centurions have benefited tremendously from his teaching and mentorship. In addition to working together with the Centurions, Dr. Sunshine and I have collaborated on a number of other worldview projects.

In this book, Sunshine offers the church a sorely needed corrective to much of the pop theology that characterizes American Christianity. Rather than being limited to the moral and spiritual realms, Christianity is a fully formed worldview, with implications for all areas of life. Sunshine demonstrates that biblical ideas left their stamp on economics, politics, science, education, and, in fact, on the entire course of Western civilization for the past 1,700 years. All of the West's distinctive achievements come from Christian foundations — a bold claim, but one echoed even by atheists, such as Germany's Jürgen Habermas. For example, the concept of universal human rights and equality comes exclusively from the biblical idea that all people are created in the image of God. This book is thus an unabashed defense of the power of biblical ideas to shape culture and of a Christianity that unites heart and mind to bring the gospel of the kingdom boldly into all areas of human life.

But if culture is shaped by worldview, as we believe, the shift in the Western worldviews away from the biblical model poses enormous challenges to our culture and the church. Ideas have consequences, and the result of the loss of the idea of the image of God as the foundation for human worth can have catastrophic consequences for human rights and human life. But just as the church changed the Roman world by living out the truths of the gospel faithfully, we today have the opportunity to do the same. This book shows how much of an impact the biblical worldview can have in transforming society. If we follow the example of those who have gone before us in learning to think biblically and to live out the full implications of the gospel, we can have the same impact on our world today.

I highly recommend this book, which is well written and is delivered in a style accessible to the laity. Church members, pastors, and teachers need to read it and then pass it on to non-Christian friends. It is a powerful and winsome apologetic for the Christian faith.

Charles W. Colson,
founder of Prison Fellowship

ACKNOWLEDGMENTS

This book is the product of a long and implausible chain of events, every one of which was necessary for the book to come to fruition. The book began as a single lecture. Alan Johnson and the Jonathan Edwards Tercentenary Commission of First Church of Christ in Wethersfield, Connecticut, asked me to speak at the Tercentenary Conference in 2003. The lecture I prepared was called "Worldview, Edwards-style" (a title supplied by First Church's communication coordinator, David Gilbert). The talk compared the worldview of Jonathan Edwards' day with our own. Paula Vining, wife of Jon Vining, the head of Prison Fellow Ministries New England, passed a copy of the recording to Charles W. Colson, the keynote speaker at the conference.

After listening to the recording, Mr. Colson asked me to teach in his newly formed Centurions worldview training program. I expanded the lecture into a survey of the evolution of worldviews from the early modern period to the present under the title of "How We Got Here." The Centurions asked me annually if I had plans to turn the talk into a book, and so I began to organize it and realized I would need to go much further back than the early modern period if the story was to make sense. The vision that emerged was certainly a "fools rush in where angels fear to tread" project, but I've lived by those words for so long that I decided to go ahead with it anyway.

Meanwhile, the Acton Institute for the Study of Religion and Liberty announced a book grant for books dealing with the origins of modern concepts of freedom. Martha Anderson, program director of the Centurions, passed along information about the grant. I applied for the grant, and the Acton Institute awarded it to me, which enabled me to devote far more attention to organizing and writing the book than I would have been able to do otherwise. It is safe to say I would still be working on the first draft without their help, encouragement, and deadlines.

Manuscript in hand, I had to find a publisher. Mr. Colson again came to my aid, putting me in touch with Stan Gundry at Zondervan, who in turn connected me with Katya Covrett, senior academic editor. In the book's first draft, Ms. Covrett and her fine team helped me correct errors, omissions, non sequiturs, and other problems too numerous to be named, and then passed it on to developmental editor Dirk Buursma, who helped me put the book into final shape for publication. The book would be far inferior without their efforts.

And those are only the main links in the story. It doesn't include the many classes I've taught over the years where parts of the book were developed, or my wife, Lynn, and daughter, Elizabeth, who plowed through early drafts of the chapters and let me know where they didn't work, or the support and encouragement of friends. The list is nearly endless. A blanket "thank you" hardly does justice to all of them, yet unfortunately that's all I can do in print. So — my heartiest thanks to all who contributed to the book.

And, of course, any errors or omissions it contains or controversies it generates are entirely my responsibility.

WHAT IS A WORLDVIEW AND WHY SHOULD I CARE?

This book is about why you think the way you do. Chances are, if you are reading this, you either grew up in the Western world or have been heavily influenced by it. And this means you probably look at the world from one of the perspectives that developed within Western culture. In other words, your *worldview* has been shaped by the Western cultural experience.

What is a worldview? A worldview is the framework you use to interpret the world and your place in it. It is like a set of glasses that you look through to bring what is happening in the world into mental focus. If you like computers, you can think of your worldview as your operating system, the thing that converts your experiences into the "ones and zeros" your mind understands — the thing that defines what inputs (i.e., experiences) mean, which of them you accept as meaningful, and which you exclude or ignore. More simply, your worldview is what you think of as common sense about the world. It is your gut-level, instinctive response to the basic philosophical questions, such as "What is real?" (metaphysics), "What can I know and how can I know it?" (epistemology), and "Are there such things as right and wrong, and if so, how do I know what they are?" (ethics).

But you do not need to be a philosopher to have a worldview. Philosophers think about these issues in greater depth than most people, but whether or not you've studied philosophy, you still have intuitive answers to the questions and therefore you have a worldview. In fact, everyone has a worldview, because otherwise it would be impossible to learn, to make decisions, to decide on values and priorities — in short, to function at all in the world.

To understand worldviews a bit better, consider the first of these questions: What is real? Is the physical universe real? Does it exist? Chances are, simply asking these questions on some level seems ridiculous to you (unless you were a philosophy major). The answer probably is, "Of course the physical universe is real! What kind of stupid question is that?" But the problem is that your answer, which seems so patently obvious to you, is not so obvious to people who hold a different worldview. So, for example, many Native Americans have historically believed that the physical universe is secondary to the world of dreams; in this culture, dreams are more "real" than the waking world. Or if you are a Hindu, you may argue that the universe is not truly real; it is simply a dream in the mind of God. Not everyone thinks of the same things as common sense, or, to put it differently, not everyone shares the same worldview.

Along with these basic sorts of questions, another aspect of worldview involves understanding what it means to be human. Where did I come from? Are we different from animals? How do I relate to other people? How do I relate to [other] animals and to the physical world? Why am I here? Does life have any purpose or meaning? What happens when I die? These are the big questions of life, and most people do not have conscious answers to these sorts of questions — just like they do not have conscious answers to the more philosophically oriented worldview questions. But whether they are aware of them or not, they do have answers, which they live out every day of their lives. What you think of other people and your relationship to them is evident in how you treat them; the same applies to animals and the physical world. Whether you think life has meaning and purpose is evident in the ways you spend your time, treat yourself, express your attitudes, and live out your priorities. So the answers are there, even if we aren't consciously aware of them. In fact, it is even possible that we may think we have a particular worldview when in fact we do not. For example, if we say we care about the environment, if that is part of what defines our self-image, yet we litter or dump our motor oil down the storm drains, we reveal through our actions what we really think and what our values really are — and thus our worldview. This is how worldviews operate — below the radar, behind the scenes, guiding our thoughts, words, and actions and only rarely being examined or analyzed.

WORLDVIEW AND CULTURE

Though our worldviews shape how we live, this is just part of the reason worldviews are important. Most of the people who grow up in a society tend to share a common worldview. In fact, for a society to function effectively or to have any semblance of stability, there must be broad agreement on at least a core set of values drawn from a common conception of what it means to be human and how we are to relate to each other, which in turn presupposes a set of beliefs about the world, truth, and morality. Even cultures that value pluralism operate from a worldview consensus that holds pluralism as a value and that sees certain kinds of differences between people as unimportant to the society. In all cases, pluralism has limits. For example, American culture allows for religious pluralism, yet we did not allow Mormons to continue practicing polygamy, nor do we allow honor killings among Muslims or *sati* (ritual suicide or killing of widows) among Hindus. So even pluralistic societies depend on a broadly accepted worldview that defines where pluralism is appropriate and where it is not. Without this agreement, a society will self-destruct.

So like people, cultures also have worldviews, and these worldviews shape the society. For example, what people believe is real determines what is taught and what is studied, as do ideas concerning the nature of knowledge; questions of ethics shape laws; concepts of humanness influence everything, from the structure of families to whether or not to hold slaves to principles of law and justice and to who has what rights.

A society's worldview can change over time, resulting in changes in the culture. Worldviews generally evolve slowly due to either their own internal logic or the force of new ideas and pressures. Sometimes new worldviews are introduced that out-compete their predecessors and become a new cultural consensus, though when that happens the result is generally something of a hybrid of the new and the old. Occasionally, worldviews are overturned in periods of social, political, or religious unrest.

What all this means is that to understand a culture or a civilization, you have to understand its worldview, since all of its successes and failures are largely the product of the basic ideas that shape the society. In fact, the society's worldview will inevitably shape the culture around its ideas, which means that the logical implications of these ideas will inevitably be followed by the culture if it survives long enough. And if you want to understand why and how a civilization changes over time, you need to track the evolution of its dominant worldview.

WHAT THIS BOOK IS ... AND IS NOT

In this book I'll be explaining the development of Western civilization from the perspective of the changes in worldview from the Roman Empire to the early years of the twenty-first century. Although this may sound like intellectual history or the history of philosophy, it is not. Since worldviews are typically held unconsciously, formal philosophical or intellectual history does not usually deal with them much, preferring instead to focus on elites who self-consciously set out to develop systems of ideas. My interest here is in the fundamental ideas that shaped the culture and how those ideas were lived out in Western society. As we will see, the intellectual elites who are studied in philosophy sometimes had a very important influence on shaping (or expressing) worldviews, but for my purposes they only enter this story to the degree that they had an influence on the broader culture.

This book is also not a formal history of religion, though since worldviews deal with foundational questions about existence, morality, and purpose, religion naturally enters the discussion. All societies in history prior to the modern West were intrinsically religious, probably because they knew that life was precarious.

Death surrounded them on all sides. If they wanted meat, they had to either kill something or pay someone to do it for them. Until around the nineteenth century, more people died in cities than were born in them (and so cities had to rely on immigration to survive), infant mortality was extremely high, and epidemic diseases and famines were not uncommon. In the Roman Empire, the average life span was around thirty years. In this kind of world, is it any wonder that people oriented their lives around supernatural forces to try to find protection from life's dangers or to look for a source of hope when death claimed them?

As a result, religion is essential to understanding worldviews. In Western history, this means particularly Christianity. In fact, in many ways the history of Western worldviews is the history of the rise of Christianity and with it the emergence of a biblical worldview, the de facto rejection of this worldview over one thousand years later by a significant segment of the cultural and intellectual elites, and the results of the movement away from a biblical worldview. Again, my concern here is not with church history per se, but rather with the impact Christianity had on worldviews and thus on culture.

The key dynamic that begins the development of a distinctly Western worldview is the interaction of Greco-Roman civilization with Christianity. To understand this dynamic, I must start with a survey of worldviews within the Roman Empire.

CHAPTER 2

THE WORLDVIEW OF ANCIENT ROME

The Roman Empire is a paradox. For the last two thousand years, the Empire has dominated Western ideas about what makes a great civilization. And there is no doubt that Rome was great. At its height, the Empire ruled territory from northern Britain to North Africa, from the borders of Persia to the Atlantic Ocean — territory conquered through the unrivaled power of the Roman military machine.

Within the Roman world, peace and prosperity reigned, with vigorous trade; literature and the arts; efficient government; and the rule of law as the hallmarks of Roman civilization. Rome's engineering achievements are still a marvel, from the great Roman roads built for the legions but used for trade and travel, to aqueducts, great temples, coliseums, baths, palaces, gardens, and government buildings. It is no wonder that the barbarian tribes beyond its borders wanted to share in the benefits of Roman rule and sought increasingly to migrate across the borders into the Empire.

But there was a dark side to Rome as well. The Roman economy and all its engineering feats were products of slave labor. The

slaves themselves came from people who had become so impoverished that the only thing they could do was to sell themselves
or their children to pay their debts, or from prisoners of war or
rebels against Roman rule. Revolts were put down with brutality
and efficiency, with rebels being tortured to death on the roads
as a warning to others not to dare to challenge Roman authority.
Nonconformity was dangerous: up to a point it was acceptable, but
beyond that point it could cost you your life. In fact, people were
killed regularly as public entertainment in gladiatorial matches
and other spectacles. Freedom was a status — if you were free, you
were not a slave — but it conveyed none of today's ideas of liberty.
At the highest levels of society, treachery, poisoning, and assas-
sination were common. And Roman decadence, gluttony, and
sexual perversion are legendary.

So what are we to make of these two pictures of Rome — the
glittering empire and the rotten core? As it turns out, both sides
of the Roman world flow naturally from the worldview of the
Empire, and when viewed from this perspective, both make sense.
The worldview originated within the context of pagan religious
ideas, and these ideas provided the foundation for Greek philosophy. In fact, Plato's philosophical approach is arguably the most
systematic explanation available of the worldview of his day. So
understanding paganism and Neoplatonism (the dominant philosophy and the form Plato's ideas took within the Roman Empire)
will thus help us make sense of the Roman worldview and why
Roman society looked the way it did.

RELIGION IN THE ROMAN WORLD

The Roman Empire had a bewildering array of religious
options, from local folk religions to pantheons of more developed
mythological systems (including the traditional gods of Greece
and Rome), to Eastern "mystery religions," and to Judaism. With
the exception of Judaism, all of these fall into the broad category of
paganism. The term *pagan* comes from the Latin *pagus*, meaning
"the countryside," and *pagani*, meaning "rural people." The term
seems to have been applied to followers of the old religions when
Christianity became a dominant religious force within the Empire.
Since Christianity was primarily an urban religion, followers of the

older religions mostly lived in the countryside, and since they were *pagani* (rural people), their religions were described as "pagan." (This same thing happened with the English word *heathen*: the people who lived on the heath worshiped the old gods.) Pagan religions had a number of characteristics in common, including a set of answers to the basic philosophical questions that form the foundation for worldviews.

TRADITIONAL ROMAN RELIGION

Paganism is most often connected to nature worship. Before the days of artificial lighting and climate control, people were much more in tune with the natural order and were abundantly aware that they were at the mercy of the elements. Crops could be destroyed or not ripen if it were too hot, too cold, too wet, too dry; volcanoes, earthquakes, floods, and storms could end their lives or condemn them to a slow death by starvation; disease could lay waste everything they had worked to build. Is it any wonder, then, that they saw in nature a source of transcendence, a force greater than themselves, which they needed to appease if they were to survive? Most pagan deities originally were connected to the forces of nature. Even Jupiter, the king of the gods, began his career as a storm deity (which is why he casts lightning bolts).

The primary function of religion was to keep the gods happy so they did not destroy the people and — for the more benign gods — to encourage them to help the people by blessing the natural world. Many pagan deities are connected to fertility, for example, and are worshiped to encourage the crops and herds to grow. So in the ancient Near East, one form of worship involved temple prostitutes having sex with worshipers to encourage Baal (a sky god) to have sex with Asherah (an earth goddess) by raining on the earth so that the crops would grow.

In the Greco-Roman world, this basic idea was extended beyond nature to human activities, including war (Mars); begging, lying, and stealing (Mercury); metalwork (Vulcan); music and poetry (Apollo); and sex (Venus). Gods were in essence the supreme rulers of a particular sphere of life or of the natural world, and worship was given primarily as a way of acknowledging the god's authority over that sphere in the hopes of avoiding the god's unwelcome and hostile attention. So, for example, before setting sail on the sea, ship captains and sailors would perform a ritual sacrifice acknowledging Neptune's authority over the sea and asking him to excuse their trespass on his domain.

In other words, for the overwhelming majority of worshipers, the gods were feared, not loved. Even where the language of love was used (as it was, for example, in Mesopotamia), it meant obeying the gods, not having an emotional attachment to them. Religious rituals were designed to appease deities, not to please them. There was little if any emotional connection to the deities, only a desire to placate them so they did not destroy the worshiper. It was all about following the proper forms and rituals and offering the proper prayers and sacrifices so the gods would not be offended by something the worshiper did or did not do.

One interesting example is that of the Roman families that frequently had shrines to their ancestors in their homes. In Rome, the father was the supreme ruler of the family, so much so that they literally had the power of life and death over members of their households. In fact, fathers had so much authority that Roman law, which was comprehensive in all other legal areas, left family law almost completely undeveloped. Why is this? Simply because the father was the law in his household. But what happened when the father died? In many families, he would join the pantheon of other heads of the family over the generations and be worshiped through the burning of incense at an ancestral shrine in the home. As the supreme authority over the household, fathers (and especially departed fathers) were the proper subjects of religious ritual.

The idea that gods were the supreme rulers over their spheres also explains why emperors were considered gods and had incense burned to their statues. It was a way of acknowledging that the emperor was the supreme figure in the political realm and of showing due loyalty and deference to him. Except for the Jews, who as monotheists were given a special dispensation not to participate in pagan religious activities, anyone who refused to burn incense to the emperor's statue was refusing to acknowledge his political authority. This was treason, pure and simple, and so any non-Jew who refused to worship the emperor was tortured and killed.

Fortunately, this was not a problem for pagans. Pagan religions did not require their adherents to worship only one god or even one set of gods. Many pagans believed that deities were local, so that if you moved to a different region, you would naturally change your gods. Adding one or more new deities to the religious system was not a problem; in fact, more educated people in the pagan world frequently thought of this as being broad-minded and inclusive. This attitude not only was seen as virtuous and cosmopolitan but also had real pragmatic value. People saw this inclusiveness as a source of strength for the Roman Empire because it helped prevent religious revolts against Roman rule. Besides, the more deities that supported Rome, the better.

MYSTERY RELIGIONS

Not all pagans in the Roman Empire were satisfied with the perfunctory worship of the traditional cults.[1] Some people wanted a closer, more intimate, more emotional connection with their deity than was possible in the standard religions of the day. As the Empire spread to the eastern Mediterranean and Egypt, new religions from these areas began to spread into the Roman Empire. While some of these functioned essentially the same way as traditional Roman paganism, others demanded far more from their worshipers. Like other pagan religions, many of these were fertility based, including Isis and Osiris from Egypt, Cybele and Hecate from the near east and Persia, and Dionysius from Greece; others were not, such as Mithras from Persia or Sol Invictus (the Unconquered Sun).

What set these "mystery religions" apart from the traditional pagan religions was that they promised their worshipers salvation and a mystical experience of deity. By learning the myths, rites, and rituals and participating in the appropriate ceremonies, a worshiper could be initiated into ever-deeper secrets ("mysteries") of the cult, attaining salvation and union with the deity by ritual participation in her or his myths. This frequently included bathing for cleansing from sin and communal feasts. For example, according to his myth, Mithras fought and slew a monstrous bull; at one level of initiation, Mithras worshipers sacrificed a bull and bathed in its blood — a rather gross image to us but undeniably powerful as a symbolic connection to the mythical actions of the deity and as a means of identifying with him.

Like other pagan religions, the mystery religions were non-exclusive. While it is unlikely that anyone would be able to penetrate the deeper mysteries of more than one cult, even those privy to the cult's deepest secrets still participated in traditional worship as appropriate. Deities did not demand or expect exclusive devotion, even in the context of mystery cults, and other gods had to get their due when moving into their sphere of influence.

NEOPLATONISM: REALITY, TRUTH, AND KNOWLEDGE

Despite the religious diversity within the Empire, a number of fundamental ideas tied all of these pagan religious options together. All pagan religions inside and outside the Empire had roots in nature worship, and these roots were shaped by the idea that both the gods and humanity were part of nature. Although this belief can be expressed in many ways, within the Empire the most systematic and popular development of this idea came from Plato's philosophy and its philosophical and religious successors.

Although many philosophical schools existed in the Greco-Roman world, Platonism towered over all of them. Even competing philosophical schools frequently drew from Platonism for some of their fundamental ideas. Plato's own writings are more difficult to understand than most other philosophers', ancient or modern, but the basic principles of his philosophy are clear enough, particularly as they trickle down to the level of worldview.

To understand Plato, we need to go back to the basic questions that make up a worldview, particularly to the questions of what is real (metaphysics) and what can we know and how can we know it (epistemology). These two areas are closely related, since in classical thought, epistemology depends on metaphysics — in other words, what is real determines what we can know.

WHAT IN THE WORLD IS REAL?

In metaphysics, one of the key questions is the problem of universals and particulars — also known as the problem of "the one and the many." The basic problem is simple. Imagine an oak tree in the summer. It has thousands of leaves on it, yet no two of them are completely identical. They are similar in shape, size, and color, but they are not exactly the same. Then if you change species of oak, the leaves are even more different. Then look at maples, aspens, willows, and rose bushes. Again, all are still more different from your original leaves. So if all of these leaves are different, how is it that we can use one word (*leaf*) to describe this whole mass of different objects? Or, to put it another way, how is the universal represented by the word *leaf* related to all the particulars, i.e., the individual leaves?

At the risk of offending philosophers, who will rightly tell you it is much more complicated than this, I give you two approaches to solving the problem. The first approach, and the one adopted by most people in the modern West, is called *realism*. This approach, which was taken by Aristotle in the ancient world, argues that the particulars in the physical world — the individual leaves — are the fundamental ground of reality and that they exist independently of the universals or ideas that connect them. Through a process known as abstraction, we distill a set of qualities out of the particulars, which then defines the universal. In other words, the universal (the Leaf) does exist, but it has a secondary existence because it is abstracted out of the particulars (the leaves).

Although realism would become the mainstream in the West centuries after Aristotle, in the ancient world the second approach to the problem of universals was overwhelmingly the most common. This approach, which was taken by Plato, argued that because the particulars (the leaves) were constantly changing — they start as buds, grow into leaves, change color, die, fall off the tree, and turn to dirt — they cannot be the fundamental ground of reality. Reality has to be built on something that is unchanging and unchangeable. Since the physical world changes constantly, ultimate reality must be based in the nonphysical world of ideas, since ideas are the only things we know of that do not change (at least according to Plato). So the idea of the Leaf (with a capital *L*), the universal, is primary. The universal Leaf, known as the form or the archetype, casts shadows, and these shadows form the leaves that we see and experience in the physical world. The particulars are real, but they have a secondary existence based on their connection with the Leaf. Since in this approach the idea is primary, it has become known as *idealism*.

Although this may seem like a trivial, academic issue, the answer to the problem of universals has much larger implications than initially meets the eye. For example, the relationship between epistemology (how we know) and metaphysics (what is real) becomes much more obvious. In Platonism, since ideas are the foundation for reality, clear thinking and logic are the best approaches to understanding the world. The effect is to minimize the significance of observation or experimentation and instead to use logic, aesthetics, and philosophical concepts to explain how and why the physical world works the way it does.

This way of thinking about nature was so fundamental for Greek thought that it even shaped Aristotle's approach to science. As a realist, Aristotle would be expected to look at the particulars — the way nature worked — and to abstract from the particulars the universals or laws that governed their behavior. Instead, Aristotle thought that logic and philosophy, not experiment, were the proper means for understanding physics and all other branches of learning. To be sure, he did some observations, but his approach to physics was based far more on logical deduction than on empirical observations. Astrophysicist George Smoot of the University of California-Berkeley put it this way:

> Although there was some degree of experience and observation in the physics of Aristotle, at its heart was a philosophical approach to science where the laws of nature are constructed to conform to a particular philosophical outlook. This basis for the investigation of nature led to some strange statements by Aristotle — for instance, that women have fewer teeth than men. Either Aristotle was not a very accurate observer, he couldn't count, or he had odd taste in women.[2]

The key here is that even as a realist, Aristotle allowed his ideas to trump observation. The reason is simply that he shared a worldview with his contemporaries that saw logic and ideas as the key to truth. This fundamental belief shaped his thought so that he did not see that his epistemology was disconnected from his metaphysics, or, to put it another way, that his approach to knowledge about the physical world was inconsistent with his belief in the priority of particulars over universals and thus of observation over logic. We will take on the question of how we learn about the natural world in more detail later, when we examine medieval science and the scientific revolution. For now, suffice it to say that the solution to the problem of universals carries over into other areas of life.

NEOPLATONIC RELIGION

Platonic metaphysics did not end with a solution to the problem of universals. Plato and especially his followers in the movement called Neoplatonism developed his idealistic metaphysics into a comprehensive system that explained everything from the nature of God to the existence of dirt.

Plato made the observation that we cannot judge anything to be better or worse than anything else without an absolute standard against which we can measure the two. Every time we make a comparison, we are comparing the particulars to the universal, the form or archetype or ideal, in the world of ideas, which gives us the absolute we use to make the comparison. But some of these areas overlap: the True (with a capital *T*) is obviously related to the Good (capital *G*); the Beautiful (capital *B*) is also connected to the Good (capital *G*), and so on. But how can there be different forms whose shadows converge to lead to the Good, the True, and the Beautiful? Plato argued that logically there must be a single archetype for all of them. He called this archetype "the One," or "God."

The Neoplatonic God is impersonal and does nothing on the basis of its will or desires, because it has none. Instead, by virtue of its existence, the One casts shadows (called emanations), and these shadows cast other shadows, which cast other shadows, and so on, each shadow becoming progressively less pure and spiritual, until finally we end with inert matter (dirt) at the end of a great hierarchy or chain of being. Thus everything in the universe is connected to everything else and ultimately finds its origin and fundamental nature in God. At this point, Platonic philosophy has turned into religion.

Neoplatonism was the most common religion among the educated classes in the Roman Empire. The goal was mystical union with the One through contemplation of the spirit. But to the Neoplatonist, even though there was only one God at the end of the chain of being, there was nothing wrong with participating in various pagan cults and emperor worship. The different deities could easily be seen as emanations of the One, and thus as aspects of the divine that were worthy of worship. This had the side effect of avoiding conflict with the imperial authorities.

In many ways, Neoplatonism was similar to Buddhism, though with important differences. Both believe in the fundamental interconnectedness of all things, though the Buddhist believes all is one and the Neoplatonist connects them through the hierarchy of being. Both have as a goal a mystical experience of fundamental reality achieved through contemplation or meditation. Both see ultimate reality as impersonal. Both permit the worship of many gods as a lower-order component of their religious belief. Both are essentially philosophies that have been converted into religions.

PHILOSOPHY AND MYTHOLOGY

Neoplatonism's connection to paganism and pagan myth is actually much deeper than simply participating in rituals, however. Many Greek and Roman myths that predate Plato share a common worldview with Platonic thought. The best example is the way creatures in the myths can be transformed into other creatures up and down the hierarchy of being. Thus nymphs turn into flowers and trees, humans become gods or animals, statues come to life, gods mate with mortals and mortals with animals to produce offspring, and so on. In fact, in classic studies of mythology such as *The Golden Bough* or Bullfinch's *Mythology*, entire sections are devoted to transformations of one creature into another. Even within the Roman Empire this was recognized. Ovid wrote a book called *Metamorphoses*, which was a collection of stories of this type.

What does this have to do with worldview? These stories are not simply tales of magic or miracles; the sheer quantity suggests that something more fundamental is at work. Rather, they are a reflection of the underlying worldview that saw continuity between the natural world, humanity, and the gods. The connections between the different levels of reality were so strong, the interconnectedness so profound, that under the right circumstances, beings could transform from one to another.

This does not mean, of course, that everything on the hierarchy of being was equal; it was, after all, a hierarchy. The closer you were to the One, a being of pure spirit, the higher your status in the cosmic order. Spirit was superior to matter (a concept called dualism), and spiritual beings were higher than material beings. Thus the gods were superior to nymphs, who were connected to physical objects, even if they were not themselves strictly physical beings. Nymphs were higher than any purely material creature. As rational beings, humans were superior to animals. As sensual beings (i.e., beings with senses), animals were superior to plants. As living beings, plants were superior to rocks.

SO WHAT DID ALL THIS MEAN FOR ROMAN SOCIETY?

The hierarchy of being was a convenient way of explaining in philosophical terms a hierarchy of value that was part of ancient pagan cultures. In other words, it was not simply a metaphysical system, but it laid a foundation for epistemology (how we know things) and ethics as well. Since we know what is superior and what is inferior, we have the basis for determining what is right and wrong. The higher up on the hierarchy you are, the more authority you have over the things that are below you and the more rights and privileges you can claim for yourself. Herbivores can demand the lives of plants for their food. Carnivores can take the lives of herbivores. Humanity can kill both. And the gods can demand whatever sacrifices they want from humans.

THE VALUE OF HUMAN LIFE

Most pagan religions practiced human sacrifice at some point in their history. Each of the three principal gods of the Celts demanded human sacrifices by a different means — Taranis by bashing the skull in with an axe or burning, Esus by strangling, and Teutates by drowning. The Druids, who presided over these sacrifices, were also well known for putting prisoners of war in wicker cages and burning them alive as a sacrifice to the gods. The Norse also engaged in widespread human sacrifices, with perhaps the best documented taking place at the temple of Upp-sala, Sweden.

The Greeks and Romans also engaged in human sacrifice in their earlier history. Greek legend tells of a number of human sacri-fices in the Mycenaean period, but according to Plutarch the Greeks sacrificed humans as late as the Persian Wars, just prior to the bat-tle of Salamis in 480 BC. The Romans did not generally sacrifice humans to the gods, but they did sacrifice them to the *manes* (spirits of the dead) during the Republic. Archaeologists have uncovered the tombs of some of these victims, including those buried alive in Rome's walls. Romans buried pairs of victims alive on other occa-sions as well, most notably in the wake of Rome's defeat by Hannibal at Cannae. The reasoning in all these cases was largely the same: the gods (or *manes*) wanted human life or at least valued it; thus, to honor the gods or curry their favor, it was perfectly appropriate to kill those whom the society deemed expendable.

By the time of the late Republic and the Empire, these practices had largely died out, and the Romans looked at the Celts as bar-baric for continuing to sacrifice human beings. But just because the Romans no longer killed people for the gods or the *manes*, this did not mean that they suddenly valued human life. They picked up the Etruscan practice of having people fight to the death in "games" in honor of the dead (another form of human sacrifice) and moved it away from funerals to turn it into a form of popular entertainment. Gladiatorial matches and other spectacles at the circus entertained the population and fed the reputation of the sponsors at the cost of the blood of the slaves who fought and died in the arena. And in daily life, the Roman authorities would act with unsurpassed brutality against anyone who dared to question or challenge their authority.

This, too, was an expression of the hierarchy of being, because even among humans there was a natural hierarchy. What set humans above animals was their rationality — it brought them closer to the world of the spirit, the world of ideas and forms. Within the value system, things that lead to the spirit are superior to things that cater to the merely material. But not all people are as rational as others. Men, for example, were believed to be intrinsically more rational than women, along with being "obviously" superior physi-cally. Men thus properly had authority over women.

But even among men, some were considered more capable intellectually than others, and in a proper world, these superior people would control society. Philosopher-kings were to rule in Plato's Republic, and each person would be given her or his proper place in society according to her or his capabilities in a hierarchy down the social order. In the real world, a nearly Darwinian "survival of the fittest" mentality prevailed. Wealth, bloodline, and power were the criteria for determining who was superior to whom. Those at the top of the social hierarchy were seen as the natural leaders of society by virtue of their superiority over the masses. In fact, the word *aristocracy* literally translates "a rule by the best." The rest of the citizens followed (with their own gradations according to how much wealth and education they had), with slaves at the bottom of society.

Slaves were considered intrinsically inferior to free people — Aristotle ranked them as "living tools," little better than animals — and thus undeserving of anything better than their lot in life. This was true of people who fell into debt, since they demonstrated that they were not capable of taking care of themselves or their families. It was true of criminals and of prisoners of war, who by virtue of being on the losing side demonstrated that they were inferior to winners.

If a slave proved worthy, he could be freed through a process called "manumission." Freed slaves held their status as freedmen as a badge of honor, since it demonstrated that they were so superior to the average slave that they were granted this status as a mark of their proper place in society. In other words, even they recognized that the society followed a natural chain based on the hierarchy of being, and now they showed that they were superior to and higher than other slaves.

WORK AND WEALTH

Another consequence of this worldview had to do with attitudes toward the economy. In the early days of the Roman Republic (prior to the Empire) and even in early Greece, the nobility owned and worked their land alongside their servants and slaves. As the Republic expanded and encountered Carthaginian and Hellenistic

Greek cultures, many of their ideas spread to Rome, and a decided shift in attitude took place among the Roman elites. Now, as had happened in Greece, contemplation of the spirit was seen as higher than mucking about with the material world. Roman nobles began developing large, slave-run plantations known as *latifundia*, in which they increasingly gave themselves over to lives of luxury, with beautiful artwork, gardens, and homes. What better way to live a life contemplating the spirit than to live in the midst of beauty? After all, is not the One the source of the Beautiful, along with the Good and the True?

Unfortunately, the luxury they sought in their quest to contemplate the spirit inexorably pulled the Romans toward activities that catered to the flesh. As often happens, luxury led to excess, in terms of both gluttony and sexual orgies. The pornographic images that adorn everything from clay oil lamps to the walls of Roman villas are ample evidence of the sexual obsession of the Romans by the time of the Empire. And the higher up the social scale, the more perverse and extreme the sexual activities often became. As evidence of this, consider Caligula, the only Roman emperor who had a biographical film about his life produced by *Penthouse* magazine.

While the elites were giving themselves over to refined living and debauchery, someone needed to be doing the work to support them. Since productive labor dealt with the material world, it was seen as demeaning, fit only for inferiors such as the lower classes and slaves. The *latifundia* of the nobility increasingly pushed the small family farms that had been the backbone of the Roman economy out of business, and agricultural production became largely a slave-driven enterprise. In the heyday of the Empire, virtually the entire economy depended on slave labor. In fact, although the Romans knew about waterwheels and other labor-saving technologies, they never used them. Why make the capital investment when you can have slaves do the work?

But it was not only private enterprise that relied on slave labor. The state used slaves to build the roads that moved goods and especially soldiers around the Empire. Slave labor also built all the great governmental buildings whose purpose was to aggrandize the emperor and the nobility. Again, the value structure of the hierarchy of being said that the inferior should serve and honor the superior. If the gods wanted temples and statues to honor them, why shouldn't the emperor and the nobility want things that glorified *them*?

To be sure, slaves and the lower classes also built aqueducts (though some were for the fountains on imperial estates), ports, sewers, and multistory apartments for the common people, partly as a way of providing employment, partly as a way of trying to prevent revolts, and partly out of a sense that Rome was the highest civilization in the world and thus should show this off at every opportunity. Still, most of the urban residents in the Empire lived in appalling squalor in disease-ridden tenements, living hand-to-mouth existence with a life expectancy of around thirty years. The great engineering and building achievements primarily and intentionally benefited the elites. They may have provided employment for the masses, but they did little else for them.

ANTINATALISM: CONTRACEPTION, ABORTION, AND INFANTICIDE

An additional consequence of the devaluation of the material world and of human life — especially of the weak — was a fundamentally antinatal outlook, particularly among the Roman elites. Augustus Caesar, the first emperor, was something of a traditionalist and was very upset that Roman nobles were not marrying and having children; he even passed laws to try to pressure the young noblemen to marry. Unfortunately, it did not work.

The Romans may have lived in an oversexed society, but many of their sexual practices were nonreproductive, not just for the enjoyment of the different kinds of physical stimulation but in a deliberate attempt to prevent pregnancy. Even when sexual activity could have resulted in pregnancy, the Romans frequently used a variety of herbal and other contraceptive measures to prevent it. When those failed, they used surgical abortion as a means of birth control. This was particularly common when the baby was the product of an adulterous affair. The abortion techniques were crude, and the Romans did not even have soap to use as a disinfectant. As a result many women died or were sterilized by the procedure or the infections that followed it.

If all else failed and a child came to be born, infanticide was always an option. Roman families would usually keep as many healthy sons as they had and only one daughter; the rest were simply discarded. In fact, the Twelve Tables, the earliest codification of Roman law, made it mandatory for the father to kill any visibly deformed child born into the family. This practice was considered essential to the health of the society and was supported by prominent thinkers such as Plato, Aristotle, and Cicero, among others.

To put this practice in perspective, in the ancient Philistine city of Ashkelon, a relatively small town, archaeologists found one hundred skeletons of infants less than a week old in the sewers under the Roman baths. The babies were unwanted or inconvenient, and so they were literally flushed down the drain.

Although some people may have discarded their children because they simply could not afford them, the wealthy did not have that problem and yet they practiced contraception, abortion, and infanticide at least as often as the poor. The only explanation is that it was a cultural trend, not one that was dictated by economics.

This antinatal culture had important consequences for the political survival of Rome. As Rome stopped expanding, the supply of slaves from prisoners of war dried up and no new workers came in. With birthrates dropping, the Romans were forced to make up the gap by permitting into the Empire more and more Germanic immigrants from beyond the borders, lured by the promise of being able to share in the benefits of Roman rule. By the late third century, the army was increasingly becoming Germanized, as was a growing percentage of the population. This resulted in a cultural change within the Empire and a transformation of what it meant to be Roman. When the barbarian tribes moved into the Empire in the fourth and fifth centuries, they were following a path that others had already laid out, and the transformation of the Latin-speaking western half of the Empire was already well under way.

Another force was involved in the transformation of the Empire, however — one that did not come from migration from the outside. An obscure Jewish sect arose in the first century that, despite its unpopularity, became a rising force that transformed the fundamental worldview of the Empire and laid the groundwork for the development of what we today call Western Civilization. That force was Christianity, the subject of the next chapter.

CHAPTER 3

CHRISTIANITY
AND THE
TRANSFORMATION
OF THE PAGAN
WORLD

I n AD 303, the Roman emperor Diocletian began a severe persecution of an unpopular religious minority in the Empire — Christians. It started with the destruction of churches and the burning
of Christian books and was followed by attacks on the clergy, who
suffered imprisonment, torture, and sometimes death. By the following year, these attacks were extended to the laity as well. Yet
just ten years after the persecution began, in 313, Christianity was
decriminalized within the empire. As time went on, it became the
majority religion and eventually succeeded in transforming Rome
politically, socially, economically, and culturally. In other words,
it shaped the worldview of the late Empire and thus changed how
people thought of themselves and how they lived their lives.

What was it about Christianity that made it such a powerful and transforming force in the Empire? To answer this question, we must begin with a look at Christianity's roots in Judaism.

JEWS AND "GOD-FEARERS"

The Jews had a unique worldview within the empire. The obvious difference between them and the rest of the Roman world was that they were radical monotheists. They believed that there was one and only one God. But in many ways, the number of gods worshiped was less important than the nature and character of the God of Israel. All of the pagan religions had origin stories for their gods. Not Judaism. The God of Israel simply was and is and will be forever. To put it another way, Israel's God was self-existent.

Furthermore, God created everything that exists apart from himself, and he is sovereign over the natural world. Rather than being a nature god or a god associated with the forces of nature, the natural world comes from God and answers to him. This may seem a bit like the Neoplatonic concept of the One, the transcendent being who is the origin of all things, which are emanations from the One forming the hierarchy of being. In fact, some Jewish thinkers, such as Philo of Alexandria, interpreted Judaism through the lens of Platonic philosophy.

There is an important difference between the Jewish and Neoplatonic concepts of God, however. The god of the Neoplatonists is impersonal, has no will, and simply throws off the emanations by virtue of its own existence. The God of Israel, on the other hand, is personal and created the world as a voluntary act. Also, the Neoplatonic universe is eternal. While the One exists, the universe does as well. The Jewish universe was created at a particular point in time.

The conception of a personal God who is creator of all things shapes the Jewish understanding of what it means to be human. The Hebrew Bible tells us that God created humanity in his image as his steward and regent in overseeing the rest of the created world. While this teaching has implications for thinking about ecology, for our purposes we need simply to note two things: first, God gave humanity a job in Eden prior to the introduction of sin into the world (more on this later); second, our unique place in the created order gives us special value before God, so that attacking a person is tantamount to attacking the God in whose image she or he was made. Thus the Jews adamantly rejected infanticide because it was murder, a position that the Roman historian Tacitus described as "sinister and revolting."[1]

The concept of the image of God roots ethics in the character of God and humanity's connection to him — another unique element of Judaism. God is not simply a personal, transcendent creator; he is holy and righteous as well, and he expects the same from humanity. In most of the pagan world, ethics was part of philosophy, not religion. It would be difficult to find strong moral standards among the gods of Greece and Rome. For example, Jupiter (Greek Zeus) regularly impregnates human women, provoking his wife Juno/Hera to jealousy and revenge against the children; Minerva/Athena turns the human woman Arachne into a spider after she outweaves the goddess in a competition; Pluto/Hades kidnaps Proserpina/Persephone and forces her to be his wife, bringing winter to the world. In contrast, the God of Israel is concerned about righteousness, and when people violate the standards he sets for them, they get judged. And not only people but nations as well, since God is the God of all the earth and is sovereign not just over the natural world but over human affairs too.

Although God is Lord over all the nations, he has a unique relationship with Israel. Out of all the nations on the earth, God chose Israel to be his own. He revealed himself and his laws to Israel and set Israel apart to have a unique and close relationship with him. The law that God gave dealt with moral issues and with government, but much of it was also devoted to ceremonies, rituals, and dietary and sanitation practices to cover sin and maintain ritual purity before God, as well as to set Israel apart as a distinct and separate people in the world. Most important, God also required all males in Israel to be circumcised, the mark of the covenant God made with Israel.

Being God's chosen people was a tremendous privilege, but it also carried with it a great deal of responsibility. Since God chose them and revealed himself to them in a unique way, more than he did for any other people, he also had very high standards for Israel. Much of Israel's national history recorded in the Hebrew Bible is the story of Israel's failure to keep the high standards of holiness God set for them and to give God their undivided and undiluted worship, and therefore it is also the story of God's judgment on them for their sins.

The Jews thus looked at the world and their place in it very differently from the way their pagan neighbors did. The Jews' lifestyle, beliefs, and religious practices would have gotten them in trouble with the Roman government except for two things. First, because they supported Roman expansion into their territory as a means of protecting them from hostile neighboring kingdoms, even to the point of helping the Romans conquer the area, the Romans gave them a special dispensation so that they did not have to participate in religious rituals (such as emperor worship) that would violate their monotheistic beliefs.

Second, the Jews had learned through the years not to mix with the Gentiles around them; this intermingling had led them to worship false gods in the past and so incur God's judgment. The Jews also believed that they would become ritually impure ("unclean") by associating too closely with Gentiles. As a result, the Jews largely kept to themselves. They did business with outsiders, but they did not generally socialize much with them or intermarry with them.

The Jews had other reasons for keeping to themselves. Many Jews believed that their unique status as descendants of Abraham and recipients of God's law made them superior to the people around them, and they had no mandate from God or other motivation to try to convert the foreigners to Judaism. So although the Jews had an exclusivistic religion — they believed there was only one true God who was sovereign over all the earth — by and large they did not try to spread their faith. This meant they were no threat to the status quo, and so Rome allowed them their own practices and left them alone (at least as far as religion was concerned). They were in effect just another weird religious group that the Empire was willing to tolerate.

There were some exceptions to the general reaction to the Jews among the Romans, however. A very few Gentiles did convert to Judaism, but there were many more who admired the Jews' conception of God and the higher moral standards they lived by.

Circumcision was a stumbling block for this group, however. The Greeks exercised in the buff—in fact, the word *gymnasium* literally means something like "a place to get naked"—so even if you were willing to be circumcised, it would set you apart from your peers when you met to exercise and socialize.

In a culture that essentially worshiped the human body, most men were unwilling to accept the stigma and personal embarrassment of circumcision, no matter how much they may have admired the Jews, and thus they never formally converted. These people, known as "God-fearers," followed as many ethical and moral standards of the Jewish law as they could and supported or hung on the outskirts of the Jewish community, but they would not accept circumcision. They did not have the same protected status as the Jews and thus followed the civic rituals such as burning incense to the statue of the emperor. This, combined with their rejection of circumcision, kept them on the fringes of Jewish society.

CHRISTIAN ORIGINS

Christianity originated as a Jewish sect in the Roman province of Judea. Judaism in that part of the world was divided into a number of competing groups, notably the Pharisees, Sadducees, and Essenes. None of these groups liked each other much, and they frequently had nasty things to say about each other. When Jesus appeared, he seems to have been seen by the Pharisees and the Sadducees at the least as trying to begin yet another sect, one that was potentially revolutionary.

Jesus' crucifixion at the hands of the Romans—a death reserved for slaves and the lowest of the low—should have ended the problem once and for all, except for the fact that Jesus' followers began preaching that he had risen from the dead and had ascended to heaven, proving him to be the Messiah, the Son of God, even God incarnate, and the only Savior for all of humanity. In other words, the early Christians were exclusivistic like the Jews, but unlike mainstream Jews, Christians also had a missionary zeal to bring the message of "salvation through Jesus Christ" to the entire world. As a result, Jesus' following grew among the Jews, spread to the Samaritans (a group that followed a religion related to Judaism but whose members were not ethnic Jews), and then jumped to the Gentile world in the city of Antioch in Syria, one of the largest cities in the Roman Empire. It continued to spread, primarily through the Jewish communities and through the God-fearers in the eastern, Greek-speaking half of the Roman Empire. Progress in the Latin West was slower, but Christianity made headway there too.

The early church used the synagogue liturgy as the foundation of its worship but added to it baptism for new members (a practice borrowed from Judaism) and the Eucharist, or Lord's Supper. In terms of organization, they met in house churches originally led by a group of elders (Greek *presbyteros*, Late Latin *presbyter*, from which we get the word "priest"), along with deacons and deaconesses who distributed alms and assisted the elders with their duties. By the end of the first century, the senior elder in the churches in a city emerged as the "overseer" or bishop of the churches both in the town and in the surrounding countryside. The church thus followed the pattern of Roman administration, which was based on cities that had political control over the rural areas that surrounded them.

The spread of Christianity raised a number of difficult challenges for the churches. After the destruction of the temple in Jerusalem in AD 70, Pharisaical Judaism became mainstream within the remaining Jewish communities. Christianity remained enough of a threat that the Jewish leaders introduced the Eighteen Benedictions into the synagogue liturgy, which among other things included a prayer for the damnation of the "Nazarenes." This was presumably an effort to prevent Jewish Christians from becoming leaders in the synagogues, since they would then be obliged to call on God for their own destruction. The introduction of the Eighteen Benedictions is indirect evidence for the appeal of Christianity within the late first-century Jewish world, since it is hard to understand why the condemnation would have been added to the liturgy if the church was not being seen as a challenge to Judaism.

From the church's perspective, however, the bigger threat came from the Gentile world, not from Judaism. As long as Christianity could be seen as a form of sectarian Judaism, Christians did not need to participate in Roman rituals like burning incense to a statue of the emperor. When more and more Gentiles began converting to Christianity, however, the Jewish community would not accept them unless they were circumcised (something the Christians did not insist on), and the Romans saw no reason to consider the Gentile Christians to be Jews either.

At first, the Romans took Christianity to be another Eastern mystery religion. Baptism paralleled ceremonial cleansing rituals, and the Eucharist looked like the ritual meals that were a common feature of mystery religions. The followers of mystery religions, however, had no objections to burning incense to the emperor; Christians could not. Since Christians were increasingly Gentiles, not Jews, their refusal to worship the emperor meant that they were guilty of treason. This was at least the official reason the Romans used most often to justify persecuting Christians.

This does not mean, however, that the Romans actually thought of Christians as dangerous revolutionaries. Christians did not rebel against Rome. They did not use force or defend themselves when the Roman authorities came for them. Nonetheless, they were an unpopular minority in the Empire. First, some of Christianity's ideas were patently offensive to Roman sensibilities. The idea of using a cross as a symbol of hope was absurd. Crucifixion was the ugliest, most degrading, and most painful form of execution the Romans could devise — a punishment reserved for slaves, rebels, and the dregs of society. Using a cross as a symbol for a religion would be roughly as outrageous and tasteless as Jews in Nazi Germany using the gas chambers at Auschwitz to represent God's love for us.

And then Christians asked the Romans to believe that their eternal destiny depended on putting their trust in a Jew (a member of an unpopular minority) living in Judea (widely considered the worst province in the Empire) who had been crucified as a rebel. This collided with not only "the offense of the cross" and anti-Jewish bigotry, but the very thing that, for a culture that prided itself on its cosmopolitan, broad-minded outlook, was the unforgivable sin: the claim of exclusivity — the claim that Christianity is true and everything that contradicts it is false. As in any society that makes tolerance its principal virtue, there were limits, and Christianity's claims of exclusivity clearly crossed them.

THE EARLY CHRISTIAN WORLDVIEW AND LIFESTYLE

To make matters worse, Christians behaved differently than their neighbors. The reason is simple: Christianity provided an alternative worldview to both the pagan and Jewish worldviews, and thus Christians acted differently than these groups. One element is the idea from Judaism that humanity is made in the image of God. This meant that, like the Jews, Christians rejected gladiatorial games, abortion, and infanticide. It also meant that the church believed that sex was reserved for marriage as part of the creation order established by God in Genesis. As early as the time of the apostle Paul, the church took a stand against homosexual activity, and the late first-century Epistle of Barnabas (probably a pseudonym) condemned nonreproductive heterosexual activity as well, since God designed the equipment to work in a specific way. The pagans did not really understand Christian views of sex; in fact, some of their writers accused the Christians of holding orgies that were even more extreme than those that accompanied pagan worship. After all, the Christians called their assemblies "love feasts," and we all know what "love" is a code word for! Christian writers refuted this and regularly pointed out the debauchery not only of their pagan neighbors but of the pagan gods as well.

But Christians took this one step further: Not only are people created in the image of God, but all people are spiritually equal before God. More than anything else, this idea separated Judaism, which was a national or ethnic religion, from Christianity. Jews and Gentiles, men and women, slaves and free, Romans and barbarians, all were welcome in the church as equals.

This idea had a number of revolutionary consequences. First, it worked, together with the ban on infanticide and the restriction of sexual activity to marriage, to increase the status of women. Because of the practice of infanticide, the Roman world had far more men than women. Estimates are that there were 130 men for every 100 women in Rome itself, and 140 men to 100 women in Italy. Paradoxically, this reduced women's status. Men viewed them as protected property, and so they had very limited freedom. And Greek thought was particularly misogynistic. For example,

Aristotle argued that women were essentially the products of birth defects. Because there was not enough "heat" in the pregnancy, they came out half-baked, with their genitals inside out. Because they were incomplete males, they were physically, mentally, morally, and spiritually inferior to men.

Although some of these ideas would creep into the church over time, Christianity initially had a much more favorable attitude toward women. Women responded to the gospel in greater numbers than men, and since girls in Christian homes were not discarded at birth, the church developed a much more balanced gender ratio than that of the Roman world. Sociologists tell us that this actually increases women's status in a group, which may help explain why women over the decades continued to be drawn to Christianity in greater numbers than men. What is clear is that they were given a freedom within the church that was denied them in the pagan world. They could take leadership roles within the church as deaconesses, and some of the wealthier women sponsored house churches. So contrary to popular belief, the rise of Christianity had a very positive effect on the place of women in society.

But the notion of spiritual equality also meant that slaves were not just "living tools" but were equals before God with even the most exalted members of society. In fact, some early church bishops seem to have been former slaves. But to take this even further, the New Testament writers talk about Jesus Christ becoming a slave for us and dying to set us free. And if Jesus set us free, should we as his followers not also imitate him by setting others free too?

The relationship of Christianity and slavery is another area that is widely misunderstood. Christians were the first people in history to oppose slavery systematically. Early Christians purchased slaves in the markets simply to set them free. Later, in the seventh century, the Franks (a Germanic people who controlled Western Germany and France), under the influence of its Christian queen, Bathilde, became the first kingdom in history to begin the process of outlawing slavery. By the central Middle Ages, the Catholic Church had all but abolished slavery in western Europe, with the exception of Muslim prisoners taken as war reparations.

In the 1200s, Thomas Aquinas declared slavery a sin. When the African slave trade began in the 1400s, it was condemned numerous times by the papacy. So it is hardly fair to blame the Catholic Church for actions taken by Catholic Portugal and Spain, which supported the slave industry in defiance of church teaching.

Along with overcoming ethnic, gender, and social distinctions, Christians were also active in taking care of the poor and the sick, not just within the church but in the wider community as well. Christians were so active in helping the poor that Julian the Apostate, an emperor who tried to return the Empire to paganism after Constantine had legalized Christianity, complained during a famine that "these impious Galileans [Christians] support not only their poor, but ours as well."[2]

Even more striking, however, was the reaction of Christians to people with contagious diseases. When life-threatening diseases struck, most people ran the other way, including physicians. They simply were not willing to risk their own lives to care for someone who was likely to die anyway. Christians reacted differently. For one thing, their faith told them that death would usher them into heaven, so they had no need to fear it. To put it in worldview terms, they had a very different answer to the question of what happens after death from the one the pagans offered. Further, they had a different answer to the question of what brings meaning to life. To the Christian, the route to a meaningful life was found in sacrificial service to others in imitation of Jesus. And Jesus was a healer.

The net result is that Christians nursed the sick at great personal risk. Dionysius of Alexandria reported that during a pestilence that devastated the city:

> *The most of our brethren were unsparing in their exceeding love and brotherly kindness. They held fast to each other and visited the sick fearlessly, and ministered to them continually, serving them in Christ. And they died with them most joyfully, taking the affliction of others, and drawing the sickness from their neighbors to themselves and willingly receiving their pains. And many who cared for the sick and gave strength to others died themselves having transferred to themselves their death.*[3]

And since even basic nursing care is effective in helping people get well, survival rates among the sick went up because of the ministrations of Christians.

All of this made the Christians nonconformists in Roman society. And in that tolerant society, nonconformity outside the bounds of tolerance was a death sentence. From the 50s AD on, Christians were sporadically persecuted, tortured, and killed, using the legal argument that they were subversives because they refused to burn incense to the emperor, and atheists because they did not acknowledge the Roman gods.

Nowhere, however, was the Christian disregard of death more evident than during these persecutions. Men and women, slaves and free, were tortured and executed in public spectacles designed to be as painful, perverse, and entertaining as possible. And Christians went to their deaths without a fight, singing hymns, preaching, and otherwise refusing to be cowed or intimidated by the abuse they were suffering. This was in many ways the undoing of the persecutions. People in the arenas saw the confidence with which Christians approached death, and this vision of boldness forced spectators to ask themselves whether they had anything they were willing to go through that kind of horror for, whether they had anything that gave their lives the confidence and purpose they saw in the despised Christians. Tertullian, an early Christian writer, said that the blood of the martyrs was the seed of the church.[4] He was right. Christianity remained an unpopular minority religion, but one that was growing and gaining at least the grudging respect of the pagan world.

APOLOGISTS AND GNOSTICS

Of course, the Christians did their best to defend themselves, but they did it with ideas rather than force. A group known today as the Apologists (from the Greek word *apologia*, meaning "a defense") did their best to refute attacks on Christianity. They corrected misunderstandings about the faith, such as the idea that they were cannibals because of the Eucharistic language of eating Jesus' body and drinking his blood, or the accusation that they engaged in orgies. They also went on the offensive against the immorality of the pagan world and pagan gods, presented arguments for the truth of Christianity based on fulfilled prophecy, and warned about the final judgment.

Beyond the specific arguments, however, the Apologists began to explain Christianity in terms drawn from Greek philosophy. In fact, Justin Martyr, one of the earliest Apologists, wore a philosopher's cloak and presented his teaching as the true philosophy — the philosophy of Jesus Christ. From there, it was a small step from using Neoplatonic terms to explain Christianity to incorporating Neoplatonic and other pagan ideas into Christianity. The most obvious example was the use of Neoplatonic ideas to discuss creation and its relationship to God. Again, Neoplatonists believed that the One was the origin of all things, but that the means by which all things were created was the *logos*, a concept that includes not just the literal meaning "word" but also the idea of logic and rationality or reason. This concept merged with the Jewish idea in Genesis that God spoke the world into existence and found its way into the prologue to the gospel of John. This led ultimately to an elaborate system of cosmology, notably promoted through the writings of Pseudo-Dionysius (dated to the late fifth century AD).

This Neoplatonic influence had a number of important consequences for Christianity. First, it encouraged a more allegorical approach to Scripture, which argued that although the literal meaning of the text was important (the particulars), what was more important was the deeper spiritual meaning that the literal pointed toward (the universals). It also meant that the church began to de-emphasize the physical world in favor of the spiritual. Thus, although the churches continued to feed the poor and take care of the sick, they began to put more and more emphasis on martyrdom and, failing that, asceticism — fasting, poverty, solitude, and especially virginity. In Judaism, there is no intrinsic connection between sexuality and spirituality, while in paganism, there is — either in the form of temple prostitution or of complete abstinence, as in the Vestal Virgins of Rome. As pagan thought began shaping Christian belief and practice, virginity became more highly valued as a permanent state of life, particularly for women. Greek misogynistic attitudes also began infiltrating the church, so that the idea emerged that women were sexually obsessed and insatiable, and only by controlling their natural urges and thus acting against their nature — in other words, by being virgins — could they live holy lives. These ideas would not be fully developed until later, after Christianity was legalized, but the crucial elements began to emerge early on.

Despite the impact of Neoplatonism, the church continued its emphasis on the goodness of the natural world and on other elements of the Jewish worldview. One offshoot of Christianity did not do so, however. Known today as Gnosticism (from the Greek *gnosis*, or "knowledge"), these groups claimed to have secret knowledge that would lead people to salvation. Many, though not all, of these groups associated themselves with Jesus, claiming to have his secret teachings that he did not entrust to the apostles. These "Gnostic gospels" date from the second to about the fifth century, well after the gospels of the New Testament were written.

Without going into detail, suffice it to say that the Gnostics tended to be extreme dualists. They believed that the physical world was not simply inferior to the spiritual but was flat-out evil. One of the most telling examples can be found in the Gnostics' attitude toward the Jewish Scriptures. In the Gnostic gospels, Jesus never referred to Judaism or the Old Testament, speaking instead from a framework drawn entirely from pagan philosophy and particularly from an extreme form of Platonism. This is rather unexpected behavior from someone who was a Jewish rabbi. What few references there are in Gnostic writings to Judaism are negative. In fact, some Gnostic texts depict the god of the Old Testament as an evil offshoot from the main line of emanations from God. This Jewish god is ignorant and wicked, as evidenced by the fact that he created the material world, which itself is evil by its very nature.

This dualism had a number of important implications for how Gnostics lived. For example, many Gnostic writings were anti-sex and anti-marriage, since both can lead to procreation, which is a bad thing since it traps an intrinsically good spirit into intrinsically evil matter. As just one example, the *Book of Thomas the Contender* is "dominated by condemnation of sexual intercourse and attachment to the flesh," as summarized by Gnostic scholar Karen L. King.[5] As a result, Gnostics tended to be even more ascetic (at least in their teachings) than the mainstream church.

Women could be leaders in Gnostic communities, but only if they abstained from sex and denied their femininity. For example, saying 114 of the Gnostic gospel of Thomas tells us, "Simon Peter said to them, 'Let Mary [Magdalene] leave us, for women are not worthy of life.' Jesus said, 'I myself shall lead her to make her male so that she might become a living spirit that resembles you males. For every woman who will make herself male will enter the kingdom of heaven.'"[6]

Although Gnosticism never became a widespread movement — it was limited to isolated communities scattered about the eastern Mediterranean and especially Egypt — the Apologists wrote treatises against them. Until recently, much of what we knew about the Gnostics came from the writings of their opponents, though recent manuscript discoveries have confirmed the accuracy of the Apologists' summaries of their teachings. As things turned out, the Gnostics' Christian veneer on pagan thought did not last long. The more robust interaction of Jewish and Greek thought in the mainstream church would win the day in dramatic fashion early in the fourth century.

CONSTANTINE AND THE LEGALIZATION OF CHRISTIANITY

Christianity's legal situation in the Empire changed in AD 313, when Constantine issued the Edict of Milan. The year before, just prior to the Battle of the Milvian Bridge, Constantine claimed to have had a vision from God, after which Jesus appeared to him in a dream and explained what he needed to do. Constantine had his soldiers paint Christian symbols on their shields, and when he won against his opponents' superior forces, he took it as a sign from God and converted to Christianity. The Edict of Milan followed in short order, making Christianity a legal religion. Contrary to the way it is often portrayed, the edict simply legalized the Christian church. It did not outlaw paganism or make Christianity the "official" religion of the Empire, though Constantine's conversion certainly made it the favored religion.

A great deal of ink has been spilled over whether Constantine's conversion was genuine or the product of political calculation. On the one hand, Christianity was a growing religion, centered in the cities, with a high degree of organization. It could thus provide an important base that Constantine could rely on. On the other hand, Christians were still unpopular, and they made up by modern estimates only about 10 to 15 percent of the Roman world — hardly an overwhelming number. Besides, many or perhaps most were pacifists, though there are indications of Christians serving in the military even prior to 313. It is thus far from clear that there was any real political advantage in embracing Christianity.

Constantine's actions as emperor have also raised a number of questions about his conversion. First of all, he seems to have confused God the Father with Sol Invictus, the Unconquered Sun — Constantine's favored deity. This was not helped by the Christian habit of portraying Jesus, using sun imagery, as the Light of the world, the Sun of righteousness, and so on.[7] Constantine also continued to use pagan deities on his coins for another decade after his "conversion" and retained the title of *Pontifex Maximus*, the title of the pagan high priest of Rome later taken by the popes.

In terms of his dealings with Christianity, Constantine got involved very early in settling problems in the church. The first challenge had to do with the Donatists, a group who believed that priests who had knuckled under during the persecutions were not true priests unless they were accepted and forgiven by a bishop who had remained faithful. The courts and Constantine ruled against the Donatists, who rioted in response. Constantine retaliated with force, a first in the history of the church. Although he revoked his anti-Donatist decrees when he saw that repression did not work, his action set a precedent for state interference and coercion in the church.

Then there was the controversy over whether the man Jesus was also an archangel (held by Arius) or God (held by Athanasius). To settle this question, Constantine convened a meeting of bishops from around the Empire at Nicea in modern-day Turkey. The meeting decided for Athanasius' position, which became the "orthodox" position in the church.

The question here is the degree to which Constantine was trying to impose his will on the church in his decisions about the Donatists and at Nicea. Was he trying to dictate the terms of

Christianity's integration into Roman society by deciding which doctrines were acceptable and which were not?

Doing so was probably not his intention. First, it was the emperor's role in pagan Rome to see that people remained on good terms with their gods. Constantine was simply following this tradition. Second, the church's only models for a Christian emperor were the Old Testament kings of Israel, who were themselves responsible for seeing to it that the people worshiped God rightly. Third, the Donatists approached him, not the other way around. When the decision went against them, they began rioting, and no government tolerates that kind of behavior.

At Nicea, Constantine actually came up to the bishops who had been tortured by his predecessors and kissed their wounds. While this could have been political theatre, it does not seem likely. Nor does it seem likely that the bishops who had held their ground under persecution would docilely allow Constantine to tell them what to do or believe. Rather, Constantine was probably trying to determine the true doctrine and to unify the church around it. It would be hard enough to win the Empire to Christianity without Christians arguing among themselves about what they were supposed to believe. Even after the Council of Nicea, Arians were tolerated within the Empire during Constantine's lifetime, and Athanasius was exiled for refusing to accept repentant Arians into the churches. In other words, Constantine did not force conformity to the decisions of the church council that he himself had convened.

Another element in evaluating the genuineness of Constantine's conversion is the fact that he sent his mother Helena to Jerusalem and the surrounding areas to try to find historical evidence and artifacts from Jesus' life. This strongly suggests that by this point, Constantine was well on the way toward a full conversion to Christianity.

People frequently point out that Constantine was not baptized until he was on his deathbed, arguing from this that he was not a real Christian. However, in this period Christians believed that baptism wiped away all your sins, but they were not clear on what happened if you sinned after you were baptized. As a result, Christians frequently waited to be baptized, with the ideal being to be baptized just before death so you did not have the chance to mess it up afterward. Eventually, theology developed to a point where this was no longer a concern, but in Constantine's day deathbed baptisms were common even among Christians who had grown up in the faith.

No matter how we evaluate Constantine himself, his actions had a profound effect on both Christianity and the Empire. The most obvious effect is that it changed the relationship of the church to the state. The transition from being a persecuted minority religion to being the favored faith of the emperor inevitably forged ties between church and state that have been a driving force in Western political life ever since. The central fact of this relationship is that the church had existed independently of the state for nearly three hundred years, and so it was well established that the church was separate from the government. What changed was that the government was willing to work with the church, to cooperate and interact with it in ways that were impossible before.

No one believed religion and politics could be separated — remember, the basic pagan concept of gods was that they were the supreme authorities in an area of life — and there were areas in which the church's interests in morality or justice, for example, collided with the interests of the state. So the question inevitably and rapidly emerged of how to balance ecclesiastical and civil institutional structures, powers, and responsibilities. At times the pendulum would swing in favor of the church, at other times in favor of the state, but this dynamic would be a critical element in Western history from that time on.

This raises the question of whether Constantine's legalization of Christianity was a good thing for the church. No doubt it opened the door for church leaders to get involved in politics, to acquire secular power, and from there to go through periods of severe corruption as they became more interested in power and wealth on earth rather than in heaven. At the same time, however, it must be remembered that though Constantine legalized and patronized the church, he neither made Christianity the formal state religion nor outlawed paganism. And for those who are critical of Constantine's actions and their impact on the church, consider the persecutions that Christians had suffered less than a decade before. It is hard to blame the church for embracing Constantine when the alternative shortly before had been torture and death.

A second area of change involved the adoption of elements of paganism into the church. Constantine, possibly out of earlier devotion to Sol Invictus, made the first day of the week ("Sun" day) a holiday in 321, though there is strong evidence that from the first century on, Christians had worshiped on this day in commemoration of Easter. But the Feast of the Nativity (aka Christmas) was set to December 25, the birthday of the sun, in part to compete with the pagan holiday of Saturnalia. Elements of pagan worship such as candles, garlands, and incense were gradually introduced into the church, though they had been avoided earlier because of their association with paganism. The Virgin Mary grew in importance, at times being connected to pagan goddesses such as Isis. The cult of saints and martyrs also grew, with Christian saints sometimes replacing pagan deities. Technically, the saints were not supposed to be worshiped, but people coming from a pagan background in which they were encouraged to pray to the saints were not likely to understand the distinction between prayer and outright worship.

The connection of all of these things with paganism would fade over time as the practices became increasingly Christianized. Of much greater significance was the ongoing and growing influence of Greek thought on the church. If anything, the trends toward asceticism, virginity, and misogyny expanded with the legalization of Christianity. The reason is simple. Prior to Constantine, people actually courted martyrdom as a way of proving the genuineness of their faith. Origen, an important theologian later in his life, had actually tried to get himself arrested as a young man during an outbreak of persecution so he could be tortured or killed for his faith. His mother heard of his plan and hid his clothes. Since Origen was ashamed to go out in public naked, he missed his chance to become a martyr. With the legalization of Christianity, the opportunity to be martyred disappeared. As a result, people who wanted to prove their faith turned to "white martyrdom" — the living of a strict, ascetic life — as the most viable alternative to actual martyrdom. People went into the desert as hermits, or they lived as celibates with limited food and sleep.

One of the more famous ascetics, Simon Styletes, spent a significant percent of his life living on top a high pillar. He would lower a basket to get food and water and never left his pillar. When that proved to be an inadequate challenge, he did time standing on one foot. And for this he earned the reputation of being a very wise man. (In all fairness, he was. People came to him to settle problems, and he gave good advice. But whether his wisdom came from standing on one foot on top of a pillar is open to debate!)

Eventually, these kinds of ascetic practices evolved into monasticism, in which people would live in community according to a "rule of life." The monasteries typically required celibacy and an austere lifestyle, though generally not as severe a regimen as the one the hermits followed. Monks and nuns would live lives of structured prayer, study, and productive labor.

These last two activities (study and labor) deserve more comment. Rodney Stark has pointed out that Christianity is a religion founded more on ideas than on practices. Yet the Bible does not directly answer a number of questions that arise naturally from its teaching, and nowhere does it include a systematic statement of doctrine or even a list of the essentials of the faith. As a result, the church historically has valued study, logic, and reason as religious activities in a way that differs significantly from paganism and even Judaism and Islam (which are religions based primarily on practice, not doctrine).[8]

For monks and nuns, study was particularly important as a foundation for contemplative prayer. As early as the fifth century, a Roman senator named Cassiodorus made copying texts and study of both Christian and pagan thinkers an integral part of life at a monastery he founded at Vivarium. Cassiodorus and others believed that all truth was God's truth, and that study was a route to spiritual development. Not all early monasteries followed Cassiodorus's viewpoint, but within a few centuries his ideas and his list of readings would provide the backbone to monastic spirituality.

Along with more obviously spiritual activities such as prayer and study, monks were also required to engage in productive labor. The Roman world may have demeaned work and pushed it off on slaves, but the monasteries did not. Although it may in part have been intended to promote humility, the idea that monks should work was based primarily on the biblical idea that God works, so we who are made in his image should work as well. In Genesis, Adam was given a job in the garden before he sinned, and thus work is not a consequence of sin but part of what we were made to do. Over time, this would lead to a strikingly different outlook on the purpose of life. As we will see later, this particular element of the shift in worldview laid the foundation for Western economic success and vitality.

The long-term, large-scale impact of this focus on study and labor as spiritual activities points to the fact that not only was Christianity influenced by the pagan world, but the dominant worldview within the empire gradually shifted because of the influence of Christianity. Nowhere is this more evident than in the attitude toward human life. As early as Constantine, new laws were passed to improve the lives of slaves. Infanticide was on the way to being banned, along with crucifixion and ultimately abortion. Gladiatorial matches also came to an end, largely because a courageous monk named Telemachus went onto the floor of the arena to try to stop the killing and was himself killed in the process.[9] The change was gradual, but the value of human life was being increasingly recognized in the Empire.

Unfortunately, however, the Empire itself was in trouble. Too many centuries of antinatalism and too much reliance on immigration to make up the gap in population combined with administrative and military blunders to leave the borders of the Empire wide open to migrating barbarian tribes. Roman authority in the Latin-speaking West collapsed under the weight of its own incompetence and the onslaught of Germanic tribes. The eventual fusion of Roman, Germanic, and Christian traditions would result in the emergence of a new culture and worldview in medieval Europe. But it would be a long, slow transition.

CHAPTER 4

THE **EMERGENCE** OF THE **MEDIEVAL** WORLDVIEW

Does this plotline sound familiar?
A powerful, advanced civilization falls because of a combination of decadence, natural disaster, and outside invasion. The survivors huddle in small communities, struggling to survive and to preserve what few scraps of culture and learning remain. Eventually, a new civilization emerges, incorporating half-remembered and often misunderstood remnants of the old empire with the very different cultural orientation that had developed since the empire's fall.

This is not the plot of the next Star Wars movie, nor is it a sci-fi or fantasy novel. It is quite literally the history of the European Middle Ages. And so, to understand medieval civilization, it is important to understand the decline of Roman authority in the West.

PICKING UP THE PIECES

Rome did not so much fall as collapse under its own weight. Germanic migrations, a corrupt and ineffectual government, insecurity within the borders, a breakdown of trade, and an economy built on slavery when the end of territorial expansion shut down new sources of slaves — all combined to destabilize Roman society. Add to that a colder and wetter climate that made it more difficult to grow crops, and this spelled disaster for at least the western, Latin-speaking half of the Empire.

The towns that had been the backbone of Roman rule shrank or were abandoned as the elites who had run them retreated to their rural estates. Literally hundreds of towns in Italy alone disappeared during this time, and in France, the entire remaining population of the city of Arles moved into the old Roman arena. Roman administration collapsed across the western provinces, and the society's center of gravity shifted from towns to the countryside.

Because of the economic stress, free peasants often gave up their land to large landowners in return for a guarantee that they could be sharecroppers on what had once been their own land. Slaves were also given their own plots of land to farm, and eventually the two classes merged, becoming serfs — semi-free peasants who were not owned as property but were tied to a piece of land they could not leave. This gave them some security — they could not be evicted — but at the expense of their liberty.

The overall economy shrank (as did the population), as the decline in trade forced the estates to become self-sufficient. This in turn meant landowners could not specialize in what they did best but had to divert resources to produce whatever they needed, whether they had a good resource base for it or not.

In the midst of all of this chaos, one institution remained standing: the church. With the civil government in free fall, the bishops were forced to pick up the pieces if any kind of administration was to continue. In many places, the bishops emerged as the political rulers of cities, not necessarily because they wanted power, but because somebody had to hold the civil administration together — and the bishops were frequently the only ones with the education, administrative expertise, personnel, and popular support to do it.

As the various barbarian tribes took over different parts of the Empire, they attempted with varying degrees of success to maintain Roman administration, though with their own personnel overseeing it. As they converted to Christianity, they frequently put bishops into their governments as well. Unfortunately, Germanic and Roman principles for governing were radically different, and as a result it took centuries before a stable system would emerge, one drawn from blending the Roman and Germanic cultures with Christianity. That system, known as feudalism, was based on personal bonds (an element of German culture) regulated by oaths (again, German) and a legal contract (an element of Roman culture). The basic idea was that the proper structure for a society was based on lordship, in which one person was owed allegiance and service from others. This applied not only in the political realm but in the economic as well (where it is called "manorialism"). As in any society, politics and economics were tied together by fundamental ideas about the "natural" way people should relate to each other.

EDUCATION AND IRELAND

However much the bishops may have tried to hold the civil administration together, they had too many balls to keep in the air. The one they dropped was education. The other needs were simply too pressing, so the old Roman urban schools largely died during the century following the collapse of Roman authority. Some monasteries did continue to provide education for monks, but not enough. As a result, the level of literacy and education went into a steep decline.

There was one exception to this trend, however, namely, Ireland. Ireland had never been under Roman rule. Its ancient culture was clan based; its religion, led by Druids, featured human sacrifice, using multiple methods to satisfy the different deities' demands. But the Druids were also remarkably well educated. It took years of hard work and study to become a Druid, including not just practicing the usual religious rituals, myths, magic, and so on, but learning about history, law, nature, music, oratory, and a host of other subjects, all studied orally since the Druids never wrote anything down.

When Christianity was introduced to Ireland in the fifth century by Patrick, it won over the populace peacefully — by means of preaching rather than conquest. Part of its appeal was undoubtedly Patrick's winsome way of presenting the gospel, but he also had a remarkable message: a God who gave his Son to die for us rather than a god who demanded we give our sons to die for him.

Not surprisingly, given a worldview that equated religious leaders with scholarship, the Irish monks set out to learn everything they could about Christianity, and with it, the Roman world in which it developed. To do so entailed reading, so the Irish learned Latin and Greek (and sometimes Hebrew as well) in order to be able to study the texts.

But there was a problem: Roman and Greek texts were written as an unbroken string of letters without capitalization, punctuation, or spaces between words. A native speaker of the language could read it reasonably easily, but it is nearly impossible to decipher this kind of thing in a foreign language. So the Irish began trying to make the texts a bit easier to read by adding word spaces, basic capitalization, and rudimentary punctuation marks. They also copied every text they could, and for important ones, such as the Bible, they produced tremendous works of art in the process.

Irish Christianity was quickly assimilated into the clan structure. Unlike on the continent, with its town-based government and ecclesiastical rule by bishops, the rural Irish culture made monasteries the center of the church, with clan leaders emerging as abbots heading the monasteries as well as being local political leaders. Irish monasteries were frequently very austere. They would sometimes be located in harsh, out-of-the-way places such as some of the rocky islands off the coast. In some cases — Skellig Michael, for example — these islands were so barren that the monks literally had to bring in boatloads of dirt so they could grow their food.

Some of the monks would engage in *peregrinatio*, or pilgrimages — unplanned wanderings in which the monk would leave his monastery, his clan, his family, probably forever, and go wherever God's wind blew him. The most famous example was Saint Brendan, who with a group of monks set sail across the North Atlantic in a leather-hulled boat, probably making it to North America and returning to tell the tale. Others founded monasteries on islands between Ireland and Scotland, such as Iona, and from there brought Christianity into Scotland, then south into England, which had by that time been overrun by pagan Angles and Saxons. Still others ended up on continental Europe, founding monasteries as they went (even founding the monastery of Saint Gall in Switzerland) and preaching in France and Germany.

And wherever they went, they established schools, since from their pagan days, the Irish thought of education as essential for a man of God. Irish monasteries became the main educational centers in Europe during the sixth and seventh centuries. These centers included the continent's major scriptoria (places where manuscripts were copied) at Luxeuil and Bobbio in France, and particularly a major school at York in England, another church founded by Irish missionaries. In fact, in the late 700s, over a century after the reintroduction of education to the continent, when Charlemagne decided he wanted to overhaul education in his empire, the best scholar he could find was Alcuin, a deacon at York. So Charlemagne sent for him, and Alcuin developed a system of schools, textual study, and copying that laid the foundation for the later widespread revival of education in Europe.

Despite Charlemagne and Alcuin's educational reform, little original scholarly work was done during the five hundred years after Roman authority collapsed in the West. Instead, scholars focused on collecting sayings and surviving snippets of information from the ancient world, on paraphrasing texts, and on copying manuscripts. About the only original thinker of that era was, not surprisingly, an Irishman, John Scotus Erigena. Erigena was heavily influenced by Platonism, and although some of his theological ideas were outside the bounds of orthodoxy, he never got in trouble for them (largely because his ideas were so complex no one really understood them). He did lay the foundation for later developments in medieval science in his book *On the Divisions of Nature*, which presented a system of understanding the natural world based on a hierarchy of being that was drawn from the Platonic tradition. He also had a bit of an acid tongue. One evening, when he was sitting across the table from Charlemagne's heir, Louis the Pious, Louis asked him, "What is the difference between a Scot (an Irishman in this period) and a sot?" Erigena replied, "About three feet" — the distance across the table. When he died, his biographers said he was "stabbed to death by the pens of his students," a description we can hope was a metaphor, though most teachers can undoubtedly relate to it.

In general, "laying foundations" is a good summary of the first half-millennium after the fall of Rome. Scholarship may have been stagnant, but it preserved the ancient texts that enabled medieval scholarship to flourish later. Charlemagne laid the foundation for the Holy Roman Empire of the German Nation, the central political authority of medieval society. Manorialism laid the foundation for the rural economy, and feudalism for the basic political system that would govern most of Europe during the rest of the Middle Ages.

Although the scarcity of written sources for this period makes it difficult to know what was going on (which is why it is sometimes called "the Dark Ages" — we cannot see into it), the same blending of Germanic and Roman cultures with Christianity that produced feudalism and manorialism occurred across the board in all areas of life during these centuries. The different strands influenced each other and gradually blended together to form a new worldview and a new civilization, which began to emerge in a more coherent form in the decades leading into the second millennium.

THE TURN OF THE MILLENNIUM

In the mid-900s, European society began a major shift in its political, economic, cultural, and intellectual realms. Prior to this, except for Charlemagne's reign, political power had been decentralized into smaller and smaller political units. With the reigns of Otto I and his successors, creatively named Otto II and Otto III, the Holy Roman Empire was reconstituted in Germany, beginning the process of centralizing political authority in Europe. The papacy, which had degenerated to the point where it was little more than a political football kicked back and forth between Roman noble families — a period frequently called the "papal pornocracy" ("rule by immorality") — was cleaned up by the Ottonians and eventually emerged as a political force that rivaled the emperor. Feudalism was restructured by the Normans in France and later England to reinforce royal power rather than to disperse it among the nobility.

While all this was going on, the climate again shifted, becoming dryer and warmer, so much so that Vikings were able to farm in Greenland. With the improvement in growing conditions, agriculture expanded, and with it the population as well. European population more than doubled between 1000 and 1300. Although about 80 percent of the population continued to live in the countryside in most of Europe, the growth in population helped spur rapid urbanization. Two thousand towns are known to have been established in the eleventh century alone, and existing towns also grew.

URBAN LIFE

Urban life spurred a growing dynamism in medieval Europe. Unlike rural society, which tied people to land and assumed a static workforce, social structure, and land holdings, urban life relied on immigration. In fact, until the late nineteenth century, more people died in cities than were born in them. Without immigration, the cities would quickly depopulate. Further, towns permitted some social mobility. Towns jealously protected their right to free serfs who had escaped from their land and lived inside their walls for a year and a day. This encouraged immigration and provided a base of workers to help fuel the economy. Once accepted as a resident in the town, a serf's upward mobility was possible, though difficult. The top of the social hierarchy was filled by members of the nobility, followed by very wealthy commoners with old money; yet it was sometimes possible to rise into more prestigious and lucrative professions over the course of generations.

Although a few farmers lived in cities, growing food was not the principal function of the towns. Instead, they were centers for manufacturing and commerce; frequently, they also became political centers as well by taking control of the surrounding rural areas and thus becoming city-states like the old Roman towns. In practical terms, this meant that the urban economy was based not on lordship and personal relations but on written contracts. As a result, towns needed a body of contract law, which led to a renewed interest in Roman law. Rome had a well-developed body of contract law, which was adapted to the needs of medieval society (with some influence from the church as well). And this revival of Roman law in its turn also tied into a growing interest in more rational legal procedures.

LEGAL DEVELOPMENTS

In the early Middle Ages, legal cases were frequently settled through an appeal to divine intervention. Trials by ordeal, by fire or water, and by combat were commonly used to determine guilt or innocence in cases where the answer was not obvious. All were based on the idea that God would protect the innocent and judge the guilty. In the new millennium, legal scholars began moving toward a more rational criminal procedure with less reliance on supernatural intervention. In some parts of Europe (especially in cities and in Italy), Roman law was revived; in other parts, customary law was codified and rationalized to provide a more systematic, written system of law and criminal procedure.

Two main approaches to holding trials developed. In the first, known as the inquisitorial system, a panel of judges decides criminal cases. One of them, acting as the "investigating magistrate," collects evidence, interviews witnesses, and presents the case in court. The other judges examine the evidence and question and cross-examine the witnesses from as many angles as possible — if need be, multiple times — on the assumption that even the most plausible lie will break down under close enough examination. This will then reveal the truth, and guilt or innocence will be established.

The other judicial approach, the adversarial system, pits the two sides in a contest against each other, the idea being that the best way to determine the truth is to let the two sides argue it out before a judge and frequently a jury. This is the system in use in the Anglo-Saxon world, including the United States, though in some ways higher appellate courts and the Supreme Court bring in elements of the inquisitorial system as well. Trial by combat did continue, particularly among the nobility or in capital cases where there was insufficient evidence for a trial, but most cases were decided using arguments based on evidence and testimony. Truth was seen as rational, anchored in the world of time and space and thus discoverable by human reason. This in itself marks a major shift in worldview in the eleventh and twelfth centuries.

Unfortunately, the recovery of Roman law had downsides. As we have seen, the Roman worldview had no concept of human rights, an attitude that was reflected in their law code. Ironically, this became a problem in the Middle Ages because the medieval adaptation of Roman law included an extremely high standard of proof of guilt. Since judges no longer relied on divine guidance but on human reason, certainty of guilt was essential to prevent miscarriages of justice. In capital cases in particular, the medieval jurists followed the Roman law of treason, which required either two eyewitnesses or a confession. Since this standard of proof was difficult to obtain in most capital cases — how many people commit serious crimes in front of two eyewitnesses? — if there was solid evidence of guilt but not enough for a conviction, the accused could be "encouraged" to confess through judicial torture. This was a revival of the Roman practice of routinely torturing slaves involved in any judicial procedure and, in cases of treason, freemen as well. When the Roman Empire was Christianized, many Christian writers argued that Christians could not serve as magistrates because it might oblige them to order people to be tortured, which Christians could not do. This led to the gradual abolition of torture in judicial procedures, especially in church courts, until well into the revival of Roman law. Not until 1228 in civil courts and 1252 in church courts do we have documentation of judicial torture in the Middle Ages.

The application of the Roman law of treason in capital cases led to a number of obvious abuses. The threshold of evidence required before proceeding to torture could be minimal, and the rules for how much and what kind of torture could be applied were often ignored, particularly in civil courts. Further, heresy (a category that in the fifteenth century included witchcraft) was defined as treason against God, and thus people accused of heresy were subject to torture by the Inquisition (church courts specifically founded to combat heresy). It does need to be said, however, that church courts were far more likely to follow the rules than civil courts, especially where witchcraft was concerned. In Spain, the Inquisition was taken over by the state in the late fifteenth century and was used as a tool for ethnic cleansing. Once again, the worst abuses were conducted by the civil government rather than the church.

SCHOOLS AND EDUCATION

Another consequence of the growth of urban life and contract law was a growing need for education. Under Charlemagne in the eighth and ninth centuries, Alcuin had set up schools in the royal palace, in monasteries, and in cathedrals. In the intervening centuries, the palace and cathedral schools had gone into a steep decline. Monastic schools located in the countryside provided most of the education in Europe. With the urban boom of the eleventh century and the growing strictness of the monasteries brought about by church reform, cathedrals once again began opening schools (or, in a few cases, expanding existing schools) in the cities.

The expansion in both civil and ecclesiastical bureaucracies further increased the demand for education, but the same bureaucratic expansion meant increasing responsibilities in the cathedrals. As a result, they could not devote the necessary resources to keep expanding the schools, and so they spun them off as more or less independent institutions known as universities, starting with the law school in Bologna (c. 1150) and the University of Paris (c. 1200). These schools provided people with the skills and credentials needed to work in church and state government, as well as offering advanced training in various kinds of law, medicine, and theology.

PLATONIC HUMANISM

Even before the universities, however, a new worldview emerged in the cathedral schools that had been anticipated in many ways by the movement away from reliance on supernatural intervention in law. Labeled "Platonic humanism" by historian R. W. Southern, this worldview was based on the idea that the world came from God and thus can lead us back to God. Without going as far as the ancient Platonic hierarchy of being, twelfth-century scholars believed that the world reflected the God who created it — the "Platonic" part of the worldview — and therefore that studying the world can tell us about God. God created the world separate from himself, and since he is rational, the world he created is also rational and subject to rational analysis. Since human beings are created in the image of God, we also are rational and thus understand the world. Though miracles can and do happen, both the world and human nature have their own integrity apart from God and can be studied and understood without recourse to divine intervention — the "humanist" part of Platonic humanism.

The assumptions behind Platonic humanism shaped the thinking and worldview of the rest of the Middle Ages. Intellectual life did not remain static, however. In particular, as Christians interacted with Muslims in Spain, they became aware that the Moors had many books from the ancient world that had been lost in the West, notably a nearly complete set of the works of Aristotle.

As Arab armies conquered Syria (which had been part of the Roman and Byzantine empires), they found Syriac translations of Greek philosophical works. These writings were translated into Arabic, and for a time they became the foundation of Muslim philosophy. Eventually, they were rejected as being inconsistent with Islam. The mullahs decided that Muslims could accept practical works from the conquered people, but speculative thought was out.

Christians, however, had long since made their peace with integrating pagan philosophy with the Bible. In fact, since the time of the early Christian writers, theologians had argued that just as the Hebrew prophets were the Jewish world's road to the truth best expressed in Christianity, philosophers were the pagan world's road to that same truth. So when Christian scholars found out about the works of Aristotle in Spain, they began to translate them into Latin, the language of the church and of scholarship. These new texts immediately caused a buzz in the scholarly community, because here was a complete, well-developed worldview that answered all of the key philosophical questions that medieval scholars had grappled with. The only question was how to integrate the "New Aristotle" into the intellectual synthesis already in place with the advent of Platonic humanism.

SCHOLASTICISM

The answer was scholasticism. Although scholasticism is usually understood to be a type of philosophy or theology, it was actually a method of study that could be (and was) applied to any subject. It was based on a few fundamental assumptions. The first is that truth is knowable to the human mind, not exhaustively but substantially. We have already seen this assumption at work in the high standards for conviction in capital cases (see above). Second, truth is necessary for society, since any society not built on truth is built on a lie and thus will fall. The more truth, the more durable the civilization. The corollary is that the best guide to truth is the past, since if you study successful civilizations, you will find truth at their core.

This fit neatly with the idea that it was possible to integrate pagan philosophy into Christianity, since both are expressions of the same truth. (The idea that there might be different truths for different people would have been seen as ridiculous, because truth was seen as that which corresponds to reality, and reality does not vary from person to person; it is simply the way God made the world and how it works.) So although we can learn new things about the world, it is safer and more reliable to build our understanding of the world on the base of ancient authorities. This attitude is best summarized by Bernard of Chartres, a twelfth-century theologian:

> We are like dwarfs on the shoulders of giants, so that we can see more than they, and things at a greater distance, not by virtue of any sharpness of sight on our part, or any physical distinction, but because we are carried high and raised up by their [the ancient writers'] giant size.[1]

Since Latin does not distinguish between an "author" and an "authority," virtually any surviving writing from the Greco-Roman world should in principle be able to be integrated into a single system. Yet, at least on the surface, these writers sometimes contradict themselves. This is where the scholastic method comes in. The method consists of five parts.

1. Ask a question.
2. List the authorities that addressed the question and divide them into categories, pro and con.
3. Using a combination of logical tools from Aristotle and surprisingly sophisticated methods of linguistic analysis, analyze the authorities with the goal of resolving as many of the apparent contradictions as possible.

4. Present the solution to the problem.
5. Argue against your solution from as many angles as possible and respond to these anticipated objections.

Scholasticism was tailor-made to allow large amounts of new material to be integrated into an existing body of knowledge. In this case, Aristotle was gradually integrated into Platonic humanism, though the sheer quantity and range of Aristotle's writings meant that, over time, Aristotle began to dominate intellectual life in Europe. Aristotle wrote about everything, from logic to poetry to politics to science, and as a result he was looked to as the source of knowledge on just about everything, to such an extent that he became known as "the Master of those who know."

THE CONDEMNATIONS OF 1277

But there was a problem. Ancient Greek thought was in some ways incompatible with the Bible. For example, the Platonists believed that the world was eternal and noncontingent, that is, it was not created by a voluntary act of the One but existed of necessity simply because the One existed. The One could no more prevent itself from causing the universe to exist than you could prevent yourself from casting a shadow while standing in full sunlight. Aristotle similarly saw the universe as the eternal result of necessary processes, with "god" being the first cause in eternity past. The Bible, on the other hand, teaches that God created the world at a specific point in time by a voluntary act. Of course, since the pagan world's concept of god was impersonal, it was impossible for anything it does to be voluntary in any meaningful sense of the word, in contrast to the biblical understanding of God.

Medieval scholars recognized this problem and needed to find some way to solve it. Some scholars suggested the idea of "double truth," that is, that something could be true philosophically but not true theologically, and vice versa. In all likelihood, no one really believed this, but it was offered as a possible answer to the problem. Another more promising solution was to suggest that there were some things that could only be known through biblical revelation, so that the ancient philosophers worked things out as best they could from unaided reason, but that ultimately we know better because God has revealed truth to us that is inaccessible to pure human reason. Although untidy to a civilization that believed that truth was an integrated whole, this approach did at least preserve the full authority of Scripture, the reliability of the philosophers in nonbiblical matters, and a strong understanding of truth as an absolute, without contradictions.

While theologians were debating this, undergraduate professors were taking matters into their own hands. Since they revered Aristotle, they assumed that anything he said was right. So as they taught, when theological issues would come up (such as the nature of the created world), they taught their students Aristotle's answers rather than the Bible's. This upset both the theologians in the graduate faculties, because the undergraduate professors were not qualified to address these issues, and the church, since some of what was being taught was heretical. The theological faculty at the University of Paris, the most prominent theological school in Europe, eventually responded to this and other problems by issuing the Condemnations of 1277. Most of the 219 condemned statements dealt with things such as necromancy and courtly love, but a number did address ideas from Aristotle as well. The net result was that Aristotle could no longer be used as an independent source for theological ideas. He could be used to support or expand on theological concepts, but those ideas could not originate with Aristotle.

The Condemnations of 1277 were a major watershed for medieval thought. Although condemning ideas would seem to restrict freedom of thought and therefore to limit intellectual development, in the Middle Ages they actually liberated thinking from its slavish dependence on Aristotle. Remember, prior to this, most scholars thought that if Aristotle addressed any issue, that pretty much settled it. But the Condemnations restricted his use in the arena of theology. This may seem like a relatively minor thing. After all, how much theology could you learn from a pagan philosopher?

Theology, however, was a much broader subject in the Middle Ages than it is today. Questions about the origin of the universe were part of theology, since they clearly had theological implications. But beyond that, theology also included studies of the natural world. Today, we call this "science," but from the Middle Ages through the eighteenth century, it was called "natural philosophy" or "natural theology." The best way to understand its significance is to look back to Platonic humanism, where the physical world was studied as a vehicle to lead us back to God. In other words, understanding the physical universe was a means of understanding bigger philosophical and theological issues, since the world is an integrated whole. As a result, medieval scholars believed it was possible to learn moral and spiritual lessons from the physical world. This, in turn, meant that studying the natural world was actually considered a branch of theology. The Condemnations thus set natural philosophy free from its Aristotelian straitjacket.

MEDIEVAL SCIENCE

Medieval science may seem like an oxymoron, but work done by scholars, monks, and craftsmen helped to set the stage for the later scientific revolution. Among many examples that could be cited, two stand out. The first was in the area of *mechanics*. To build the great cathedrals of the thirteenth and fourteenth centuries, medieval architects needed to develop a solid understanding of statics, the branch of mechanics dealing with stationary objects. Medieval scholars also worked on basic questions of dynamics, the branch of mechanics dealing with moving bodies. Aristotle had a complete (though incorrect) theory of dynamics. With the Condemnations of 1277, medieval natural philosophy began to develop in new directions. For example, an early form of inertia was suggested, as was the idea (correct, as it turns out) that falling bodies move with uniformly accelerating motion.

A second example is in the area of *cosmology*. Nicholas Oresme, a fourteenth-century Franciscan, and Nicholas of Cusa, a fifteenth-century cardinal, both suggested that the earth could move around the sun rather than the other way around. Oresme argued that this would solve several problems in astronomy, though he also said that we knew this was not actually the case. Cusa went further, arguing that it was just as valid to have the earth go around the sun as the sun go around the earth since rest and motion were both relative, as was the center of the universe. Significantly, neither got into trouble with the church.

WORLDVIEW AND NATURAL PHILOSOPHY

At this point, it is helpful to reiterate the worldview ideas underlying the study of natural philosophy in the Middle Ages. The medieval mind assumed that the rational God created a rational universe and that human beings, made in the image of God, were rational as well and could understand the universe. Although they believed that miracles could occur, they also believed that God did not need to intervene actively for the world to function normally. God created it to operate in a certain way, and the rules that governed its behavior could be discovered by human investigation. Contrary to the assumptions of classical thinkers (including Aristotle), the best method of learning about the world was not deductive reasoning but direct study and examination of the world. The importance of this shift is hard to overstate, since it laid the foundation for the tremendous success of Western science in later centuries.

The impact of this worldview can best be seen in a comparison between Western Europe and the Islamic world. Although the medieval period is often described as a golden age for Muslim science, this is only partially true. Medieval Islam excelled in a number of important areas. As we have seen, they preserved and spread the writings of classical thinkers, notably Aristotle, and expanded technology and ideas from Asia into the Mediterranean basin, including, for example, numerical notation from India (so-called Arabic numerals) and cotton weaving from China. But the mullahs soon prohibited studying speculative thought (including philosophy) from non-Islamic sources. For example, the prominent Sufi scholar Abu Hamid al-Ghazali argued in his book *The Incoherence of the Philosophers* that Muslim philosophers who in any way called into question the teachings of the Qur'an or of Islam were infidels. This may sound similar to the Condemnations of 1277 except that al-Ghazali added that killing infidels was obligatory for all good Muslims. This kind of thinking put a real damper on philosophical development.

As a result, Muslim scholars excelled at practical learning such as geography, astronomy, and medical practice, as well as mathematics (including inventing algebra). What they did not do, however, was develop *science*, in the sense of explanations of *why* the physical world works the way it does. This highlights the second difference between orthodox Muslim thinkers, such as al-Ghazali, and the Condemnations of 1277. Islam teaches that Allah directly controls everything and can do as he pleases with the world. Seeking explanations of physical processes was thus either not possible or inappropriate. So, for example, al-Ghazali argued that the idea that there were natural laws was blasphemous because it denied Allah's freedom to govern the universe as he saw fit. Similarly, Ibn Rushd (known in Europe as Averroes) was dismissed from his position under the emir of Al-Andalus (Spain) because his rationalistic arguments collided with the emir's orthodox beliefs.

The Condemnations, as we have seen, had opened up inquiry into the physical world as a legitimate enterprise within the Christian worldview. Al-Ghazali and other orthodox Muslim thinkers effectively shut it down. As one example, consider reactions to the Black Death during the fourteenth century. Islam taught that since Allah controlled all things, disease was not spread by contagion but by the will of Allah, who alone determined who lived and who died during an outbreak of disease. As a result, Ibn Khatimah, a Muslim physician living in Spain, had to argue that plague was not caused by a contagion. The Arabs had believed in contagion before Islam, but now they knew better. It is open to debate whether he believed what he said, but it is clear that he believed he *had* to say it to keep from attracting unwanted attention from the religious and civil authorities. Ibn al-Khatib, another Spanish Muslim physician, argued that plague certainly was contagious. He was imprisoned in 1374 for holding non-Islamic views. A mob of people broke into the prison and lynched him, apparently in part because his views of contagion were non-Islamic.

While other Muslim scholars wrote plague tracts without generating the same kind of hostility, Ibn al-Khatib's fate is illustrative of an important worldview difference between Islam and Christianity. In Europe, plague may have caused popular hysteria, but the church and the scholars agreed that it was a natural event and sought to find both the physical explanation for the plague and a cure. The church opposed efforts to scapegoat Jews for causing the plague, pointing out that they were dying from it just as Christians were. Church and government officials also rejected the idea, put forth by groups such as the Flagellants, that the plague was a direct judgment of God on a corrupt society. Instead, they argued it was a natural phenomenon.

The most common explanation is found in the *Paris consilium*, written in 1348 for the pope by the theological faculty of the University of Paris. The *Paris consilium* explained that, although God was ultimately behind the plague because he is sovereign over everything that happens, the immediate cause was purely natural. Following Aristotle's and Hippocrates' theories of disease, they argued that a conjunction of Saturn and Jupiter caused the earth to release noxious vapors, and those vapors caused the plague. This in turn meant that to avoid infection, people needed to breathe purified air. So, for example, to keep from becoming infected, Pope Clement VI sat between two roaring fires (which proved successful, but not for the reasons he thought it did). Other people carried flowers on their shoulders or in packets to sweeten the air, a practice which eventually produced the corsage.

We know that this *Paris consilium* explanation is wrong, but however fanciful it may look to us, it shows a degree of faith in natural causation. While acknowledging God's ultimate control over all things, it does not view this control as being exercised arbitrarily: God works rationally, through secondary causes that we can search for and find. In the long run, the contrast between this view of the universe in the Latin West and the idea that Allah directly and immediately controls everything that happens in the world explains why the West would later outstrip the Muslim world in the development of science. The basis for Western success was already in place with the contrast in worldviews in the Middle Ages.

Interest in the details of the natural world was not limited to scholars. Medieval art became progressively more realistic as the intellectual activities of the scholars began to spread and influence aesthetics. The anonymous sculptor at the cathedral in Naumburg, Germany, began producing exceptionally realistic sculptures in the early 1200s, a good two hundred years before Italian Renaissance artists began to produce comparably realistic work.

The statue of one woman, Uta by name, was so beautiful that Adolf Hitler promoted her image as the picture of the ideal Aryan woman. Since the sculpture of her husband (Ekkehard) next to her was not so attractive, Hitler promoted another sculpture, known as the Bamberg Rider (possibly by the same artist), to be Uta's male counterpart.

Shortly after the Naumburg sculptures were made, similarly realistic sculptures began to appear on the cathedral in Reims, France. The same sculptor may have done these as well, but whether or not he did, these sculptures mark the beginning of a trend toward increasing realism in art. Illuminations in France; miniatures, portraits, and altarpieces in the Low Countries; and a host of other artwork mark an increasing appreciation for the physical world in shaping aesthetics and artistic technique in the late Middle Ages. Significantly, this movement predates the Italian Renaissance, and even where the two overlap chronologically, there is little evidence of the influence of Italian artists on artists north of the Alps. If anything, the influence is the other way around, as oil paint and the techniques for using it spread from the Low Countries to Italy.

Along with areas such as law, education, and natural philosophy, the Middle Ages led to enormous changes in economics and politics that once again laid the foundation for the subsequent development of Western civilization. This is the subject of the next chapter.

CHAPTER 5

MEDIEVAL ECONOMICS AND POLITICS

Just as it is with any other worldview, Platonic humanism and its successors had implications for much more of life than simply scholarship and law, particularly as additional ideas from Scripture were incorporated into them. One of the most important areas was their impact on economics.

THE MEDIEVAL ECONOMY

In this case, the emphasis on the goodness of the physical world as a creation of God that reflects his character was further strengthened by the idea of the intrinsic goodness of work. God worked in creating the world; therefore we as his image bearers should also work. Besides, according to Genesis, God put Adam to work tending the garden of Eden before Adam sinned. So work is a good thing.

THE ROOTS OF CAPITALISM

In keeping with Genesis, the medieval mind thought of work as production, either in agriculture or in manufacturing. As we have seen, monks in the monasteries were required (in principle) to engage in productive labor. But because they were also to live austere lives (again, at least in principle), they could not spend the income from their labors on conspicuous consumption. They could and did give to the poor, but what were they to do with the rest? If productive work was good, then investing the profits to increase production would also be good. And so, ironically, the stricter the monastic order, the more austere the lifestyle, the harder their work — the richer they became. The key was reinvesting profits to increase production, one of the central principles of capitalism. But without the initial concept, drawn from the Bible, of the inherent goodness of the physical world and of labor, this idea would not have emerged in the West any more than it did in any other region of the world.

Another key component of capitalism is property rights. The medieval world under the influence of Christianity had a much stronger emphasis on property rights than other cultures had. Even serfs had property rights. They may not have been allowed to leave their land, but they could not be evicted either. The same could not have been said of slaves in slave-based economies. Similarly, much of biblical law in the Old Testament focuses on rules for property ownership, so much so that not even kings could take land that belonged to a family. As a result, Thomas Aquinas argued that property was a fundamental right, and William of Ockham contended that since property is a right, it is more fundamental than laws and thus cannot be taken away arbitrarily by the government. This type of thinking set a standard that provided protection of personal property that was higher than in non-biblically based cultures. When this is combined with the biblical idea that people are entitled to enjoy the fruits of their labor, it provides a firm foundation for the idea of private property.

To understand the importance of these ideas, consider the case of Ali Pasha, the commander of the Ottoman fleet at the Battle of Lepanto (1571). This battle was won decisively by a coalition of Christian powers and prevented the Ottomans from extending their power into the western Mediterranean. When Ali Pasha's flagship was captured, his entire personal fortune was on board. Similar treasures were found on the galleys of other Muslim commanders. Even though Ali Pasha was the supreme commander of the Ottoman fleet and a powerful member of the nobility, he thought it necessary to keep his treasure close to prevent it from being confiscated by the sultan, should he become displeased with the admiral for any reason. This kind of arbitrary confiscation would have been illegal anywhere in the Christian world in the absence of a legal judgment because of the insistence on private property rights, based on biblical teaching about ownership and the right to enjoy the profits of your labor.

These same ideas of property rights, God's call to engage in productive work, and the reinvestment of profits also carried over into manufacturing. Although the most basic form of production was agriculture, craft work and manufacturing were also recognized as legitimate forms of production. Someone had to make the tools needed to work the fields, including the large and complex wheeled plows needed to cultivate the fertile but dense clay soils of the northern plains. Someone had to make mills, horseshoes, harnesses, houses, furniture, clothes, arms, and armor.

THE GUILD SYSTEM

As towns developed, craft industries grew larger, making products not just for local consumption but for export. To regulate the more important crafts, a system of guilds evolved in the towns. Each guild covered a single craft. Their main responsibility was setting rules of production and, to some extent, sale. So, for example, all shops in a guild might have to be on the same street to allow buyers to compare products and to make sure the rules of production were followed. The guilds also set production standards; for example, a chandlers guild (candle makers) would set a minimum weight for the candles and a minimum percent of animal fat in the wax. To do so was particularly important for crafts that would be exported, since the reputation of the town's products could be ruined if one shop exported inferior goods. Guilds set employment rules (the number of apprentices and journeymen who could be in a single shop, for example), and they regulated the entry of new masters into the guild and controlled the number of shops in the town. Contrary to what is often said, however, no guild was permitted to set prices; pricing was handled by competition. The object of all this was to maintain as level a playing field as possible between the guild shops. Some craftsmen would excel, but the intention was to prevent one master from competing unfairly and thus taking business from another.

In addition to regulating competition, there was another, less obvious reason for these rules. Guild members believed that their work was a calling from God, that they were following the command to "tend the garden" in a different way from the farmer, and thus that their work was being done to the glory of God. Production standards were set not simply for sound economic reasons, but because quality workmanship was seen as a legitimate end in itself. Whenever possible, guild members would leave identifying marks on their work, not so much for advertising or so that problems could be traced to their source, but as a sign of pride in their work.

And they had good reason for pride. Medieval craftsmen had production techniques we are hard-pressed to match today. At The Cloisters in New York City, which has the blue set of The Unicorn Tapestries, you can see that one of the tapestries has a brown background on the bottom rather than the royal blue of the others (and of the upper part of the tapestry). That tapestry was damaged, and when it was restored, modern dyes were used. Unfortunately, though they matched the color at the time, in a few decades the blue turned to brown. The medieval colors have remained true for nearly six hundred years. The point? The guild masters knew their craft, excelled in it, and took justifiable pride in their work. Further, each craft had its own patron saint, a sign that the craft itself was blessed and approved by God. In fact, guild members had to attend Mass together on the feast day of their patron saint. They also took care of the widows and orphans of guild masters, in keeping with well-known biblical commands about caring for the powerless. So the guilds represented not just a professional trade association but the union of religion and business in the spirit of the Platonic humanist worldview.

THE MEDIEVAL INDUSTRIAL REVOLUTION

Another little-known element of medieval production is the amount of technological innovation that occurred during the period. In agriculture, the heavy wheeled plow, the horse collar and horseshoe, and the scythe all contributed tremendously to the productivity of the fields. Waterpower was harnessed to grind grain, a technology that originated in the monasteries, incidentally. But once the waterwheel was developed, it was quickly adapted for other purposes, from operating the bellows in smithies to "fulling" cloth to making paper. In the textile industry, the spinning wheel replaced the distaff and drop spindle, making production of thread quicker and easier. New types of looms were invented that allowed weavers to produce much more cloth with no more work and to maintain and even increase the quality of the product. In metallurgy, new types of furnaces were developed that made smelting iron easier. It was even discovered that putting limestone in the furnaces with the ore resulted in a greater yield of iron. In the fifteenth century, Europeans actually developed the blast furnace.

The idea that ties nearly all of these inventions together is that while work is good, drudgery is not. Great ingenuity, effort, and expense went into producing labor-saving devices so that people could spend their time using their creativity rather than doing menial, repetitive tasks. The technologies were seen as enhancing work, making it more meaningful and valuable, not as taking it away. They also increased production, of course, but this was also recognized as good, fulfilling more effectively the vocation to till the garden as described in Genesis.

THE GROWTH OF TRADE

With urbanization and the expansion of production came the expansion of trade. Just to be clear, a medieval merchant was not a shopkeeper. Merchants dealt with long-distance trade and wholesaling and did little or no retailing. Because of the expense and danger of travel, they emphasized luxury goods, especially items that were high in value and low in bulk, such as spices, silks and other luxury cloth, furs, amber, and so on. Low-end and bulk commodities simply were not worth the effort. Merchants had their own guilds and were typically among the wealthiest and most influential non-nobles in the towns.

The problem, however, involved the meaning of work. Craftsmen and farmers produced things; merchants did not. In what way did merchants improve on what they sold? All they did was move it from place to place. They were certainly entitled to recompense for their expenses and for their time and labor, and to some profit as well, but how much should they legitimately make on trade, especially compared to the profit made by the producer, who, after all, did the *real* work? And yet merchants were wealthy — wealthier than almost any of the craftsmen they worked with. In fact, they frequently dictated to the crafts guilds what they should produce based on what the merchants expected would sell. This makes perfect sense from a business perspective, but it makes the *real* workers — the crafts guilds — subservient to people who provide a service (transportation of goods) without actually producing anything. And because of the medieval understanding of work, people found this troubling.

THE PROBLEM OF INTEREST

In tandem with the debate about merchants' profits was a debate about the emerging financial services industry. By the late tenth century, monasteries that had been producing profits from their land began lending money to feudal lords and charging them interest in the process. No doubt they saw this lending practice as simply another way of reinvesting their profits, but as the church moved to clean up abuses, this practice was called into question. The Bible prohibits lending money at interest. The law was intended to protect people who had become destitute and needed to borrow money to survive. Lending money at interest was seen as taking unfair advantage of your neighbor's misfortune, and thus was banned. Church reformers applied these laws more broadly to prohibit all lending at interest ("usury") between Christians, which had the effect of making commercial investment much more difficult.

With the growth of population, urbanization, manufacturing, and trade, however, some form of lending and other financial services became necessary. One solution involved the Jews. Since they were not subject to canon law, they could lend money at interest and were frequently forced to do so by kings and nobles, who then also felt free to default on those loans when convenient. But even within the Christian community, mechanisms were developed to pay interest on loans but to disguise the fact that this was happening.

For example, one system involved bills of exchange. In a bill of exchange, a borrower received one currency and paid back the loan in a different currency at some specified later time and in a different location (usually Bruges, the main money market in Europe). So, for example, you might receive a certain number of Florentine florins and agree to repay in English pounds six months later in Bruges. But since exchange rates were not fixed, by changing the currency you could manipulate the exchange rate to collect more than you lent, effectively charging interest without making it obvious that you were doing so. Bills of exchange were used for other purposes as well, such as currency speculation or simple purchases, but here they were especially important as a means of getting around canon laws against usury. Church officials probably knew what was going on but turned a blind eye, though it is unclear whether they did so because they knew it was necessary, would benefit from it, or couldn't prove guilt.

Eventually, the church would come to terms with both merchants and moneylenders. Theologians and canon lawyers came up with the idea of "just price," that is, the idea that prices needed to be fair while still allowing profit — not exorbitant profit, but profit nonetheless. Although impossible to enforce, this concept proved useful for justifying mercantile activity. And by the thirteenth century, theologians began to distinguish between consumption loans and investment loans. Consumption loans benefit only one person, and thus no interest can be charged for them; investment loans, however, have the potential to benefit both lender and borrower, and under these circumstances interest can be charged.

A number of specific reasons were given to justify interest — potential for default, loss of opportunity to use the money for profitable investments, and so on. But the bottom line was that canon law and theology evolved to suit the new circumstances of the age, expanding the concept of work and to some extent the legitimacy of profit.

WEALTH AND POVERTY

We may not conclude, however, that the church gave unqualified support for the emerging capitalist system. In fact, the church emphasized poverty as a greater good than wealth. Monks and nuns, who were considered to be following the highest road of spirituality, were required to take vows of poverty. After all, Jesus himself said, "Blessed are you who are poor" (Luke 6:20) and commented that "it is easier for a camel to go through the eye of a needle than for a rich man to enter the kingdom of God" (Luke 18:25). The legacy of austerity from the early church and the early influence of Neoplatonic otherworldliness further contributed to a distrust of this world.

In the early Middle Ages, poverty was rampant (except among the higher nobles, who believed they deserved their wealth), and no one except monks thought of poverty as a good. In general, only wealthier individuals tend to see anything positive about poverty. As the medieval economy grew and people prospered, salvation anxiety grew as well. To be sure, members of crafts guilds saw their work as a divinely approved calling and thus felt justified in enjoying the fruit of their labors. Merchants could not make the same claim, however, and thus were especially susceptible to wealth-induced worry about the state of their souls. For example, Saint Godric of Finchale (c. 1065 – 1170) began as an impoverished beachcomber and gradually built up his business until he became a wealthy merchant. He then gave away his wealth and became a hermit. For this, he was canonized after his death.

Similarly, in the thirteenth century, Saint Francis of Assisi, the scion of a merchant family, gave away everything he had and gathered a group of followers to live a life of "apostolic poverty." The idea here is that Jesus and his followers were poor and so clergy should be as well. Francis and his followers begged each day for their food for that day. They did not accept money, since they believed that living a hand-to-mouth existence was the best way to truly live by faith. In some ways, this approach harks back to the early monastics, who looked for more and more extravagant forms of asceticism as a means of proving their faith. Francis's ideas became so popular that other emerging groups such as the Dominicans, who did not emphasize apostolic poverty, had to become "mendicant" orders (in other words, they had to live by begging) to meet the popular concept of what a holy life should look like.

Francis may have wanted his followers to live by begging for the sake of their personal sanctity, but his actions were also intended as a criticism of the wealth and power that the church had accumulated. To understand how the church had become so powerful, we need to look at concepts of government — secular and sacred — and the worldview behind them.

MEDIEVAL POLITICAL THEORY

Medieval political theory and practice is a messy, complicated subject that includes multiple kinds of governments — manorial, feudal, royal, imperial, urban, and ecclesiastical — and competing ideas about the proper division of power between church and state, among other things, all of which were in flux during the thousand or so years that made up the Middle Ages. From a worldview perspective, the key to understanding the arguments and debates is found in the writings of two men who did more than anyone else to shape political thinking during the Middle Ages: Saint Augustine and (not surprisingly) Aristotle.

AUGUSTINE AND *THE CITY OF GOD*

Saint Augustine lived in the late fourth and early fifth centuries, in the declining years of the Roman Empire. He was a converted Neoplatonist who eventually became a bishop at Hippo Regius in North Africa. He spent much of his career trying to deal with challenges to orthodox Christianity from Manichaeism (a descendant of Gnosticism), Donatism, and Pelagianism. Many of his letters and writings deal with practical political and legal issues related to these problems. His most important work on politics, the massive book *The City of God*, was written in response to a different threat — a pagan revival buoyed by the sacking of Rome by the Visigoths. The pagans believed Rome was sacked because it turned away from its ancient gods. In *The City of God*, Augustine argued that the problem with Rome was not that it had become too Christian but that it was not Christian enough.

To understand Augustine's views on politics, we must begin with his views of human nature. According to Augustine, when God first created Adam and Eve in the garden of Eden, they were innocent but capable of sinning if they chose to do so (Latin, *posse peccare*). Once they ate the forbidden fruit, they and all of their descendents were so affected by sin that they could no longer prevent themselves from sinning (*non posse non peccare*). Jesus' death and resurrection made it possible for his followers to decide not to sin (*posse non peccare*), and those who go to heaven will no longer be able to sin (*non posse peccare*). What all of this means is that right now, we are in a world dominated by evil on both the individual and the institutional levels.

Augustine argued that there were two cities in the world. The first and most obvious is the City of Man — a city dominated by love of self and built around the lowest common denominator, namely, self-indulgence. In this city, virtue is completely absent. People may have good habits, enforced by social forces or coercion from the state, but true virtue is impossible since people ultimately love themselves more than others. They are incapable of not sinning. To prove his point, Augustine quoted Roman social critics who bemoaned the same problems as Augustine did. The difference is that the social critics claimed that this was something new, while Augustine saw it as present throughout Roman history, and indeed in any earthly empire.

In this environment, government is essential to prevent a complete moral breakdown and anarchy. Its existence is justified by the need to restrain evil. But the government itself is based on self-love and is therefore more interested in self-aggrandizement and maintaining power than in promoting the good. Government is, in fact, organized oppression; in a word, it is evil — a necessary evil, but evil nonetheless. Even Christian emperors were part of the City of Man, and though Augustine paid a certain amount of lip service to their goodness, he clearly saw them as part of the corrupt, self-centered world.

In contrast to the City of Man, the City of God is characterized by love of God and therefore love of neighbor. All true goodness and virtue reside here, along with everything that makes human society possible. Such things are only found among the people who belong to Christ, who are capable of not sinning and thus practicing true virtue. Nonetheless, despite the need for virtue in society, actual human societies belong to the City of Man. Augustine commented that Cain, the first murderer, founded a city; the righteous Abel, whom Cain murdered, did not. In the end, the City of Man, with its vast accomplishments and even vaster abuses, will come to naught; only the City of God and its values will endure.

But we need not conclude that the two cities must always and necessarily be at war. First, the City of Man always seeks its own stability and equilibrium, which is essentially a kind of peace, even if misshapen by greed and selfishness. To attain stability, government legislates at the level of the minimum standards needed to preserve society. The City of Man thus emphasizes toleration as the means to preserve peace in the Empire. The City of God is also seeking peace but of a different sort. Though on pilgrimage in this world, it can support the City of Man in its quest for "peace," with the goal of furthering God's mission in this world.

The two cities also use the same resources and social structures and seek protection through the same laws, but they do so for very different purposes and with different means. The City of Man uses terror from the enforcement of laws to compel good behavior and to promote a peace and stability in which good people can live their lives unmolested by the wicked. In contrast, the only weapons that the City of God has against evil are penitence, grace, and mercy. Indeed, one role of the magistrate is to use terror to encourage penitence, thus bringing the two cities closer.

Ultimately, in practice, the two cities can act to support each other. The City of God can encourage the City of Man toward the good without itself taking on the responsibility of making laws, and the City of Man can promote good behavior through the courts (hopefully leading to penitence), defend society, and promote peace so that the City of God can flourish.

Augustine's vision of government is thus profoundly pessimistic, based as it is on the idea that in the absence of grace, humanity moves always toward selfishness and evil. Yet at the same time, despite worldly government's corruption, he does carve out a space where a Christian can serve in the government and even gives the government a role in suppressing evil and encouraging repentance. His ambivalence toward government is not simply theological — his understanding of Scripture gave him both the idea of original sin (our inbred tendency toward evil) and the idea that we are to obey the government — but also historical. The church had for centuries existed as a despised and sometimes persecuted minority. In his day, however, the Empire was led by Christians. The church thus had to be separate from the state, but at the same time there needed to be some theological framework for understanding how the two could work together in the new circumstances the church was facing after Constantine.

CHURCH AND STATE

Significantly, Augustine never identified the City of God with the church, despite giving it his unqualified support in other ways. The church would not be identified with the City of God until Pope Gelasius I at the end of the fifth century. He argued that the church and emperor had separate functions that reinforced each other, though he also argued for the "spiritual" superiority of the priestly side over civil government and for the primacy of the pope over the entire church, a relatively new idea at this point. Later theologians and popes (beginning in the late tenth and eleventh centuries) would run with these ideas, arguing that just as the eternal is superior to the temporal, so the church is superior to the state and the pope as the head of the church is supreme over all earthly monarchs.

Some theologians argued that popes could appoint and depose rulers at will, since the job of the ruler was to enforce righteousness and only the pope could decide what that was and thus determine if the ruler was legitimate. The identification of the church with the City of God was also one of the roots of the idea of the infallibility of the church and especially of the papacy. Since error, sin, and corruption are found in the City of Man, it was only logical to think that the church as the City of God was free from these evil influences.

Direct papal involvement in secular government began in the eighth century, when the pope was given a large territory in central Italy over which he became a secular ruler as well as the presumed leader of the universal church. This, of course, fit in with the earlier bishops' practice of stepping in to take over the administration of the towns when Roman rule collapsed, as well as the monarchs' habit of bringing bishops into their administration. Add to this the fact that administrative units in the church had typically coincided with political units, and you have a recipe for conflict over ecclesiastical and political authority.

Needless to say, emperors and kings had a different take on political theory and the relationship of church and state. Constantine, for example, had called into session the Council of Nicea; and in the late eighth century, Charlemagne said that it was his job to rule, and the pope's job to pray for him. When the conflict between pope and emperor exploded in the eleventh century, imperial theorists appealed to Byzantine tradition and, increasingly, Roman law. They placed the emperor below the laws of nature and reason but above human legislation and in a separate, God-ordained sphere that had its own powers and prerogatives independent of the church. The Augustinian distinction between the City of God and the City of Man was also employed, with the argument that power in the secular world — not simply political power, but wealth as well — could not properly be exercised by clerics.

THE WEALTH OF THE CHURCH

The church hierarchy, on the other hand, thought it was perfectly appropriate that they be wealthy. They would cite passages from Augustine that declared that all of the world properly belongs to the righteous, and thus claimed that wealth should flow to the church as the City of God and the seat of righteousness. Further, the pope, as the vicar of Christ, who is the King of kings and Lord of lords, needed to display the glory of the God whom he represented. Kings do not send beggars in rags to represent them as ambassadors; they send people who can show the grandeur and power of the kingdom that sent them. In the same way, God should be represented on earth in a way that displays the majesty of his kingdom.

Unfortunately for the church, many people did not see this issue the way the church hierarchy did. Virtually all medieval reform movements (as well as heretical movements) saw the wealth of the church as a fundamental problem. With political power, land, and influence, the church had grown very wealthy, with members of the higher clergy and even some monks living in luxury. It was easy for poor people to resent the fact that they had to pay tithes to a rich bishop and for wealthy people to turn their own salvation anxiety into attacks on the wealth and power of the church. Saint Francis's insistence on poverty was just one example. Although he was careful to emphasize his loyalty to the church, he was clearly critical of its wealth and its secular power. As a result, the emperors courted Franciscan theologians as part of their intellectual defense against the popes.

ARISTOTLE AND POLITICS

With the renewed interest in Aristotle, new weapons were added to the imperial arsenal against the claims of the papacy. Aristotle had argued that communities arose organically, and as they developed into self-sufficient bodies, they established governments and laws as expressions of "natural law" — the moral law that was part of nature. These communities worked toward the common good under the direction of the ruler, and each part made its own distinctive contribution toward this goal.

In its Christianized version, this model argued that even with the effects of sin, the natural ends and functions of society were not lost, and thus this society was legitimately pursuing the good. The practical upshot is that secular government was a proper element of the natural moral order created by God, not dependent on the papacy for its legitimacy. Aristotle thus offered a far less pessimistic view of society than Augustine held, one that appealed not just to emperors, kings, and nobles but also to the guilds that dominated urban life. In all of these cases, they saw themselves as following a divine calling, which integrated quite naturally into the idea of the sanctity and goodness of the community.

At the same time, however, theologians had to wrestle with the effects of sin on government. Once again, Aristotle helped them, having argued that there were three basic types of government, each of which could exist in positive or negative forms:

- The first pair is *monarchy and tyranny.* Both are characterized by rule by a single individual, though in a monarchy this individual rules for the common good, whereas a tyrant rules for self-interest. A strong point of monarchies is that they can respond quickly in an emergency, but their weakness is that if the monarch makes a mistake, no one can correct it.

- The second pair is *aristocracy and oligarchy*. Both have to do with rule by a small group or council, again with the distinction that aristocracies work for the common good, while oligarchies pursue their own selfish interests. The strength of the aristocracy is its ability to deliberate to make wise decisions; its weakness is that it can be slow to act in an emergency.

- The last pair is *republic and democracy*. A republic is rule by representation; a democracy is literally rule by the mob, through direct decision making by the populace. Democracies are a degenerate form of government because they are inevitably susceptible to falling under the control of a demagogue, a charismatic leader who can sway people to her or his own ends rather than to the common good. Republics are buffered from this danger by the representatives who run the government, yet this system of government also retains the great advantage of buy-in from the citizens.

ORIGINAL SIN AND GOVERNMENT

Although Aristotle was a pagan, his warnings about degenerate forms of government were remarkably similar in some respects to Augustine's analysis of human sin and the selfishness that characterizes the City of Man. Even the positive forms of government had their weaknesses, signifying another element of human fallibility. Christian Aristotelian political thinkers were thus left with a problem: How do we design a form of government that takes advantage of the strengths of the various types of government while avoiding the weaknesses?

One potential answer was the idea of *limited government*. Given the doctrine of original sin — all people tend to do evil — giving unlimited power to anyone was a recipe for disaster. As a result, all medieval governments had constitutional limits on their powers, with a system of checks and balances in place. These checks typically came from a "mixed" government drawn from at least two of the types of government that Aristotle had defined. So, for example, kings (monarchial principle) always had a royal council or court (aristocratic principle) to advise them and to help them avoid mistakes. Towns, which were typically a form of republic in the Middle Ages, always included councils of the wealthiest citizens or nobles (aristocratic principle) and sometimes a de facto prince such as the Doge (chief magistrate) of Venice (monarchial principle) as well. By setting up "mixed states," the hope was that the strengths of one system would counteract the weaknesses of the other and that the effects of sin would be minimized by keeping arbitrary power out of any one person's hands.

LIMITED GOVERNMENT IN THE CHURCH

As an aside, the church had some limited elements of mixed government as well, but they were derived from a different theoretical base. The early church elected its leaders — a practice that continued in some areas of the church. Monks and nuns traditionally elected their abbots and abbesses; in fact, monasteries were the first communities in history in which all members had an equal say in elections. Once an abbot or abbess was elected, however, in keeping with their vow of obedience, the monks or nuns did not have the right to supervise or challenge their leader's decisions, at least in principle. (In practice such challenges did happen occasionally. Monks periodically revolted and threw out their abbot if they did not like their food, for example, but this was rare.) Similarly, the important clergy in the cathedrals elected their bishops, again at least in principle. In this case, secular rulers and the pope usually had a great deal of influence over who was eligible to run for the office. Even the pope was elected by the College of Cardinals, who were technically the priests of the city of Rome.

The underlying principle is a distant echo of the idea of spiritual equality of all believers — the belief that the members of a community within the church are equal and thus should all have a say in selecting leaders. These elections are also an example of one of the most fundamental principles of medieval law, namely, that those who are affected by a new policy, regulation, or law have a right to a say before it is implemented. The members of the community thus have a right to weigh in on who will be their leader.

After the elections took place, however, the republican principle disappeared. The church was extremely hierarchical and was based on the monarchial principle, especially from the eleventh century on. Bishops and popes had courts (Latin, *curiae*) that they worked with, but except for the constraints of canon law, bishops could run their dioceses as they saw fit, subject to review by their spiritual superiors. As the top of the hierarchy, papal decisions were not subject to review. Popes could even issue dispensations for violations of canon law, so there were few, if any, theoretical constraints on papal power and authority in the church.

After a period in which there were multiple people claiming to be popes, each supported by different sets of kingdoms, a movement grew to place the pope under the authority of a general council of the church. Although this movement succeeded in ending the schism and establishing a single pope, he and his successors were able to undermine later councils and to declare heretical the idea that a general council was superior to the pope.

NATURAL LAW AND INALIENABLE RIGHTS

Another check on civil government involved the idea of *rights*. Although we typically associate the idea of inalienable rights with the Declaration of Independence and one of its primary influences, the theories of British political philosopher John Locke, the idea itself comes from medieval political theory. As beings created in the image of God, humans have a number of natural rights that the state itself cannot violate. As we have seen, they include the right to property. The right to life is also assumed, and there are some tentative moves toward a limited idea of liberty — mostly in the form of limitations on the jurisdiction of civil and ecclesiastical government, so that the "liberties" of different groups are preserved. So, for example, the Magna Carta states that the English church is to be "free" and its "liberties unimpaired" by the crown, and confirms the "liberties" of the city of London.

The concept of natural law lent further support to the emerging idea of inalienable rights. In this context, natural law refers to the idea that God wove moral laws into the fabric of the universe. Living (or ruling) according to those laws leads to goodness in this world, while violating them will lead to chaos and evil. Legislation must conform to the dictates of natural law, since "an unjust law is no law." This provides a foundation for criticizing government and finds its echo in Thomas Jefferson's argument that the pursuit of happiness (by which he meant goodness and virtue) is an inalienable right. As we have seen, even at their most imperial, kings were below the laws of nature and reason, so even *they* needed to act in conformity to natural law.

SUMMARIZING THE MEDIEVAL WORLDVIEW

Far from being a stagnant, backward era, the nearly thousand years that made up the Middle Ages were in fact a dynamic period that laid the foundation for Western civilization. From this too-brief summary of the period, several worldview ideas are obvious.

- The medievals assumed that the world was real and that it was created by God with its own integrity but that it also mirrors God's nature and character.
- We, as beings made in the image of God, can understand the world, and thus we can learn both by studying the world itself and by using our reason to interpret the world and its significance.
- Since the world was created by a good God and reflects his nature, it is also inherently moral. We can learn moral lessons from the universe, and our laws must conform to natural moral law.
- Since we are made in the image of the God who "worked" in creating the world, we are meant to work as well. We each have a calling, which we are to carry out for the glory of God.
- Since the world is good, our use of the world's resources for production is good as well and is sanctified by God. Thus we are free to enjoy the fruits of our labor and to reinvest our profits to further increase production.
- Though the world is good, there is also evil in it, and this evil finds its home in the human heart. As a result, governments are necessary to restrain evil, though they themselves are corrupt and need to be restrained through limited government, checks and balances, and the higher laws of nature and reason.
- Ultimately, however, nothing in this world can solve the problem of the heart. The solution to our problem is found

in grace, penitence, and forgiveness, with the church — identified with Augustine's City of God — as the sole vehicle through which we can achieve salvation. The institutional church may have had its problems, but to the medieval mind it was the only game in town when it came to salvation. So we are to work hard in our calling, seek virtue and righteousness, and tie into the church's sacraments and rituals as the means to achieve heaven, the goal and purpose of our lives.

The basic elements of this worldview would remain in place long after the end of the Middle Ages, though it would be modified in important ways in the succeeding centuries. In fact, a series of major problems emerged through the early Modern period (the sixteenth through eighteenth centuries) that would challenge important elements of this worldview. The next chapter discusses these challenges.

CHAPTER 6

THE **BREAKDOWN** OF THE **MEDIEVAL MODEL**

The medieval worldview evolved over centuries through economic expansion, political centralization, church reform, and the recovery of Aristotle. Through all these changes, a number of basic ideas drawn from the Bible, the church fathers, and the classical past remained relatively constant as guiding principles for society. Even the Black Death, an outbreak of plague that killed 30 to 40 percent of the population of Europe, failed to shake the worldview.

Starting in the late 1400s, however, Europe was jolted by a series of movements and discoveries that threatened the underlying pillars of medieval thought. The Italian Renaissance, the Protestant Reformation, the European discovery of the Americas, and the rediscovery of an ancient form of skepticism set the stage for momentous changes in the European worldview.

TOO MUCH INFORMATION: THE ITALIAN RENAISSANCE

People often describe the Italian Renaissance as the beginning of the modern world, a time of light and discovery when people threw off the ignorance, superstition, and darkness of the Middle Ages and took on a more progressive, optimistic, rational, and secular approach to life — a time when "the world is bright, and all is right, and life is merry and gay," to quote Arthur and Guenevere in the song from *Camelot* titled "What Do the Simple Folk Do?"

This view of the Renaissance is wrong on all counts (or almost all — the Italian sun is bright). First, as we saw in the last chapter, the medieval world was not as static and bleak as this caricature suggests. A great deal of development and creative energy penetrated all areas of life. Second, as we will see, even though they did not realize it, Renaissance thinkers had far more in common with the medieval worldview than they did with either the ancient or modern worldviews. Third, Renaissance thought was hardly progressive and forward looking. The very word *renaissance* means "rebirth" and refers to a rebirth of classical civilization, of ancient Greece and Rome. In other words, they used the ancient past as the measuring rod for everything. How is that progressive?

As for optimism, one of the themes of Renaissance writers was *the decay of nature*:

- Everything in nature dies and decays;
- human societies exist in the natural world;
- therefore all human societies (including ours) will die and decay.

After all, Rome fell, so why should we escape? Renaissance writers may have been positive about their society's accomplishments, but they never expected them to last.

What about science? The Renaissance was the golden age of magic theory for explaining the physical universe.

Secular? Most of the art was religious (it was either paid for by the church or intended to be displayed in a church), and all of the major writers and thinkers saw the world as anchored in God, with God providing a standard of values for the society.

If virtually everything we have been taught about the Italian Renaissance is wrong, what was it really about? The Renaissance was born in the fourteenth century, an era that was arguably the worst in European history. It was shot through with problems — economic decline, continent-wide crop failures, the Hundred Years War, the papacy being moved to Avignon, multiple popes, and, of course, the Black Death. In this context, people began to think that the world had gone seriously wrong and that something better had to be out there. In southern Europe and especially in Italy, they had right in front of them evidence of a better world — the remains of Roman monumental architecture, roads, aqueducts, and artwork.

To make a long story short, Italian thinkers in the fourteenth century began to argue that Rome was the epitome of civilization, and when Rome fell, civilization ended. Quite naturally, then, these writers looked to Rome and Greece as sources of values and standards for just about everything — art, literature, education, philosophy, military organization, political structures, and so on. As Europe began to recover from the devastation of the fourteenth century, Renaissance thinkers began to believe that civilization was making a comeback and began to talk about ancient civilization (which was still the standard by which all things were measured) and "modern" civilization. Everything that came between was a blank — the "dark ages," an era of barbarism when civilization simply did not exist. This is where the term *Middle Ages* comes from. Have you ever wondered what the Middle Ages were in the middle of? To Renaissance historians, it was that empty period between two eras of civilization, the ancient and the modern. This was their self-image, and it carries over into our thinking about the Renaissance today.

Of course, as we have seen, medieval scholastic thinkers also looked to the ancient world as a source for truth, but Italian Renaissance writers were far more obsessed with classical civilization than their northern counterparts. This could be taken to ridiculous lengths. For example, given the scholastic method, northern scholars focused their education on *logic*; the Italians (following ancient Roman precedent) believed that *rhetoric* should be the centerpiece of education. The greatest Roman rhetorician was Cicero, and so they tried to model everything they did after him. Some, even in the church, went so far as to refuse to use any words Cicero had not used himself. This was a real problem, since Cicero was a pagan. How do you talk about Jesus Christ when Cicero did not use his name? As a result, the "Ciceronians" would substitute "Jupiter" for Christ, since Jupiter was the king of the gods. Some Ciceronians went even further and refused to use any *form* of a word that Cicero had not used. For example, if there was no example of a word as a possessive, they refused to use it as a possessive.

Even those who did not go to these extremes, however, used classical sources differently from the scholastics. Rather than trying to integrate the texts into a larger body of knowledge or mining statements out of them that could be used as building blocks for logical constructs, the Italian scholars studied them as independent literary works in their own right, analyzing grammar, vocabulary, rhetorical devices, and so on, to come to an understanding of what the author actually meant rather than trying to fit him into an existing logical system. After all, the ancients were the real masters. Why try to integrate them into the thought of the ignorant, barbaric people who came after them?

This obsession with the ancient world meant that Renaissance thinkers wanted to get their hands on everything they could from the ancient world — coins, statues, art, chunks of buildings, everything. They were especially interested in manuscripts of ancient works, the older the better. Their systematic effort to rediscover ancient texts only brought them as far as the era of Charlemagne, when the oldest surviving copies of most ancient texts were made, but many forgotten texts were recovered nonetheless. With the influx of Greek refugees fleeing the expansion of the Ottoman Empire into Byzantine territory, knowledge of Greek language and literature grew as well. Some scholars learned Hebrew and Arabic and even studied magical texts believed (incorrectly) to come from ancient Egypt (the so-called "Hermetic" tradition), with the goal of incorporating all of these into one coherent system of thought.

THE GRAND SYNTHESIS

And therein lay the problem. Renaissance thinkers were still far more medieval than modern. They believed with the medievals that truth existed and could be known with certainty. They also believed (obviously) that the best guide to the truth was the past, and that a unified system of truth could be found by studying past authors, aiming at a grand synthesis of all human knowledge.

For example, Marsiglio Ficino, one of the most influential scholars of the fifteenth century, combined Plato and other ancient writers with Christianity, while giving Christianity priority in the system. He developed a form of the ancient Platonic hierarchy of being that placed man (yes, I mean adult males) in the middle position of the hierarchy. This made man a microcosm of the universe, since, like God and the angels, he was a spiritual being who had eternal life, but, like animals, he was also a physical being bound by time. This gave man his unique "dignity."

Ficino also believed that when you love something in this life, you exchange souls with it; it is thus important to love the right things. If you love gold, you lose your soul since gold has no soul to give you. If you love a woman, you are endangering your soul since women are fickle and are unlikely to reciprocate your love. But if you love the right person — by implication, a man — and the love is reciprocated, you exchange souls and thus are safe. (There is a reason why many Renaissance figures are thought to be homosexuals, namely, entrenched misogyny. It may be that for some, life was, in fact, "merry and gay.") And such love can lead you by analogy to love of God, the ultimate purpose of life, by progressing up the hierarchy of being.

Ficino's younger protégé, Giovanni Pico della Mirandola, took these ideas one step further. Pico was a brilliant scholar and linguist who was fluent in Italian, Latin, and Greek and was one of the first Christians in the era who had a good working knowledge of Hebrew and Arabic. His synthesis was built from all available sources (pagan, Jewish, Christian, and Muslim) without giving Christianity a privileged position in the system — a fact that got him into some trouble with the church.

Pico argued that man has no fixed place in the hierarchy of being at all, but that by his choices he can determine his own place. If he chooses to love gold, he becomes quite literally lower than the animals; if he lives for his appetites, he is a beast; if he loves God, he can ascend higher than the angels. This, in Pico's system, is what gave man his unique dignity. Pico described this by quoting the ancient Greek philosopher Protagoras: "Man is the measure of all things." To Pico, this meant that we have it within our ability to span the entire created world by our choices and our love. This phrase, which has been taken as a summary of Renaissance humanism, is not a statement about people setting their own standards of right and wrong or being autonomous from God. Rather, it is embedded in a system that is anchored in God and in which there are clearly right and wrong choices. In other words, it is hardly a secular system of thought.

The problem for Pico was that his system left little room for original sin or the role of the church and the sacraments in mediating salvation. When he published his "900 Theses," in which he laid out his system and challenged any and all comers to debate them, the Inquisition in Rome, where Pico was living, indicated that they would be very interested in discussing the theses with him. At that point, Pico decided that Florence would be a much healthier place to live and skipped town.

Ficino and Pico generated the two best-known of the Renaissance syntheses. Each includes a complete worldview — metaphysics, epistemology, ethics, the meaning and purpose of life, and so on. They are not complete philosophical systems but rather are more poetic descriptions of the world, focused on the dignity of man. It is not clear how many people bought into these worldviews, however.

THE FATAL FLAW

Pico's problems with church doctrine point to a larger underlying problem that applies to both Pico and Ficino, namely, that the various systems of thought that went into their syntheses were not really compatible with each other, and as a result, these scholars' methodology made their goal unattainable. Earlier on, the thirteenth-century scholastic theologians had taken on a similar project to that of the Renaissance thinkers, producing massive works, such as Aquinas's *Summa theologica*, to bring the "sum" total of knowledge together into one work. The scholastics soon discovered that this project was too big and the sources too contradictory to produce a true synthesis. By the fifteenth century, they had largely given up on writing any more summae and instead concentrated on more limited topics in works called *quodlibet* (Latin for "whatever").

Renaissance thinkers did not know about or were uninterested in these earlier attempts to systematize all knowledge — they refused to read the barbaric Latin of the scholastics — and so they continued with the earlier medieval goal of building a grand synthesis. Now, however, instead of having just the texts available to the scholastics, they had far more Roman, Greek, Jewish, Muslim, and "Egyptian" sources to try to integrate into the mix. If the scholastics could not do this, there was no way the Renaissance thinkers could, especially since their major tool was rhetoric, not logic. And just as had happened with the scholastics, the next generation of Renaissance scholars stopped trying to build the grand synthesis, realizing that the sources they had were too many and too contradictory to bring together into a single system.

This in turn posed other even more basic questions. If a grand synthesis was impossible because the sources were contradictory and there was no way to reconcile them, what was the point of scholarship? The original goal had proven to be impossible, so what should scholars be trying to accomplish? And what does the failure to find the grand synthesis say about the nature of knowledge? People still believed that truth was absolute and knowable, but how do you find it if past authors could not agree on it? The assumption for centuries had been that ancient writers all told of the same truth from different perspectives and with different vocabulary, but if they truly contradict each other, how do you determine who (if anyone) is right?

In essence, the Renaissance was a victim of its own success. They had accomplished their task of recovering the surviving knowledge of the ancient world, and vast amounts of new texts had been made available. But at the same time, the overwhelming amount of new material caused their broader intellectual project to collapse under its own weight. Of course, the scholastics had weathered this kind of disappointment earlier, and it might be that Renaissance thinkers would have as well, had this been the only problem they were facing. As it is, however, it was only the first of the challenges Europe faced during this period.

KILLING FOR THE PRINCE OF PEACE: THE REFORMATION AND THE WARS OF RELIGION

A second major challenge faced by Europe in the early modern period was the Protestant Reformation, a movement that began as a theological challenge to blatant abuse within the church but ended up splitting the church in the Latin world into multiple competing factions. The details of how and why this happened need not concern us here.[1] Suffice it to say that new methods of study from the Renaissance led to new answers to old questions, so much so that the new approaches to theology could no longer be accommodated within the Catholic Church.

The Protestant challenge began with questions of salvation. Protestants argued that we are saved by faith, not works; Catholics believed that both faith and works were necessary for salvation. Protestants also believed that if we are saved by faith, the sacraments are not necessary to obtain forgiveness of sins; in Catholicism, the sacraments are the principal means by which our sins are forgiven.

The Protestants also believed that the only reliable way of answering theological questions was the Bible. They took the Renaissance tendency to look for truth in the oldest available texts to its logical conclusion. The earliest, purest source for Christianity was the Bible, and so it was to be the sole authoritative source for "faith and practice." Protestants thus rejected the church, the papacy, and tradition except insofar as they reflected what the Bible taught. Catholics believed that both Scripture and tradition were sources of authority, and that tradition guided the interpretation of Scripture. This approach functionally makes tradition primary since it is simultaneously an independent source of authority and the gatekeeper to the Bible.

PROTESTANTISM AND WORLDVIEW

Protestantism raised a number of important worldview issues beyond those concerned with how we can know religious truth. Among other things, it elevated the secular world to equal importance with the church. Protestants insisted that all believers are priests. Pastors had a role in the community that differed from that of laypeople, but not one that was qualitatively different from other professions. The idea of one's profession as a sacred calling — an idea that was at the root of the guild system — became more central to religious life, since the call to be a craftsman was no less important in the eyes of God than the call to be a pastor. Both were essential to the proper ordering of the community.

Further, in Protestant territories the church and state were much more tightly integrated than in Catholic areas. Each Protestant state had its own church, answerable to no one outside itself. The church's structure generally paralleled the state's, with bishops heading the churches in territories run by a prince, and councils running the churches in the republican cities. In most Protestant areas, the church was actually a branch of the state, with pastors as paid civil servants.

In the old war between pope and emperor, the emperor won hands down in Protestant areas. But despite this cozy relationship, Protestant reformers were always careful to draw boundaries between ecclesiastical and civil responsibilities. They were eager to avoid the "illicit usurpation" of civil authority by the church, which was one of their complaints about the Catholic Church. Conversely, they did not want the state interfering too much in purely religious matters, which were best left in the hands of the pastors and theologians to whom God gave those responsibilities within the community. At the same time, in some places, the lines between civil and ecclesiastical functions blurred, particularly in areas of social welfare and sometimes when it came to enforcing moral standards in the community.

REVITALIZING CATHOLICISM

One of the reasons Protestantism grew so fast was the state of the Catholic Church in the early sixteenth century. Virtually every level of the church, from pope to parish priest, was riddled with corruption. Of course, there were many sincere clergy, but the problems were nonetheless widespread and were magnified in the popular imagination. The only reason the church did not face a significant challenge earlier was that it held a monopoly on a product everyone needed, namely, salvation. Once Martin Luther broke that monopoly, the floodgates opened and Protestantism spread rapidly.

For its part, the Catholic Church tried to stem the tide with only limited effect until it began a systematic program to clean up its act. The church began to enforce moral standards across the board among the clergy. Bishops were required to live in their diocese and preach; priests were educated; the papacy and the curia took their responsibilities to the church more and more seriously; missionaries were sent to Asia, North America, South America, and to Protestant areas in Europe. The effect of all this was a revitalized Catholicism, and some areas reconverted.

THE CONFLICT INTENSIFIES

The rise of Protestantism and the revitalization of Catholicism raised important questions for people in the sixteenth century, the most pressing of which had to do with which of the competing churches was right. In an era of trust in absolutes, people thought that making the wrong choice could cost them their souls. By the same token, most people believed passionately in their churches and saw dissenters as superstitious idolaters or heretics. This posed a particularly acute problem for rulers, who almost invariably believed that religious unity was a practical necessity for a state's survival, and further that it was their divine responsibility to support the true church. The most notable example in Protestant areas was England, where Henry VIII viciously attacked anyone who disagreed with him, and Elizabeth I banned Catholic priests from the kingdom (largely because some had been implicated in plots to assassinate her).

In several Catholic kingdoms, monarchs either initiated or were embroiled in full-scale religious wars during the second half of the sixteenth century. Charles V, the Holy Roman emperor, fought the two Schmalkaldic Wars in an ultimately futile attempt to force Protestant territories to return to Catholicism. Later, Charles's son Philip II of Spain fought a civil war in his possessions in the Netherlands that was triggered by a combination of anti-Spanish nationalism and religious dissent. Eventually, the Netherlands would be partitioned, with the north becoming independent (and Protestant) and the south remaining as part of the Spanish Empire (and Catholic).

In France, an interminable series of wars of religion were fought between the Catholic monarchy, the ultraconservative Catholic League, and a strong Protestant faction headed by many high-ranking members of the Protestant nobility. The wars in France were unusually destructive, not simply because they lasted so long (from 1562 well into the seventeenth century) but also because the two sides had radically opposing worldviews and thus truly hated each other. Popular Catholicism in France was obsessed with reports of signs and portents, apocalyptic expectations, and fear of the antichrist (i.e., Protestants), a state that historian Denis Crouzet calls "eschatological anguish."[2] The Catholics believed God expected them to fight for him and to exterminate the heretics. The Protestants, on the other hand, rejected this *Weekly World News* approach to religion, preferring a more rational worldview drawn from Calvinism and seeing the Catholics as ignorant and superstitious.

These differing outlooks and the fear or contempt of the other side led to major atrocities during the wars. The biggest of these was the Saint Bartholomew's Day Massacre (1572), in which Protestants in Paris during a truce in the Wars of Religion were butchered in the streets. When word spread, copycat massacres occurred throughout France. The best estimates are that about 2,000 were killed in Paris and perhaps 20,000 across the kingdom, making it the worst mass murder in history prior to the twentieth century. Eventually, by a dynastic accident, the head of the Protestant side (Henry of Navarre) inherited the throne of France. To secure his position, he converted to Catholicism and then issued an edict that allowed limited Protestant worship and provided safeguards for the Protestant community. This action stabilized the situation until his son's reign (Louis XIII), when there was yet another relatively brief religious war.

POLITICAL THEORY

The Wars of Religion helped spur two rising developments in political thought. The first, in the wake of the Saint Bartholomew's Day Massacre, was a systematic exploration of *resistance theory*, that is, dealing with the question, "When is it legitimate to resist the government?" The key issue was determining under what circumstances a legal king would become an illegitimate tyrant who could be deposed or even killed.

The second political development was in many ways the opposite of resistance theory. In the face of the challenges posed by religious division, some thinkers began to suggest that the only solution was to put more and more power into the hands of the king and to insist on unconditional obedience to him, an idea known as *absolutism.* Just as a soldier has no right to decide whether or not a war is legitimate but must submit to the decisions of his superiors, so too people must submit to the ruler, whether or not he was right.

The idea of the *divine right of kings* was developed to support absolutism: God placed the king on the throne, so he was answerable only to God. Everyone else must submit to the king's decisions, since to do otherwise is to resist the person whom God has placed over the kingdom. The hope was that this would enable the king to force obedience on those under him and thus prevent civil war. This idea was in marked contrast to the medieval idea of *limited government.* Even kings are subject to original sin, and so they cannot be trusted with unlimited power. Instead, there should be constitutional limits on royal power. Absolutism tended to be associated with Catholic powers, with the result that particularly in the Anglo-Saxon world Catholicism was associated with tyranny. It was also a factor in some of the religious wars of the seventeenth century.

ABSOLUTISM, RELIGIOUS WAR, AND ITS EFFECTS

One place where absolutism came into play in a religious war was in the English Civil War. Parliament was led by Puritans — Calvinists who wanted to see England become more thoroughly Protestant and to eliminate many of the "high church" practices that had been brought over from Catholicism. They also wanted to limit the power of King Charles I and William Laud (the archbishop of Canterbury), both of whom exhibited absolutist tendencies and leaned too far toward Catholicism for Puritan tastes. When Laud pushed a prayer book on the kingdom that was far too "papist" for the population, war broke out. Eventually, the parliamentary side won. The archbishop and the king were executed, and Oliver Cromwell became the Lord Protector of the Commonwealth.

The king's son, Charles II, spent his time in exile in France in the absolutist court of Louis XIV. After Cromwell's death, Charles II was restored to the throne of England, and religious uniformity was enforced in the kingdom. Charles II's son, James II, was Catholic, however, and England was not ready for a Catholic ruler. Louis XIV persecuted French Protestants and was seen as a tyrant, and Parliament feared that James would follow his lead. When James not only tried to appoint Catholics illegally to high positions in the government but had the temerity to have an heir, he was deposed in the name of preserving English liberties in a relatively bloodless coup (three battles in England, and fighting in Scotland, which hardly counts) known as the Glorious Revolution. James's daughter Mary and her husband William of Orange were brought in, and they quickly established a limited monarchy, with carefully defined parliamentary rights and religious toleration for Trinitarian Protestants. The principal theorist of the Glorious Revolution was John Locke, whose ideas developed out of earlier medieval constitutional political theory and the resistance theory inspired by the Saint Bartholomew's Day Massacre.

The most devastating war of the period, however, was the Thirty Years' War (1618–1648). This war pitted Catholic Spain and the Holy Roman Emperor against Protestants in the Empire, the Danes, the Swedes, the Dutch, and even Catholic France. It was a very complex, messy affair, and although dynastic rivalries, the conflict between absolutism and constitutionalism, and a host of other political considerations played a part, it was ultimately triggered by religious differences between the emperor and some of his Protestant subjects. The details need not concern us, only the effects. To this day, the Thirty Years' War is still remembered in Germany as the most devastating war ever fought there (including World Wars I and II). Almost every territorial unit within the Holy Roman Empire lost 30 percent or more of its population, agricultural production was set back for a century or more, widespread inflation and personal and state indebtedness took place, and people were exhausted by the war.

The practical result of all this turmoil was that people began to ask a number of dangerous and daring questions that cut at the heart of their worldviews. Was it truly possible to be so certain about the truth of one version of Christianity over another that it was worth going to war over it? Was religious uniformity so essential to society that it was worth killing people and devastating the country over it? These questions challenged the assumption of medieval and early modern epistemology that truth was knowable and necessary for society, especially in an area as fundamental as religion. When these questions were combined with the problems created by the Italian Renaissance, which focused on finding truth and the goal of intellectual life, we have all the ingredients for generating an epistemological crisis all by itself. But there were other worldview challenges to deal with as well.

THE PROBLEM OF ARMADILLOS: THE NEW WORLD

While the Renaissance and the Reformation were changing the face of European culture, the discovery of the New World raised a host of other questions of a different sort. Once again, however, we need to dispense with a few myths about the era. When Columbus sailed, the key question facing his backers was not the shape of the world. Anyone with any education at all knew that the world was round. Not only was this information (and a number of arguments to prove it) preserved from ancient Greeks, but the entire system of physics developed by Aristotle depended on the earth being a sphere at the center of the universe. (Yes, Aristotle's physics was still in use despite the Condemnations of 1277, since on this point it did not raise any theological problems.)

The issue was not the shape of the world but its size. Everyone assumed that there was only one land mass — Eurasia and Africa — and that if you set sail west from Europe, you would not run into anything until Asia. The danger was that if the ocean was too large, you would run out of drinking water before you arrived and the crew would die of thirst. Most people believed this to be the case, and so no one sailed. Columbus, however, knowing the legend of Saint Brendan, thought the ocean had to be small enough to make the voyage. He consulted with a Florentine cartographer named Paolo Toscanelli, who convinced him that it was only about 5,000 miles to Asia across the Atlantic. Armed with this information, Columbus was able to get the backing to set sail. Unfortunately, Toscanelli's calculations were off by about 10,000 miles. Had Columbus known the real numbers, he would never have left Spain.

So where do we get the idea that people thought the world was flat? Washington Irving — the man who wrote the short stories "The Legend of Sleepy Hollow" and "Rip Van Winkle," among other things — wrote a biography of Columbus in which he wanted to make Columbus out to be a great man. Since he could not very well say that Columbus was a hero because he had bought into bad numbers from Toscanelli, Irving decided to say that he was a brilliant visionary who was the first to realize that the earth was round, playing on the stereotype of medieval ignorance. Irving was a great writer of fiction, even as a biographer.

No, the problem raised by the New World was not the shape of the earth. It was something far more disturbing. When Europeans arrived, they found armadillos. And llamas and alpacas. And bison and beavers. And a host of other animals not known in the Old World. They also found people here. Lots of them, something like nineteen million in Mexico alone.

Now this was a real problem because it raised questions about the truthfulness of biblical history. The Bible says in Genesis that Noah built an ark and put two of every kind of animal in it to protect them from a global flood. He and his three sons and their wives got on board as well. The flood came, all human and animal life was destroyed, and then Noah and his family let all the animals out to reproduce and replenish the earth. All people were descended from Noah's family, and all animals came from those that were on the ark.

So here is the problem: given all the animals that were known to exist in Europe, Asia, and Africa, the ark would have been pretty crowded as it was. Now a whole group of new animals had to be fit onto the ark as well. Where would you put them all? And where did the people already in the Americas come from? As they understood it, Noah's three sons were already accounted for — Shem in the Middle East, Ham in Africa, and Japheth in Eurasia. Whose descendants were the Native Americans? (They did not know about land bridges at the Bering Straits or this might not have troubled them as much.) So the very existence of all of these new animals and people was hard to reconcile with biblical history — and if the Bible is the Word of God, how can it be wrong about something like that? If it is wrong here, how can we really rely on it in other areas?

But there was a deeper problem. Christians had believed from the beginning that Jesus Christ was the only means of salvation for the world, which is why it has always been a missionary religion. Now, however, here were millions upon millions of people who for untold generations had never had even the remotest chance of hearing the gospel. Christian theology suggested that they would all end up in hell, but was that fair? How could a good God do something like that? Did he not owe these millions of people at least a chance to become Christians? In other words, the existence of the Native Americans raised troubling moral questions about fundamental Christian doctrine and the goodness of God, along with questions about the historical veracity of the Bible. The medieval worldview was thus placed under even more stress, both epistemologically and ethically.

THE TODDLER FROM HELL: PYRRHONICAL SKEPTICISM

As if all of this were not enough, Renaissance scholars discovered one ancient thinker whose ideas would shatter what remained of medieval epistemology, ethics, and everything else it touched — an ancient Greek skeptic named Pyrrho, brought to light through the writings of one of his followers, a Roman author named Sextus Empiricus.

Pyrrho was in many ways an anti-philosopher. Where most philosophers were interested in finding truth, Pyrrho was not. Instead, he seemed determined to show that knowing anything with certainty was impossible — though he knew it would be foolish to actually make that claim. When academic skeptics would assert that it was impossible to know anything, Pyrrho would respond, "How do you know that?" You see, the statement that you cannot know anything is itself a claim to know something, so it is self-contradictory. If it is true, it is false.

Rather than making any positive statements, Pyrrho would ask questions. In fact, his epistemology was summarized by the question "What do I know?"—to which he never gave an answer. His questions were designed to show that the things we think and believe are without any sure foundation. He was rather like a toddler who keeps asking, "Why?" until an adult gives up and says, "Because!" But "because" is no answer, and Pyrrho would not go away. His point was that we cannot have certainty, and in the absence of it, the best course is to suspend judgment and neither affirm nor deny anything as objectively true.

Sextus Empiricus wrote attacks on numerous groups in his works, employing the arsenal of Pyrrhonical questioning to dismantle all claims of knowledge. This left a blueprint for using the technique in other areas as well. When his work was rediscovered, a copy was sent to Henri Estienne, a well-known printer of that day. Estienne had been in a depression, but when he read Sextus, his mood lightened immediately. As far as he was concerned, it was the funniest thing he had ever read—he did not take a word of it seriously—and so he published it as a cure for melancholy. Other people realized it was no joke, however, and began to toy with it in their own thinking.

One important person influenced by Pyrrhonism was Michel de Montaigne, the sixteenth-century French writer who first employed the term *essay* (meaning "attempt") to describe short pieces of writing. The idea was that he was "attempting" to describe himself and his thinking. Pyrrhonism makes an appearance in some of Montaigne's essays, particularly in his social criticism. For example, in his essay "On Cannibals," he outlines the supposed cannibalistic practices of peoples in the New World in some detail, but then asks whether this kind of practice should be condemned and whether it is any worse than the horrors Christians inflict on each other in Europe. The belief of European and Christian superiority to the "savages" in the New World is questioned, but it is neither affirmed nor denied.

Montaigne and other Catholic writers also used Pyrrho as a support for Catholicism. Remember, a fundamental question in many people's minds was which version of Christianity was true, and each side marshaled the strongest arguments it could to defend itself and to attack its competitors. Pyrrhonical methodology, however, could be used to show that neither side was certain. In light of this, moving from one uncertain opinion to another did not make much sense, so the best thing would be to stick with tradition and remain Catholic.

Later, in the seventeenth century, the Jesuits would attempt to use Pyrrhonism even more extensively. Protestants believed that Scripture alone was to be used as a source of authority in the church. The problem was that Protestants disagreed with each other about how to interpret it in a number of key places — which left the Jesuits an opening.

The Jesuits would start with something like, "How do you know the Bible is true?" The usual response was that it was confirmed by the witness of the Holy Spirit in their hearts. The Jesuits would respond with something like, "How do you know it is the Holy Spirit and not something you ate?" This would force the Protestants to develop a more reasoned response, which would again be subjected to attacks that used Pyrrhonical questioning. Then the Jesuits would move to, "Even if we give you Scripture, how do you know you're interpreting it correctly?" The response again typically relied on the illuminating work of the Holy Spirit, to which the Jesuits would reply, "But you can't agree among yourselves what the text means! Why is the Holy Spirit telling Luther one thing, Zwingli another, and Calvin something else? Can't the Spirit make up his mind? We don't have that problem, of course, because we have church tradition to show us what the text actually means." From there, they would move to the thorniest biblical passages and seeming contradictions they could find and throw them out as problems, using Pyrrhonical arguments against any reply that might be made. The idea was to force the Protestants back to the comforting certainty of the Catholic Church and tradition.

Some Catholic theologians, when they observed this Jesuit tactic, tried to warn them off. They argued that this method would turn people away from the Bible and Christianity altogether rather than bring them back to Catholicism. The Jesuits didn't listen, however, and the net result was that they did, in fact, undermine faith in the Bible.

As a tool, Pyrrhonism was devastating to religion since it was designed to lead people to suspend judgment on any question of belief. It was equally devastating to all other areas, since the same technique that undermined religious belief could also be used to demolish not simply faith but the kind of certainty about truth that was universally recognized as the very definition of knowledge. And without knowledge, there is no metaphysics or ethics, since we cannot know anything about either reality or morality and thus must suspend judgment about them and about the meaning and purpose of life as well. Pyrrho believed, evidently, that living without committing oneself for or against any belief would lead to inner peace. In reality, this mind-set produced huge amounts of turmoil in Europe and set out a challenge that the seventeenth-century world could not ignore.

The Western worldview in the early modern period thus faced an unprecedented series of challenges. The Renaissance called into question both the method that had been accepted for centuries for finding truth and the very goal of intellectual life. The Reformation broke the unity of the church, the anchor that had held the medieval world together, as Latin Christendom fragmented into many competing churches. The Wars of Religion led many to question whether religion was as central to society as had been believed. The New World raised questions about biblical history and reliability, as well as about the justice and morality of God. And Pyrrhonism was like an acid that corroded everything it touched, leaving in doubt the very possibility of knowing anything at all.

The key issue in the midst of all of these challenges is *the question of knowledge*: What can we know, and how can we know it? What was needed was an entirely new paradigm for knowledge, even though a new approach would inevitably ripple through the rest of the worldview. While all these challenges were undermining much of the old worldview, the foundations for a new epistemology were being laid in the sixteenth century with the beginning of the scientific revolution. This is the subject of the next chapter.

CHAPTER 7

A NEW PARADIGM OF KNOWLEDGE

While the Renaissance, the Reformation, the Wars of Religion, the implications of the New World, and Pyrrhonical skepticism were breaking down the medieval worldview, especially in terms of what can be known and how we can know it, in the background a different movement was laying the foundation for a new worldview by gradually developing a whole new paradigm for knowledge: the emergence of science from Christian natural philosophy. While a number of fields were developing during this period, including anatomy and physiology and chemistry, the changes in cosmology and physics are the most striking and will serve here as an example for the scientific revolution.

THE TRADITIONAL MODEL OF THE UNIVERSE

To understand the reasons for the changes in cosmology, we need to look at the model of the universe inherited from the ancient world.

The universe was believed to be made of four basic elements — earth, water, air, and fire. According to Aristotle, everything in the universe has a natural tendency to seek its proper place. Earth, as the densest element, naturally sinks to the center of the universe and forms a sphere, the perfect shape. Water, the next densest, follows, then air, and then fire, starting at the orbit of the moon. Of course, the earth is not a perfect sphere, nor is it uniformly covered with water. The problem is that below the level of the moon, things do not work perfectly. We are in the realm of terrestrial mechanics, the physics of imperfection. From the moon outward, the universe does operate perfectly according to the laws of celestial mechanics.

To explain the motion of the stars and planets, an Egyptian cosmographer named Ptolemy devised a model of the universe that was still in use into the early modern period. He began with a stationary earth at the center of the universe and then argued that the heavenly bodies were on a series of crystalline spheres that nested together like a series of Russian dolls. The closest spheres each contained a planet, including the moon, Mars, Venus, the sun, Jupiter, and Saturn. (Uranus, Neptune, and Pluto are not visible to the naked eye.)

Why were the moon and the sun considered planets? The word *planet* comes from the Greek *planaō* meaning "to wander." All of them "wandered" around the field of the fixed stars, which were found on the outermost of the nested spheres. The stars never moved in relation to each other, but the planets (including the sun and moon) did. Each night, the sphere of fixed stars rotated around the earth, and its motion induced the next circle to move, which moved the next, and so on down to the moon. This explained the motion of the stars and planets in the night sky.

Or it almost did. The problem was that when you do the calculations, using simple spheres for the planets does not accurately predict their position. So Ptolemy force-fit things into the system to make it work. He added epicycles — circles that contained the planets and rotated around a point on each of the spheres, which in turn rotated around the Earth. That helped, but it still did not make it observationally accurate. So Ptolemy added deferents — off-center epicycles — and then added equants, which was a way of varying the speed of the planet as it moved around on its epicycle.

To make a long story short, by adding all of these things together, Ptolemy came up with a system that "saved the appearances" — in other words, that accurately predicted the position of the planets. It was a remarkable achievement, particularly since it was done with no calculators or computers, no calculus or algebra, and by using Roman numerals. (If you don't think that makes a difference, try dividing CLXIX by XIII without converting them to Arabic numerals.) It was particularly impressive because it worked well for over a millennium.

Unfortunately, by the sixteenth century the model was beginning to be the worse for wear. As accurate as it was, it was not perfect, and the gradual accumulation of errors over centuries meant that dates for seasons were shifting, and it was becoming harder and harder to predict solstices, equinoxes, and phases of the moon accurately. This, in turn, meant that it was difficult to predict the date of Easter, which in the Latin world was fixed as the first Sunday after the first full moon after the spring equinox. Since the church calendar was built around the date for Easter, the difficulty in predicting equinoxes and full moons was becoming a serious problem. So in the interest of calendar reform, people were beginning to revisit the Ptolemaic system to try to tweak it into accuracy.

THE COPERNICAN REVOLUTION

In this context, Nicolaus Copernicus began his work. Copernicus was a brilliant Polish mathematician, scholar, and clergyman. After getting his education in the north, he traveled to Italy to pursue advanced study in the "New Learning" of the Renaissance. While there, he developed a love for ancient Greek thought, notably that of Pythagoras — a philosopher, mathematician, and sun worshiper.

COPERNICUS AND HELIOCENTRISM

When Copernicus began working on cosmology, he found a number of features of the Ptolemaic system distasteful. He believed that in the heavens, everything should move in perfect, uniform, circular motion, so he was offended by Ptolemy's equants, which varied the speed of planets. Further, given the centrality of the sun in Pythagoras's thought, Copernicus believed that it would be appropriate if the sun were in fact the center of the universe. So he began working on a heliocentric system, placing the planets on spheres moving out from the sun, with the moon on a sphere going around the earth. When he did the math, he found out it did not work accurately enough. So he added epicycles. When that didn't work either, he added double epicycles — something Ptolemy had not done, but which was necessary to eliminate the equants. In the end, Copernicus came up with a system that once again "saved the appearances" and was easier to use than Ptolemy's.

Copernicus's system did have a few disadvantages, however. First, although it allowed for simpler math to predict planetary motion, in some ways it was more complex than Ptolemy's. It had more circles in it, for example. Also, although it was more aesthetically pleasing than Ptolemy's (at least to Copernicus), it raised enormous problems for physics. All of physics in this period was based on Aristotle, and the starting point for Aristotle's physics was the idea that things tend to move to their natural position and stay there, meaning that a stationary earth was essential if the system was going to work. If the earth was not the center of the universe, everything scholars thought they knew about physics would have to be discarded, making it impossible to explain anything. So to accept Copernicus was to give up the intelligibility of the universe in return for a prettier system. It was not a trade-off most natural philosophers would be willing to make.

Copernicus himself knew that the model would cause problems, and thus he was reluctant to publish it. We often assume, in light of events nearly a century later, that he was worried about attacks on his model based on theological considerations. That fear may have been a part of it, but he was equally aware that it would be attacked not just by biblical scholars but by natural philosophers as well.

A Lutheran pastor named Andreas Osiander finally convinced Copernicus to publish his book in 1543. It was greeted with a yawn. It raised no outcry, and no one attacked Copernicus for the book. There were several reasons for this non-reaction. First, Osiander added a preface saying that the book was only a mathematical model — that it was not in fact intended as a physical model of the universe, but only as a means of simplifying the math for predicting planetary movement. This was a bald-faced lie, as anyone who read the book would know, but the preface probably forestalled criticism. Also, the book was so complex mathematically that few could actually follow the argument, so it was largely left unread. It is also worth noting that less than a century earlier, Nicholas of Cusa had suggested a heliocentric universe, and a century before that Oresme had done the same thing — and neither of them had gotten into trouble for it. So Copernicus need not have worried. The book did not generate the opposition he had expected.

Although Copernicus is often seen as one of the founders of modern science, his motivation and methodology were far removed from what we think of as science today. He was a natural philosopher who believed that his model of the universe needed to be linked to aesthetics and to other philosophical ideas. And he was still operating within the Christian worldview that argued that the world was rational and beautiful because the God who created it was rational and beautiful, and that we (as rational creatures) could understand God's creation. Copernicus was thus as far from a secular rationalist as could be, as his lack of concern for explaining the physics of his model shows. He was far more interested in the aesthetic than the scientific.

TYCHO BRAHE AND JOHANNES KEPLER

Copernicus was not the only one who was trying out new models of the universe. One of the more popular systems during the seventeenth century was devised by Tycho Brahe, a volatile Danish nobleman who had lost his nose in a duel. He had several false noses made, including one composed of solid gold. But in addition to his nose collection, Tycho also had an interest in astronomy. He believed that the sun and moon went around the earth but that the other planets circled the sun, a model known as geoheliocentrism, or the Tychonic system.

Tycho was convinced that the problem of cosmology and calendar reform could be solved with better data, so he convinced the king of Denmark to give him an island on which he could build an observatory. He bought the most accurate scientific instruments ever made so he could observe stars and planets and record their positions. He worked diligently at his observations and as a result became the greatest observational astronomer to that point in history. But once he had his tables of planetary positions, he needed to find someone to do the math for him to prove that his system was correct. As it turned out, his mathematician actually contacted him to ask to use his data — and now Tycho had his man.

The mathematician's name was Johannes Kepler — a brilliant all-around scholar, a committed Lutheran, an equally committed Copernican, and a Pythagorean. He had written a book called *The Cosmographic Mystery*, in which he came up with a geometric explanation for why there could only be six planets — and he had the ratios of their orbits worked out. The only problem in his explanation was Jupiter, which was close to where his model predicted it should be, but not close enough. He thought the problem was bad data, so when he heard about Tycho, he sent him a copy of his book and asked if he could use his data on Jupiter. Tycho thought Kepler was a nutcase, both for believing Copernicus and for making the argument he made in his book, but the Dane also recognized a bona fide mathematical genius when he saw one. So he hired Kepler but told him to forget Copernicus and use the data to prove Tycho's theory. And to make sure Kepler did not go off to do his own work, Tycho gave him the data for Mars and told him to start there.

Kepler tried using the data with Tycho's system, but no matter how he tweaked the variables, he couldn't get it to work. So he switched to heliocentrism, and things improved dramatically, but it still wasn't perfect. The observations were off by a small amount, but that amount was still outside the known margin of error for Tycho's instruments. Most people would have said it was simply observational error — Mars's orbit was only out of round by about .5 percent — but Kepler believed that God had given him Tycho's data, and so it was his responsibility before God to use it to the fullest extent possible.

Kepler's next step was to jettison circular motion and try using an "egg shape" for the orbits. But eggs are not a mathematically defined shape, so he decided to use an ellipse to approximate it. When he did that, the data snapped into place perfectly. He went on to figure out that planets do, in fact, vary in speed during their orbits, and he developed ratios connecting minimum and maximum speeds as well as the average radius of the orbit with the time it takes to orbit the sun.

Kepler knew he would be on shaky ground with most of his readers. Among other things, he rejected the two most important motivations for Copernicus — circular motion and constant speed — so he would not be popular among the few natural philosophers who had accepted heliocentrism. As for the majority who did not, they may have recognized Kepler's mathematical genius and his work as a cosmologist, but they still rejected his theories. Again, without the earth at the center of the universe, there was no foundation for physics. Kepler was not concerned about that, though. It had taken 6,000 years (the apparent age of the earth in the Bible) before anyone understood how God had made the cosmos, so Kepler could afford to wait a century to be proven right. It was a good thing he had this attitude, or he would have been sorely disappointed at the reception of his ideas. It would be fifty years before anyone would accept all of his laws of planetary motion, which today we know to be true.

Once again, it is important to note the influence of Kepler's Christian faith. He believed that God had created the universe by using geometry, and through the use of geometry human beings could discover what God did. In this way, following the long tradition of blending the Bible and philosophy, he was able to combine Christian natural philosophy and Pythagoreanism, adding to the mix a rigorous empiricism that refused to compromise on the known reliability of the data, based on his commitment to using to the full the gifts that God had given him.

GALILEO AND THE CHURCH

One of the Copernicans who ignored Johannes Kepler's work was the Italian Galileo Galilei. Unlike Copernicus and Kepler, Galileo based his arguments for Copernicanism on observation, not mathematics. Also unlike Copernicus and Kepler, Galileo wrote for a popular audience, which drew considerably more attention to his work and made it considerably more controversial. On top of that, Galileo had a penchant for making people who disagreed with him look like fools, a practice that earned him quite a few enemies, including some important and powerful figures in the Catholic Church.

Galileo was the first to use a telescope to observe the heavens, and he claimed that his observations proved heliocentrism. His detractors disagreed, and frankly, they were right to do so. For example, Galileo observed mountains on the moon, proving that it was not a perfect sphere. This does not prove that the earth goes around the sun, however. Galileo also noted that Venus went through phases, as the moon does. This might indicate that it went around the sun, but not necessarily, and even if it did, most astronomers accepted the Tychonic system in which Venus actually did go around the sun. Either way, however, Venus's phases do not prove that the earth goes around the sun.

Galileo observed a comet that went through the orbits of the planets, proving they were not on crystalline spheres. This was old news. Tycho had proven the same thing decades earlier. Galileo also discovered that Jupiter had moons, proving that more than one thing in the universe could have "planets" orbiting it. Again, this was the case in Tycho's system, and in any event it still does not prove that the earth goes around the sun. What Galileo had was interesting and suggestive, but it was not *proof*, and it was not strong enough to warrant throwing out all of physics.

ASTRONOMY AND THE BIBLE

Galileo's opponents were the first to bring up the problem of biblical passages that suggest a stationary earth and a moving sun, possibly because they were theologians, possibly because Galileo had so annoyed them that they were grabbing anything they could to throw at him. Galileo's response was classic natural philosophy: God created two books, nature and Scripture. Both were difficult, and the insights gleaned from one should be used to help understand the other. He suggested that the biblical passages needed to be reinterpreted so that they could be true while still leaving room for holding to heliocentrism. In fact, he spent a great deal of time and effort trying to show that the relevant passages made better sense *literally* in a heliocentric universe rather than in the traditional geocentric one. His opponents disagreed, marshaling their own biblical and scientific evidence against him.

Unfortunately, the Catholic Church had painted itself into a corner. While allowing that *proof* of heliocentrism would mean that they would need to reinterpret Scripture, they also argued that in the absence of proof they could not do so. Further, the Council of Trent, meeting in part as a response to Protestantism, had forbidden interpreting the Bible contrary to the ways it had always been interpreted in the church. Although this was intended to counter Protestantism, it was pulled out here to argue against heliocentrism because all the relevant passages had traditionally been read as describing a geocentric universe.

HELIOCENTRISM AND HERESY

Once the issue was forced, the church decided that calling heliocentrism a *fact* was heretical, while holding it as a *theory* was not. Galileo agreed to abide by this decision. Later, however, one of his friends became pope, and Galileo approached him to ask permission to write a book about the controversy between geocentrism and heliocentrism. The pope agreed, as long as Galileo did not advocate heliocentrism but simply presented the arguments for both. He also suggested that God could have made a geocentric universe that was nonetheless set up to have all the appearances of heliocentrism. Galileo agreed to the terms and wrote his *Dialogue Concerning the Two Chief World Systems*.

The dialogue included a supporter of heliocentrism, a supporter of geocentrism, and a neutral third party named Simplicius, who was essentially the village idiot of the piece. (Galileo claimed that Simplicius was named after a popular Aristotelian natural philosopher, though in point of fact no one by that name has ever been identified. Instead, the name points to the fact that the character was a simpleton.) Needless to say, Galileo's heliocentrist got the better of the argument. In the end, however, Simplicius presented the idea that God could have made a geocentric universe that was set up to have all the appearances of heliocentrism. All sides agreed to this wise statement, and the dialogue came to an end.

When the book was published, Galileo's enemies saw it as a violation of the ban on teaching heliocentrism as fact. They took it to the pope, who was naturally incensed that Galileo had not only advocated heliocentrism but had also put the pope's words into the mouth of the village idiot. Galileo was put on trial for heresy again. He was condemned, forbidden to write or teach on astronomy, and put under house arrest on his estate.

RELIGION AND SCIENCE?

More than any other, this incident has been used as a poster child for the supposed battle between religion (that is, Christianity) and science. Nothing could be further from the truth. First, this stereotype ignores Galileo's habit of making unnecessary enemies and his betrayal of the pope in the *Dialogue*. Personal animosity and political values were at stake in the conflict, along with interpretation of Scripture and emerging ideas in natural philosophy. It wasn't as simple as religion versus science. These other issues may help explain why Galileo attracted so much hostile attention while other Copernicans did not.

Further, both sides used both science and Scripture in this debate. The conflict pitted one view of science and religion against a different view of science and religion. Galileo always claimed loyalty to the Catholic Church and was concerned to present his views as compatible with the Bible. He would reject categorically the idea that he was irreligious or that science and religion were at war. Like Copernicus and Kepler, he was working as a Christian natural philosopher. In fact, even after Galileo's condemnation, other Catholic scholars, including the Jesuits who had attacked Galileo, continued to do original and important research in natural philosophy, once again highlighting the fact that the church was not intrinsically opposed to scientific advancement.

Nor did Galileo's house arrest end his own work in natural philosophy. He knew well that in order for heliocentrism to be accepted, he needed to establish a new foundation for physics to replace Aristotle's. As a result, Galileo worked on several branches of dynamics — the study of moving bodies — to try to build that new foundation. Aristotle had believed that the density of an object determined how fast it would fall. Galileo did experiments which demonstrated that objects fell at the same rate, and then worked out that they fell with uniformly accelerating motion — that is, the speed increased at a constant rate. This was not a new idea — it had been suggested in the Middle Ages — but Galileo was able to devise experiments that provided strong evidence for it.

Next Galileo worked on a more general theory of moving bodies. Aristotle had believed that the natural state of objects was rest, and in order to move objects, you needed to apply a force. As soon as the force was removed, the object would stop or would seek its natural position. This idea made it difficult to explain ballistics — for example, why a thrown rock continues to fly after it leaves your hand. Aristotle explained this by saying that as the rock moved forward, the air it displaced moved around behind it and pushed it, thereby providing the force needed to keep it in flight. Galileo's approach to the general problem of motion began with the medieval idea of impetus. He suggested that, contrary to Aristotle's view, both rest and motion were natural, and that to change the state, you needed to apply a force. Again, he devised experiments to show that this was the case.

Then Galileo began to work on ballistics, trying to determine the math behind cannonballs and other thrown or launched objects. Using observations, he noted that falling objects (such as water flowing out of a horizontal spout) traveled in a curve; the problem was how to analyze that motion. He came up with the idea of separating the vertical (downward) motion from the horizontal motion and analyzing each independently. Horizontally, the object in flight moved at a constant speed, since no force was acting on it to change its motion; vertically, it fell using uniformly accelerating motion. Together, these two types of motion defined the curve. This analysis was correct and was truly a groundbreaking idea, even if built from medieval precedents. It is arguably Galileo's most important contribution to physics. In particular, it was a critically important contribution to Newton's theories of gravity and motion.

ANSWERING PYRRHO

While all this was going on, the challenge of Pyrrhonism continued. There were numerous attempts to solve it — including the approach taken by Pierre Bayle, a French Protestant refugee living in the Netherlands. Bayle was the editor of *The News of the Republic of Letters*, a journal that acted as a clearinghouse for new scholarship. He embraced Pyrrhonism, arguing in essence that the Pyrrhonical arguments were airtight, and that we had to accept the idea that all knowledge is fundamentally built on unproven and unprovable assumptions. Certainty is thus not possible. As a result, Bayle rejected the medieval and early modern insistence on absolute knowledge and focused instead on the role of faith as the foundation for epistemology: Since we cannot prove our most fundamental ideas, we must instead take them on faith. Bayle saw this as a positive, particularly with respect to religion; others, however, thought (and continue to think) that he was trying to use Pyrrhonism to undermine religious belief.

DESCARTES AND CARTESIANISM

Other thinkers were not as ready as Bayle was to give up on certainty. The most famous was René Descartes, a French Catholic and a lawyer by training. Descartes was troubled by the arguments of the Pyrrhonists, so he decided to try to come up with a foundation of truth that would be immune to their attacks. He began by systematically doubting everything he could to try to find a kernel that could not be doubted. Eventually, he reached the idea that the only thing he could not doubt was that he doubted. From this, he derived his famous principle, "I think, therefore I am" (Latin, *cogito ergo sum*), the point being that if there was doubt, there was thought, and if there was thought, there had to be someone doing the thinking. This has been the subject of endless jokes (Descartes goes into a café and orders a coffee. The waiter asks him if he would like a pastry to go with it. Descartes replies, "I think not," and promptly vanishes), but it was actually a serious attempt to address a real epistemological problem. Interestingly enough, when Saint Augustine wrote to counter the academic skeptics, he used essentially the same argument. Descartes claimed to be unaware of this, however.

In any event, armed with the *cogito*, Descartes went on to build an entire system of thought that he claimed was necessarily true because he had proven his own existence. The next step was, "I exist, therefore God exists." While this may sound egotistical, it does not really mean that Descartes is God. Rather, the idea is that things do not just come into existence out of nothing. Instead, if something comes into existence, something else must have caused it. Since Descartes knew he was not eternal, something else must have made him — and this something Descartes called "God." Descartes' third step was, "God exists, therefore clear and distinct ideas must be true." If God was the creator, he must be the guarantor of truth as well. As a result, he would not deceive us, and so ideas that are "clear and distinct" are automatically true.

At this point in the argument, Pierre Bayle replied that Descartes *might* be onto something with "I think, therefore I am," but that proceeding to the existence of God was certainly open to doubt. And Bayle and Descartes' other critics rejected his argument on clear and distinct ideas even more quickly, for precisely the same reason. In other words, Bayle argued, quite reasonably, that Descartes was cheating. But once Descartes developed his argument for clear and distinct ideas, he got the bit between his teeth and developed a purely deductive explanation for the entire universe. And since this explanation was deductive, its conclusions were certain as long as its starting premises were true, which was precisely the point of his "refutation" of Pyrrho. Descartes thought he had certain premises from which he could deduce the rest of his system.

Descartes believed that all that existed in the universe was mind and matter; further, he believed that matter was "extension," that is, anything that took up space. Everything that happened in the physical world was caused by the physical interaction of particles of matter, which collided, pushed, or stuck to other particles of matter. This idea, called mechanical philosophy, was very popular in Descartes' day because it eliminated any reference to magic.

Renaissance thinkers of the previous centuries had developed elaborate systems to explain the physical universe, based on hidden (Latin, *occultus*) connections in the fabric of the world. These connections could cause "action at a distance." For example, if the stars or planets aligned in certain ways, it instantly affected you, even though there was no physical connection between you and the stars. Or think about a voodoo doll. You have a doll made to look like someone. You stick a pin in it wherever you are, and the person jumps wherever he or she is. The occult connection between the doll and the person is the conduit that enables you to produce action at a distance.

Mechanical philosophy was intended to eliminate any recourse to magic in explanations of the physical world, just as scholars in the central Middle Ages had developed more rational systems of criminal justice and relied less on miracles or demonic activity to explain natural events.

Unfortunately, however, Descartes' deductivism had its limits. For example, since matter is extension, Descartes believed the idea of a vacuum was nonsensical, and thus if there is volume, there is matter. Another French Catholic natural philosopher named Pierre Gassendi had a different approach in which he worked to reconcile Christianity with a theory taken from the Epicureans that the physical world is made up of atoms and the space between them. Vacuums are thus present in the "gaps" between atoms and can be produced in other places as well.

PASCAL, PROBABILISM, AND PROGRESS

The disagreement was ultimately resolved by yet another French thinker, Blaise Pascal. Pascal was a mathematician and thinker who, among other things, was one of the founders of probability theory. A conservative Catholic, he wrote on theological and philosophical issues in addition to his work in mathematics and natural philosophy. Pascal designed an experiment to test whether a vacuum could exist. He used a barometer. To make a barometer, you take a long tube, sealed at one end, and fill it with liquid (originally water, but later mercury); you then cover the opening, turn it over into a bowl with more of the liquid, and uncover the submerged opening. Some of the liquid from the tube will run down into the bowl, leaving empty space at the top. The question is, What is in that empty space? According to Gassendi, it was a vacuum. Descartes said it was filled with tiny particles of matter that boiled off from the sides of the tube. Pascal set out to find the answer.

If Gassendi was correct, then the weight of the liquid in the tube was the same as the air pressure on the liquid in the bowl — this is what supports the column of liquid. However, the higher you go into the atmosphere, the less air there is above you, and as a result the less weight on the liquid. If this is correct, the column of liquid should be higher at sea level and lower the farther up you move. To test this, Pascal made a barometer and put it on a cart. He took measurements of the height of the column at the base of the mountain, drove the cart to the top, and took more measurements there. He then returned to the bottom and measured it again. The column of liquid behaved as Gassendi's theory predicted, and so Pascal argued that Gassendi's theory was more probable than Descartes'.

This was an enormous step forward. The experiment did not disprove Descartes — it was possible that his explanation was correct — but it lent substantial weight to Gassendi's ideas. On the basis of probability, the odds were clearly in favor of the latter. This represents an extremely important epistemological shift for Western thought. Traditionally, knowledge was thought to be certain, and best found in the past. Like his predecessors, Descartes continued to insist on the certainty of knowledge, but though he respected past authors, he did not consider them definitive; for him, truth was better found in the present. In effect, Descartes straddled the medieval and modern divide, with one foot on each side. Pascal, on the other hand, gave up both assumptions. He did not insist on certainty as necessary for knowledge; probability was good enough.

This idea was known as probabilism, and as it took root, it effectively disarmed Pyrrho. Probabilists did not look for or expect certainty; thus Pyrrhonical questioning, which was designed to undermine certainty, was not a threat to their epistemology. Further, though Pascal also respected the past (especially in theology), he did not believe it was authoritative except perhaps in matters of religion. Truth in the natural world could better be found in the present or in the future, through experimentation and observation, rather than in the conclusions of past authors.

This in turn set the stage for the quintessential modern concept of progress. The idea that we can and should know more than our predecessors — that things will improve and keep improving — had simply not occurred to thinkers prior to this. They all believed that the past was the gold standard for truth, knowledge, and all aspects of society. Now all of that had changed. Truth was found in the present or in the future, people would learn more and improve on the past, and society was increasingly believed to be on an upward trajectory toward a more knowledgeable and better world.

With the shift in epistemology and the concept of progress, the critical elements were in place that would lead to the rise of the modern world. The ascendancy of this new way of looking at the world was cemented by the remarkable success of Sir Isaac Newton, whose work in physics was in many ways the culmination of the scientific revolution and the ultimate evidence of just how effective the new approach to knowledge could be.

SIR ISAAC NEWTON

Isaac Newton had a troubled childhood. He was born prematurely; his mother said that at birth, he would have fit in a quart-sized mug. His father died when he was young, and his mother remarried. Newton was raised by his maternal grandmother. He disliked his stepfather so much that in a list of sins he made when he was nineteen, he confessed to wanting to burn his stepfather's house with his mother and stepfather inside. When his stepfather died, Newton's mother moved back and tried to turn him into a farmer. This did not work out well, which fortunately the family recognized. Newton was sent back to school, where he was inspired by Descartes' writings (among others) to begin studying geometry seriously. From there, his work in natural philosophy was to make him the preeminent scholar in England.

It is hard to overstate the importance of Newton's work. He made groundbreaking discoveries in mathematics, including inventing calculus. He laid the foundation for modern studies of optics, proving, among other things, that white light can be broken into colors, which can then be recombined to form white. He also discovered that color is a characteristic of light; it is not a quality that is intrinsic to objects. But far and away his most important contribution was the work he did in physics and gravitation. His laws of motion and his theory of gravity provided the alternative physics that Galileo had been searching for. It laid a new foundation for mechanics — one that worked not only on earth but also in the heavens. His was the first theory that unified celestial and terrestrial mechanics. The same principle of gravitation plus the three laws of motion explained why apples fell from trees, why Kepler's laws of planetary motion worked, and why planets stayed in their orbits. It was a remarkable achievement by any measure.

So how did Newton manage to accomplish all of this? The most important point is that his work did not occur in a vacuum. He knew about mechanical philosophy, as well as Descartes and his theories. He studied Copernicus, Kepler, and Galileo, along with Robert Hooke and a host of other scientists. But he added experimentation and mathematical analysis. In essence, Newton's work confirmed and extended the work of many other early modern natural philosophers, to a large extent through mathematizing mechanical philosophy and converting it into experimental science.

That, at least, is the official answer. It is correct as far as it goes. But there was another side to Newton's work that also influenced what he did and how he did it. If anything, Newton was more interested in theology and occult studies than he was in mathematics, physics, and natural philosophy. In terms of religion, Newton devoted an enormous amount of time to biblical studies, applying the same methods he used in natural philosophy to his analysis of the Bible. In other words, he looked at what other people had done, formulated his own ideas, and "tested" them. It must be said that not all of his ideas were completely orthodox, particularly with respect to the Trinity. (In this area, he was either unorthodox or perhaps closer to the Eastern Orthodox position than to Western ideas.) He was particularly interested in the book of Revelation in the New Testament. He worked very hard at developing an interpretive schema that would align with history and tell him the date of the end of the world.

For Newton, this kind of speculative theology was not a separate activity from his "scientific" work. Both were expressions of his desire to understand God through both of the "books" God gave us — nature and Scripture — albeit using new methods leading to new conclusions in interpreting both. Newton's worldview was in some ways similar to the medieval movement away from supernatural explanations of the natural world, but the medieval approaches still saw divine intervention as necessary to explain some things. Even John Calvin in the sixteenth century argued that the only explanation we have for why the seas do not cover the land is that they are restrained by the hand of God. But Newton did not believe ongoing divine intervention was needed. His natural philosophy was designed to discover how God designed the world to operate as well as to reveal the character of God and his plans for the world.

Yet at the same time Newton had not given up on magic theory and the old idea of occult forces hidden in the natural world. Newton's writings on alchemy and the occult were so extensive that twentieth-century economist John Maynard Keynes, who acquired and read Newton's papers on these subjects, said that "Newton was not the first of the age of reason. He was the last of the magicians."[1]

Newton worked extensively on alchemy, possibly poisoning himself in the process and causing a nervous breakdown. He also revived the old idea, rejected by the mechanical philosophers, of action at a distance, which was central to Renaissance magical explanations of the natural world. In fact, one of Newton's major contributions to science — his theory of universal gravitation — is in effect action at a distance. What mechanical explanation can be offered for why the sun's gravity holds the planets in their orbits? What is the physical connection that makes gravity work? There is none. Today, we can talk about curvatures of space time, but in the seventeenth and eighteenth centuries, no one knew anything about this. Gravity looked like action at a distance — magic pure and simple — and so Newton's ideas were initially rejected by mechanical philosophers. He attempted without success to find a mechanical explanation for gravity, though his occult studies suggested that he himself was not personally troubled by action at a distance. When he failed to find an explanation, he said it was his job to describe what happened, not to explain it. This was a cop-out, but it is where he left it.

Newton and his predecessors not only established a new system of physics but also laid the foundation for a new epistemology in Europe. It was not totally clear what that epistemology was — there were different interpretations about how Newton did his work — but the general outlines were becoming clearer. It began with a rejection of certainty spurred by Pyrrho, with probability considered good enough to work with. Although the past was respected, scholars increasingly believed that they could build on and improve on past authors, and even prove them wrong. The ancients were no longer "authorities" but merely people who wrote down ideas that might be right or might be wrong. Study, analysis, and, where possible, testing became more important than simply citing Aristotle. In short, the idea of progress emerged, and with it, a greater optimism about human potential.

This change in epistemology would inevitably affect the rest of the worldview, since epistemology, ethics, and metaphysics are all interrelated. At the same time, all of the key figures in the scientific revolution were self-consciously working as Christian natural philosophers, with a worldview which said that a rational God would create a rational world, one that we as rational creatures made in the image of God can understand. Unlike the worldviews of other cultures, this fundamental concept made the emergence of science possible.

Ultimately, however, the kinds of problems discussed in the last chapter and the new developments in natural philosophy led to a movement away from the fundamentally Christian worldview of the leaders of the scientific revolution. With the coming of the Enlightenment, other worldviews began to have a greater influence on Western civilization, though without displacing Christianity.

CHAPTER 8

ENLIGHTENMENT AND REVOLUTIONS

Although the medieval worldview placed a new emphasis on rational explanations of the physical world, it still left plenty of room for supernatural intervention and "occult" (from the Latin for "hidden") forces behind physical phenomena. People believed in witchcraft, magic, and charms and thought it was possible to summon demons to obtain secret knowledge. Medicine, as we have seen, was built around astrology, which was believed to affect nearly all of human life.

These ideas continued into the Renaissance. Although the Renaissance is frequently associated with the birth of science, it was actually the golden age of magic theory, much of which was drawn from the newly recovered Hermetic tradition. Explanations of even mundane physical phenomena relied on occult forces that could be manipulated through the use of rituals and symbols.

By the early seventeenth century, however, scholars were rebelling against this way of looking at the world, whether because of the failures of the Renaissance, the disruptions caused by the Reformation and the Wars of Religion, or for other reasons. The society shifted its focus toward rational explanations of the world, continuing and extending trends that had begun in the later Middle Ages. The scientific revolution was motivated in part by a desire to get rid of magic and to understand the world entirely in mechanical terms, as a closed system of cause and effect devoid of nonphysical forces. This approach, known as "mechanical philosophy," tried to explain all natural phenomena as the products of collision, pushing, and other kinds of mechanical contact on the part of the particles that made up the material world. Although natural philosophers would continue to draw moral and spiritual lessons from the physical world well into the eighteenth century, they turned away from relying on the spiritual world to explain the material.

A similar trend toward reason occurred in religion. As we have seen, Calvinism spread rapidly, especially in France, because it represented a more rational approach to religion than popular Catholicism. In the seventeenth century, the newly emerged Protestant churches quite naturally began to draw up doctrinal statements (remember, Christianity is a religion of doctrine), a process that historians call "Confessionalization." This movement, which began in the late sixteenth century, saw a growing emphasis on the use of reason to develop and explain the theologies of the various competing Christian churches across Europe.

At the same time, in the wake of the Wars of Religion, many people began to think of religious passions as politically and socially dangerous. Although Confessionalization served to differentiate churches, there was a countermovement that pushed for an approach to religion that was less dogmatic, less passionate, more reasonable, and more tolerant. In the process, the more extreme representatives of this group began to develop a new worldview known as deism.

THE RISE OF DEISM

To understand deism, it will be helpful to start with the orthodox Christian conception of God. In historic Christianity, God's nature can be described in part by three pairs of terms:

- God is infinite — he transcends space, time, and number — while at the same time he is personal. As a Trinity, he is relational by nature and therefore can have relationships with people.

- God is the creator of the universe and also its sustainer. Its continuing existence and operation depend on his supporting activity.
- God is transcendent — he is utterly beyond the universe and anything the human mind can conceive — yet he is also immanent, that is, immediately present with us at all times.

GOD AND CLOCKMAKERS

Deists generally accepted the first term in each of these pairs while rejecting the second. In other words, God is infinite but not personal; he is the creator but the universe operates on its own without any involvement by God; and he is transcendent but not immanent.

The standard metaphor that deists used was that God is like a clockmaker. A good clockmaker makes a clock and winds it up, and it runs. If a clockmaker were to make a clock that required his intervention periodically — to move the hands or to manipulate the mechanism in any way other than winding it up — we would dismiss him as a poor clockmaker. In the same way, if we accept God as perfect, all-powerful, and transcendent, then why would he make a universe that required his manipulation? If God intervenes in any way in the world, he is less than perfect because it would mean that the world he made is less than perfect. So to suggest that God acts in the world is insulting and diminishes his glory.

DEISM AND CHRISTIANITY

This idea has enormous implications for Christianity. First, it means that the biblical accounts of miracles are false, because God cannot perform miracles. Also, it is impossible for Jesus to be God, since that would be about as extreme an intervention on God's part as could be imagined.

But even beyond these sorts of things, the fundamental principles of deism spill over into all areas of religious life. For example, sacraments do not convey grace or spiritual power — in fact, the very idea of grace is problematic — and God cannot answer prayer because to do so would require him to interfere with the world he created. People should give thanks to God and be grateful for his gifts, though there is no particular advantage or disadvantage that comes from doing so; it is simply appropriate. And that is about it in terms of religious activities.

Deism also raises important questions about evil in the world. If there is evil, then God is not good since everything in the world was created by him and is exactly as he intended it. (Orthodox Christianity argued that the world was created by God, but it was marred by human sin and thus is not the way he created it.) To a deist, then, evil cannot actually exist; the world must be good and right because that is how God had to have made it. To quote Alexander Pope, "Whatever is, is right."[1] That is, since God created everything, however the world is, is how it is supposed to be.

While Protestantism relied on the Bible and Catholicism on Scripture and tradition, deists believed that reason was the only guide to truth in any area of life, including religion. This exclusive emphasis on reason came in part from growing doubts about the reliability of the Bible. Although deists generally respected the Bible's ethical teachings, they obviously did not accept its miracles, answered prayers, and interventionist view of God.

Along with the questions raised by the Reformation, the Wars of Religion, and the New World, the Jesuits' use of Pyrrhonical arguments against Protestants helped undermine faith in the Bible, as critics of this approach predicted it would. Then a major debate in Pierre Bayle's late seventeenth-century journal, *The News of the Republic of Letters*, challenged Mosaic authorship of the Torah, thereby undermining biblical history, the authority of the Law and the Ten Commandments, and the inspiration of the many passages in both the Old and New Testament (including Jesus' own words) that attributed the Torah to Moses. This debate led a number of important figures away from orthodox Christianity toward deism, or at least toward a less orthodox, "liberal" Christianity. This group included John Locke, whose political theory I will discuss later in this chapter.

NEWTON'S GOD?

By the eighteenth century, Enlightenment thinkers began pointing to Isaac Newton as an example of what could be accomplished through the use of reason. According to them, Newton took the accumulated experience of his predecessors, added some of his own work, and thought really hard about it, and voila! He was able to unravel the mysteries of the universe. Again, to quote Alexander Pope, "Nature and Nature's laws lay hid in night: God said, 'Let Newton be!' and all was light."[2]

If Newton could accomplish all this with the physical world, could reason not guide us equally well to religious truth? (Of course, the deists conveniently ignored Newton's work in theology and the occult when they made him the patron saint of Reason; they were really more interested in using Newton as a prop for their own religious ideas than in exploring Newton's.) Deists believed they could sift through the world's religions as a record of the collective experience of humanity and find the most "reasonable" points to include in their religious system. They generally ended up with a God who was simultaneously a God of reason and a reasonable, tolerant God who did not demand much of us in the way of doctrine or ritual. Deists were, in fact, generally very tolerant of anyone except for people who were strongly orthodox and made this known. Such people were frequently ridiculed as being old-fashioned, "enthusiastic" (a bad thing in the period), ignorant, closed-minded, and intolerant.

Some people normally associated with deism would take the premises and the use of reason even further. John Tolland, for example, in a book titled *Christianity not Mysterious* (1696), argued for a rational religion with no place for mystery but did not define God as a creator distinct from the creation. Tolland instead identified god *with* the creation and coined the term *pantheism* (Greek for "all [is] god") to describe this belief.

CHRISTIAN DEISTS

Significantly, though, as the title of Tolland's book implies, deists typically saw themselves as Christians. They may have disagreed with the church, with the Bible — with any sense of organized religion, in fact — but they still kept many aspects of the

Christian worldview in place. For example, they generally accepted foundational ideas of political and economic theory drawn from the Christian tradition such as inalienable rights and specifically property rights. Many of their ethical ideas were also drawn from Christianity (though in terms of their own personal morality this was not always the case). Even the concept of reason was rooted in medieval Christianity's belief that the world is governed by rational laws that human beings could discover.

Since our worldview determines what we think of as reasonable, deists coming out of a Christian tradition naturally brought much of the Christian worldview with them. So most deists in the period can actually be described as "Christian deists," not because they held to traditional Christian beliefs, but because so much of their thinking was drawn from Christian sources.

THE AGE OF REASON

Even beyond the deists, much of eighteenth-century thought was centered on using reason in all areas of life. Inspired by Isaac Newton, other thinkers began looking for laws to explain not simply the physical world but other aspects of human life and experience as well.

ADAM SMITH

Arguably the most important of these was Adam Smith, a Scottish moral theologian by training and a probable deist. Smith's book *The Wealth of Nations*, published in 1776, laid the foundation for what is now called "classical economics." Building on a growing desire for free trade in Britain and the Americas, Smith argued that contrary to the common economic theory and practice of the day, interference in the economy, whether by government action or guild regulations, ended up decreasing the wealth of the country rather than increasing it. Regulations added to the cost of production, lessening efficiency and raising prices, which in turn lowered demand.

Smith argued that the economy would grow in efficiency and productivity if allowed to operate freely, as if guided by an "invisible hand." The fundamental idea was that people inevitably act out of self-interest. If prices and costs were allowed to float, people would migrate away from industries that did not produce money toward those that did; with the increase in producers, prices would drop and the economy would balance itself. Those who are efficient — whether through machinery, division of labor, or other methods — would win more of the market share and make more profits since the difference between their production costs and the price of the product would increase. Those who were less efficient would potentially be driven out of business. In other words, the economy functioned best if competition was allowed to run its course and determine winners and losers without constraints set by either government or guilds.

Smith's work was groundbreaking in many respects. His theories opened the way for the first time to entrepreneurs, who have become the engine driving the most successful Western economies ever since. His scheme dismantled the ideas of the mercantilists, who emphasized maintaining a positive balance of trade and the accumulation of bullion, and of the Physiocrats, who emphasized land ownership rather than labor.

At the same time, Smith's work built on earlier precedents in the medieval and early modern cities and especially in the Netherlands, which had the least restrictive economic policies of any early modern state. Just as Newton took the medieval desire to develop a more rational explanation for the universe to a much more systematic, logical, and intellectually satisfying conclusion, Smith took many of the premises of the medieval economy — the value and goodness of labor, private property, reinvestment, and so on — and brought them to a more systematic and logical conclusion, albeit one that was divorced in many ways from the moral elements of medieval thought. Smith did not think highly of the morality of businesspeople since he believed they were motivated entirely by greed rather than compassion, which was the foundation of his moral philosophy, yet he recognized that their greed could be used for the good of society. In the Middle Ages, people were more concerned with the personal moral implications of economic policy.

Smith's work also set the stage for further developments in economics. For example, Thomas R. Malthus, an Anglican cleric, developed an analysis of population trends. He thought that all populations tend to overreproduce until the available resources can no longer sustain the increased numbers. At that point, nature will step in to correct the imbalance through starvation, disease, or war (yes, war is a response of nature, according to Malthus) and thus reduce the population to a sustainable level. The process then repeats. (Malthus's conclusion was that aiding the poor is a mistake, since if you do, they will have more children, bringing on the "crisis" sooner and more severely. This is not the kind of argument you normally expect from a clergyman, but in an era that believed in reason and natural law, it seemed to make sense.)

ECONOMICS, POLITICS, AND WORLDVIEW

Allowing markets to work without government interference was an idea whose time had come. Adam Smith is considered the father of classical liberalism. Edmund Burke, the father of classical conservatism, may have disagreed with Smith on many points, but he agreed that government regulation was bad for the economy.

If the fathers of both classical conservatism and classical liberalism agree on such a basic point in economic theory, it suggests that the idea was deeply rooted in the era's worldview. Not surprisingly, then, these ideas had political as well as economic implications. Since politics and economics are both governed by assumptions about the "natural" way people ought to relate to each other, the same cultural context that led to free market capitalism also contributed to the rise of representative democracies. In essence, elections are the equivalent of applying the ideas of the free market to politics. Just as when you buy a product, you are "voting" the product and vendor into business and "voting against" their competitors, so when you vote for representatives in an election, you are "buying" their politics and not that of their competitors. (In Anglo-Saxon countries, the legal system was also built around the concept of competition within the court of law, where the two sides in the adversarial system competed for the votes of the jury.) It is thus no accident that as representative democracies emerged in the wake of the American Revolution, they tended to institute economic policies based on free market principles.

Although in the long run Adam Smith's work would arguably have the biggest impact on Western society, other thinkers were trying to apply reason to solve human problems as well. Collectively, these thinkers are often called *philosophes* (French for "philosophers"). The term is actually a misnomer. *Philosophes* were not philosophers but social critics who believed that traditional ways of doing things stood in the way of solving the problems of society. They believed that through the use of reason based on collective human experience, we should be able to come up with likely solutions to problems, and that these solutions should then be tested to see if they worked. In other words, they advocated using Newton's method and applying it in society as well as in natural philosophy.

The *philosophes* prized intellectual independence and original thinking, though they could be savage in their opposition to those who criticized them or their ideas. In his masterpiece *Candide*, for example, the French *philosophe* Voltaire not only presented a sweeping satire of society, religion, culture, and human nature but also took time to target a theater critic who had disliked one of Voltaire's plays. That he should attack this critic in a work of this scope reveals a petty, vindictive streak in this otherwise brilliant satirist and thinker.

Nonetheless, despite this kind of verbal counterpunching, the ideal of intellectual independence meant that there was no single program promoted by the *philosophes*; some programs were relatively conservative, others quite radical. Politically, some liked the idea of an "enlightened despot," an absolutist prince who was guided by Enlightenment ideas in his state. Frederick the Great of Prussia attempted to fill this role. Others supported constitutional monarchy. Still others wanted a republic, and some even wanted democracy — direct control of the government by the people.

PHILOSOPHES AND RELIGION

Many Enlightenment thinkers were particularly interested in attacking religion. Although some *philosophes* were deists, others such as David Hume in Scotland and Baron d'Holbach in France were atheists, something that would have been inconceivable a generation earlier. For these thinkers, human reason was supreme. If something did not meet their standard of reason, it could and should be rejected. Since the traditional proofs for the existence of God did not seem reasonable or compelling to them, they rejected the idea of God altogether.

The arguments of Hume and others would pave the way for philosophical naturalism in the nineteenth century; in the eighteenth century, however, most intellectuals were still holding a theistic or deistic worldview. Nonetheless, many of the eighteenth-century *philosophes* wanted to break the church's influence on society. Church and state were still closely intertwined, whether in Protestant countries with their state churches or in Catholic countries where the monarchies had close ties to the church hierarchy.

In France, these ties were particularly strong. The church even had a formal role in the rather anachronistic institutional structures of the state, and it enjoyed special privileges and rights not extended to other religious groups. This drove the *philosophes* to vicious verbal attacks on the church; Voltaire, for example, took as an unofficial motto the phrase *écrassez l'infâme!* ("crush the infamous thing," meaning the Catholic Church). To be fair, he wasn't particularly enthusiastic about Protestants of any stripe either, but in France, he saw the Catholic Church as a particular problem.

THE ENLIGHTENED WORLDVIEW

In terms of worldview, then, this group of Enlightenment *philosophes* saw the material world as the only one that mattered. Even the deists believed that God was aloof and uninvolved in the world. Knowledge came exclusively from human reason and could be expected to grow and improve over time, based on the further accumulation of experience. Morality was cut off from revealed religion and instead was based on the dictates of reason, at least in principle. Personal moral standards grew much looser. The Genevan-born philosopher Rousseau, for example, had a number of illegitimate children, all of whom he abandoned. (In view of his track record, it is something of a mystery why some people continue to see him as having made important contributions to the discussion about the proper way to raise and educate children.)

At the same time, however, ideas of inalienable rights and other elements of political, economic, and social morality were imported from earlier Christian ideas, albeit with some modifications. Even as they rejected Christianity and the role of the church, these thinkers often maintained a great deal of residual Christianity within their worldview. This should come as no surprise, because even the framework they used for reason was rooted in medieval and early modern society, which itself was a product of the blending of the Bible and classical civilization.

CHRISTIANITY IN THE ENLIGHTENMENT

None of this meant that Christianity had lost its role as a cultural and intellectual force during this period, even if its place in society was changing. In the wake of the Wars of Religion, religion was seen by many to be a dangerous and divisive force, and anyone who was too serious about it was condemned for their "enthusiasm." Nonetheless, in many countries reform movements pushed toward a deeper experience of the Christian faith.

In France, a seventeenth-century movement called Jansenism advocated a return to a strict Augustinian theology and an austere lifestyle as essential to a truly Christian life. Since this suggested that the king would go to hell — given the decadence and opulence of the royal court — Jansenism was seen as politically dangerous. As a result, it was attacked by Cardinal Richelieu, the Jesuits, and other members of the church hierarchy as heretical and "crypto-Calvinist."

The Jansenists found powerful support in Blaise Pascal, the mathematician and natural philosopher who pioneered probabilism. Pascal had a conversion experience that led him to Jansenism, and he spent his considerable literary talents trying to defend the movement by deflecting attention to the Jesuits. Ultimately, he failed, but the fact that an early Enlightenment thinker such as Pascal was involved with as conservative a movement as Jansenism speaks volumes about the vitality of traditional Christianity, even as its ideas were starting to come under attack.

In Germany in the same period, a reform movement led by Jacob Spener argued that the Lutheran churches had become excessively rationalistic and had reduced the faith to assent to a system of theology. Known as pietism, this movement advocated renewed study of the Bible, vibrant personal faith and devotion, and living out the faith in daily life. Some pietists rejected doctrinal statements, philosophy, and other things that were central to the established churches, and thus they were ejected from those churches. Younger theologians, however, picked up their ideas and carried them throughout Germany, though the lack of cohesive leadership meant that different groups took the basic ideas of pietism in different directions, some of which would influence other reform movements in the eighteenth century.

In the American colonies, a major religious revival broke out in the Dutch Reformed churches in New Jersey in 1726. Known as the Great Awakening, the revival spread to the Presbyterian and Congregational churches and peaked in New England in the 1740s. Later, it spread to Virginia and the southern colonies as well. Like pietism, the Great Awakening emphasized personal experiences of conversion and evidence of a changed life. Its leaders, however, including Jonathan Edwards and George Whitefield, believed doctrine to be important as well and sought to tone down what they saw as the excessive emotionalism and experientialism of some involved in the revival. But also like pietism, the Awakening divided churches over whether or not the experiences of the "converted" were valid or necessary for true Christianity.

Jonathan Edwards is remembered today mostly for a single paragraph out of his sermon "Sinners in the Hands of an Angry God." This is unfortunate, not only because the quotation is taken out of context and misses the point of the sermon, but because Edwards was the first and arguably the greatest major thinker America has produced. His works included important treatises in philosophy, psychology, and theology; a piece on entomology; and a history of the Great Awakening.

His essay on entomology, written while he was still a teenager, is particularly revealing. He was interested in how spiders "fly." After close observation, he concluded that they let out some silk and are picked up and carried on the breeze. He speculated that spiders probably enjoy flying as much as they can enjoy anything, and he suggested that his observations helped explain where all the baby spiders go after they hatch in the thousands from the egg clusters. Since the prevailing breeze blows out to sea, the spiders as they fly are carried over the ocean, where they fall in and become food for fish. He then offers this conclusion: the "pleasure and recreation" of the spiders became the means of their destruction, which provides an important moral lesson for us.[3]

To our ears, this argument may seem quaint or even rather bizarre, but as George Marsden pointed out in his biography of Edwards, the transactions of the Royal Philosophical Society, the preeminent scientific organization in the eighteenth-century world, are full of moral and spiritual lessons drawn from studies of nature.[4] In other words, even in the eighteenth century, the intellectual elites were still thinking in terms of natural philosophy and theology as they studied the world. These kinds of lessons were hardly the secular thinking of a deist, a rationalist, or an atheist; instead, they demonstrate the ongoing influence of an essentially Christian worldview on the intellectual elites of the day.

The Great Awakening was also accompanied by a revival in England, led by George Whitefield and the Wesley brothers. The Wesleys especially were influenced by the pietists via the Moravian Brethren, who had been given sanctuary in Germany by Spener's godson, Count von Zinzendorf. Whitefield and the Wesleys not only preached personal conversion but also advocated for social justice issues. They were accused of "enthusiasm" by the powers that be in the Church of England, eventually causing John Wesley to split off to form a new church, the Methodists.

But even in the Church of England, the Wesleys continued to influence important segments of society. The best-known example of this is William Wilberforce, a key figure in the so-called Clapham Sect, whose conversion to "evangelicalism" (in this context, Christians who held to a high view of Scripture, emphasized personal conversion, and believed that Scripture should be applied to every area of life) moved him to lead the battle in Parliament to abolish the slave trade (a fight that took twenty years) and then slavery itself (which took another twenty-six years). He was inspired in this work in part by the last letter John Wesley ever wrote, which encouraged him to pursue this battle, but only with the help of God. In addition, Wilberforce helped establish the Bible Society, the Royal Society for the Prevention of Cruelty to Animals, and over sixty other charitable and moral organizations for the "reformation of manners" (i.e., reform of society) in England.

CHURCH AND SOCIETY

In the midst of Enlightenment rationalism and deism, a Christian worldview was thus alive and well and even thriving in many parts of the Western world. It had evolved in some ways, particularly in its view of the role of religion in public life. Up to this point, it had always been assumed that being religious was a good thing, and that a good Christian would be the best citizen, as Augustine argued. In the wake of the Wars of Religion, however, these ideas were no longer seen as true by many, especially those in positions of authority in society. People who were *too* religious were seen as potentially dangerous. In polite society, "proper" religious practice focused either on the acceptance of correct doctrinal formulations or on following the correct liturgical forms. Too much intensity in religious life was discouraged, even by the clergy.

Important segments of the population were not content with a merely formal religion, however. Yet the established churches placed serious roadblocks in front of them as they sought to restore what Wilberforce called "real Christianity." The reformers were thus forced on the one hand to emphasize the importance of personal commitment to the gospel because they could not count on the churches to encourage it, and on the other hand to argue that Christians have social responsibilities, that Christianity has implications for all of life, and thus that personal change should result in social change and societal reform as well. These ideas were not new; they had been part of the Christian worldview for centuries. What was new was that these ideas increasingly had to be asserted in opposition to both the state and the church itself.

WORLDVIEW AND REVOLUTIONS

The late seventeenth and eighteenth centuries saw three revolutions — one in England, one in America, and one in France. Each was influenced by the new thinking that developed in the period, but each also had very different results.

The first was the Glorious Revolution of 1688 in England. As we have seen, this revolution was triggered by the perception that Catholic government was inevitably tyrannical, a perception reinforced by Louis XIV's outlawing of Protestantism in France through his revocation of the Edict of Nantes in 1685. Protestant England was unhappy with their Catholic monarch James II and his attempts to circumvent Parliament by putting Catholics in high positions in his government, and then having an heir, another Catholic king, waiting in the wings. As a result, James II was deposed and his daughter Mary and her husband William of Orange were invited in (with troops!) to take the throne, the last successful invasion of Britain from the continent.

John Locke provided the intellectual justification for this revolution. His ideas grew out of, among other things, the Protestant resistance theory developed from the Saint Bartholomew's Day Massacre in France (1572), medieval ideas of inalienable rights, and the doctrine of original sin and the resulting argument for limited government and against the divine right of kings and absolutism. Locke argued that governments exist by contract with the people to preserve their God-given inalienable rights to life, liberty, and property. Where the government does so, the people are duty bound to obey it. If, however, the government fails to protect those rights, the people can legitimately revoke the contract with that government and set up a new contract with a government that will preserve their rights.

In keeping with this concept, once William and Mary were securely in place, they worked out a system for a constitutional monarchy, with Parliament given a number of new rights, privileges, and responsibilities secured by the Bill of Rights (1689). Significantly, all the disputes between James II and the Parliament were settled in favor of the latter. That same year they also issued the Toleration Act, guaranteeing freedom of worship to all Trinitarian Protestants, despite the status of the Church of England as the "established" church. Both of these were expressions of the idea that the government exists to preserve the liberty of the people, the inalienable right that James II as a Catholic was seen as undermining.

THE AMERICAN REVOLUTION

The second revolution took place in the British colonies in America in 1776. The causes of the American Revolution are many and varied, and historians and politicians argue about them constantly. Although taxation without representation is usually cited as the main reason for the revolution, that issue actually came as the seventeenth accusation against the king of England in the Declaration of Independence. One critical element was royal interference with the colonies' right to govern their own affairs. For example, several colonies had passed laws abolishing slavery, but the monarchy had vetoed them. In some cases, the monarchy changed the terms of government within the colonies to place them under governors appointed by London.

The leaders of the revolution saw these and other actions by the government as violations of their liberty and, in some cases, their property. Following the logic of the Glorious Revolution, they therefore had a right to end their allegiance to Britain. In fact, in the Declaration of Independence, Thomas Jefferson indirectly refers to John Locke with his appeal to "life, liberty, and the pursuit of happiness." Locke placed property as the third inalienable right, but to Jefferson, the pursuit of the good life, by which he meant a life of virtue, was even more fundamental. Of course, property enabled one to pursue this kind of life and so was also important, but Jefferson wanted the focus to be on virtue. In any event, after the Revolution and a brief period under the Articles of Confederation, the new country adopted the Constitution and the Bill of Rights as the fundamental law of the land.

ENLIGHTENMENT, CHRISTIANITY, AND THE CONSTITUTION

The origins of the Constitution and Bill of Rights are also debated hotly, and the issue has become highly politicized. The key point for our present purpose is the worldview of the framers. One side argues that they were deists, rationalists, and secularists in the mold of the Enlightenment; the other claims they were orthodox Christians.

There is no question that Enlightenment thought — particularly John Locke's political thought — influenced the founders. And some of them were heavily influenced by deism. Probably the most broadly influenced was Thomas Jefferson. Jefferson went so far as to take a pair of scissors and cut out of the Bible everything he found unreasonable, including all cases of supernatural intervention. He then read the rest for inspiration. At the same time, however, he considered himself a Christian and expressed concerns about divine judgment on the nation — something a consistent deist wouldn't have done since God does not intervene in the world. Overall, however, in terms of worldview, there is little question that Jefferson leaned heavily toward deism. On the other hand, though he was the primary author of the Declaration of Independence, he was in Europe during the Constitutional Convention and the passing of the Bill of Rights, so his views are hardly relevant to those documents.

Benjamin Franklin, who is rightly viewed by all sides as one of the least religious of the founders, strongly advocated prayer at the Constitutional Convention, noting that prayer in the Continental Congress during the Revolution had resulted in the protection and guidance of Providence and urging the Convention to follow that precedent in their own deliberations. (As it turns out, the motion failed because the Convention did not have enough money to hire a minister to lead the prayers.) Clearly, Franklin had some kind of religious belief and wasn't a pure deist because he believed that Providence intervened in the world in answer to prayer.

The same can be said of George Washington. Several people had reported walking in on him when he was on his knees fervently praying. In fact, only a very small minority of the two hundred or so people considered to be founding fathers in America could be fairly described as deists or free thinkers.

The rest belonged to a variety of orthodox churches — Congregational, Presbyterian, Anglican, Baptist, and others (though some of the founders who were members of these churches had somewhat unorthodox views). Many were ministers or had earned divinity degrees. And if you take the time to read what they wrote, both for public and private audiences, it is clear that they thought they were establishing a government based on biblical principles, including the ideas of *inalienable rights* (which had roots in medieval theology) enshrined in both the Declaration of Independence and the Bill of Rights, *limitations* on the reach of the federal government to the enumerated powers in the Constitution, and *checks and balances* within the government to prevent human sinfulness from corrupting the government, even representative government (which they saw as being rooted in Jethro's advice to Moses in Exodus 18). To be sure, they rarely cited chapter and verse from Scripture in their political discussions, but their priorities and overall approach to government were firmly grounded in a Christian worldview.

In fact, in a ten-year study undertaken at the University of Houston, researchers examined 15,000 documents (many unrelated to politics) from the founders and determined that 34 percent of the quotations came from the Bible, the highest of any source. The next highest was the French political philosopher Montesquieu at 8.3 percent, then the English legal scholar William Blackstone at 7.9 percent. John Locke came in at 2.9 percent.[5] (Blackstone's commentaries on the law, which guided the Supreme Court for over a century, also include a great deal of Scripture and argue that the Bible is the foundation for all law.) Whatever else can be said, it is clear from this study that the intellectual world of the founders was heavily influenced by Scripture.

LOCKE, ORIGINAL SIN, AND THE CONSTITUTION

In their discussion of politics, the founders emphasized the idea drawn from the Bible that only godly men of character should be elected to government, since the forms of government were only a shell; the substance of government and the only defense against corruption were the people who were elected to office. This emphasis on the danger of corruption, drawn from the doctrine of original sin, contrasts sharply with John Locke's ideas about how to prevent abuse in government. Locke believed we are blank slates at birth, with no preprogrammed structures in our minds. Our experiences are stored in our mind, which organizes and makes sense of them. A proper education would provide a child with many and varied experiences that will make her or him smarter, more capable, and, if the experiences are carefully selected, more moral. This idea was very popular among Enlightenment thinkers, in part because it suggests the possibility of human perfectibility. Among other things, it denies the doctrine of original sin.

This rejection of original sin helped shape Locke's political thought. Locke believed that good laws would hold in check even bad people in government. Developing and, if necessary, elaborating the proper governmental structure was thus critical — proper structure in all its details was essential to preventing tyranny. For example, the Fundamental Constitution of the Carolinas, which seems to have been drafted by Locke in 1669, is almost twice the length of the United States Constitution because of its attention to detail.

This contrast in length illustrates the fundamental difference in attitude between Locke and the American founders on this point. Although the founders believed that proper governmental structure was important and that they could help prevent corruption through the system of checks and balances, they did not have Locke's faith in the perfectibility of humanity, nor did they follow him in rejecting the idea of original sin. Thus they did not elaborate the system of government in as much detail as Locke did, but instead argued that the key to keeping the government from turning into a tyranny was the quality of the people elected to office.

AMERICAN GOVERNMENT AND THE ECONOMY

The American emphasis on the importance of personal morality for political leadership carried over into economics as well. Although the country was founded on free market principles in keeping with its system of representative government, the founders were also concerned about "sharp" business practices that would take advantage of workers or customers and the effects of unrestrained greed. Although they did not think it was the job of the government to regulate those areas, they did believe that social pressures and "voting with the feet" would restrain businessmen from excessive profits gained through exploitation of the public or their workers, and that in any event, people who did such things should be disqualified from political office.

Unfortunately, this idea has sometimes been misapplied, so that anyone who becomes wealthy in business is believed to have done so through taking advantage of either workers or customers. While sometimes the case, frequently it is not, but it has contributed to the strong streak of populism that arises periodically in

America, pitting the masses against the wealthy and penalizing the successful in the name of equality of outcomes rather than equality of opportunity.

On the other hand, exploitation of workers occurs and has occurred, with the most extreme example in American history being slavery. The founders recognized this tendency, and in keeping with the long tradition of Christian opposition to slavery, most of the signers of the Declaration of Independence were abolitionists. Once the Constitution was ratified, half of the states voted immediately to outlaw slavery. Unfortunately, however, not all did, with tragic results that have come to expression in the Civil War and the legacy of racism in our society.

EUROPE AND AMERICA

The Bible was not the only source for the Constitution, of course. Among other things, for example, the elected branches of the federal government represent the three good types of government outlined by Aristotle: the President embodies the *monarchial* principle, the Senate the *aristocratic* principle, and the House of Representatives the *republican* principle. The federal government is thus an Aristotelian "mixed state," with the different branches providing the checks and balances needed to counteract the weaknesses of the others. In fact, the Constitution was greeted by progressive thinkers in Europe as an ideal system of government. They concluded with some amazement that the colonists were able to do what the best political thinkers in Europe had been unable to do, namely, to design a balanced, mixed government.

In point of fact, the European reaction to the Constitution was more correct than they knew. The colonists were able to pull off a new model of government in a way that Europeans simply could not. One of the advantages the Americans had was that they did not have a long-entrenched system of government or a centuries-old aristocracy or monarchy to deal with. The Americans were free to develop a system of government that drew from the best of the British model while getting rid of institutions such as the nobility and the monarchy that they judged as not helpful.

This hadn't been an option for England's Glorious Revolution because of both the long-established social and political structures and the experience of the civil war and Commonwealth, which resulted in regicide and social turmoil and failed to produce durable institutions to replace the monarchy. And unlike the French Revolution, the Americans felt no compulsion to remove all traces of the past and start from scratch with something new and opposite from what they had previously.

THE FRENCH REVOLUTION

This brings us to the French Revolution, the last and most extreme of the three. If anything, the causes of the French Revolution are debated even more hotly than those of the American Revolution, largely because it was a major turning point in European history. Suffice it to say that the Revolution was triggered by a fiscal crisis. Louis XVI's government was bankrupt and saddled with an inefficient system of taxation that exempted the nobility and the clergy (the wealthiest members of society) from paying any direct taxes. Any attempt to reform the system was opposed by the nobility (of course), using the Enlightenment argument (adapted from medieval legal theory) that taxes could only be imposed with the consent of the governed. Since the nobility did not agree to the tax reform, any attempt to impose new taxes on them amounted to an unlawful attack on property, and thus was tyranny. (Of course, the nobility conveniently ignored the fact that no one had asked the peasants or urban workers if they consented to taxation, but the nobles figured that since these groups had always been taxed, their opinion didn't count.)

When the Revolution broke out, the "third estate" (non-clergy and non-nobles) rapidly took control. From there, things got even more complicated, with the Revolution passing through a moderate phase to a very violent, radical phase, and back to a more moderate period. The worldviews varied in each of these phases and were often obscured by the various governments' attempts to deal with simultaneous crises in many areas of society. But all phases were products of Enlightenment thought.

THE FIRST MODERATE PHASE

In the first moderate phase of the Revolution, the goal was to produce a written constitution for France and to set up a limited monarchy. In fact, at one point the strategists thought they had accomplished this, but the king reneged on the deal, sneaking out of Paris and attempting to join the foreign armies moving in to stop the Revolution. Unfortunately, Louis XVI was caught and returned to Paris, where he and his family would later be executed for treason.

Beyond the constitutional monarchy, the moderates also wanted to produce a freer, more equitable society. Some of these ideals would be enshrined in the "Declaration of the Rights of Man and Citizen" (and yes, they meant adult males; women participated in the Revolution but were not given equal rights with men). These goals, however, proved to be difficult to balance. For example, the revolutionary government was committed to respecting property rights — a holdover from medieval Christian ideas that was nonetheless embraced by most Enlightenment thinkers — while simultaneously ending hereditary privilege and titles of nobility that were themselves a form of property. The peasants wanted all old dues and obligations abolished, but if that were to happen, the National Assembly would lose the support of the nobility. In the end, a compromise was reached that *looked* as though it supported the peasants while actually taking away some of their traditional rights to compensate the nobles for their losses.

This compromise helped stabilize one problem, but there were other problems to be faced as well. The National Assembly realized that it needed to assume the debts of the old government if it were to have any hope of legitimacy (and if it were to be consistent with its own economic principles), but the insolvency of the government meant that the National Assembly had no means whereby it could pay the debt. To raise money to try to keep the government afloat, the National Assembly decided to target the Catholic Church.

THE FIRST ATTACK ON THE CHURCH

This attack was inevitable. Much of the French Enlightenment showed itself to be virulently anticlerical, and the National Assembly embarked on a program to break the power and influence of the Catholic Church in the country. Because the political districts in the kingdom corresponded to the Catholic diocesan structure, the revolutionaries introduced an entirely new system of organization for the state built around a new level in the government called Departments. They introduced new secular holidays to replace the old ones, which were invariably religious. Then to ease their financial troubles, they confiscated nearly all of the church's land in the kingdom. When the pope objected to this and condemned the Revolution, the National Assembly responded by making all priests paid agents of the state and insisting that they take an oath of allegiance to the Revolution. Priests who refused the oath were subject to arrest and, at times, execution.

THE RADICAL PHASE: THE REIGN OF TERROR

Even after confiscating the church's lands, the government was still insolvent. Inflation was out of control. There were food shortages and hoarding, and in general things went from bad to worse. This led to the radical phase of the Revolution, when the Jacobins, the most extreme party in the National Assembly, teamed up with the Paris mob to stage a coup and take over the government.

ROBESPIERRE AND ROUSSEAU

The Jacobins were led by Maximilien Robespierre, an ardent follower of Jean-Jacques Rousseau, whose thought was built on John Locke's teaching that people were born as blank slates and learn through experiences, which the mind organizes for itself; there are no preset structures in the mind, and especially no original sin. For Rousseau, people were perfectible if given the right education and experiences; and so he wrote *Émile* and *La Nouvelle Héloïse* to explain the proper way to educate boys and girls.

But this idea also led Rousseau to utopianism — to the belief that the right organization of society would bring about perfect equality and freedom. Rousseau outlined his scheme in *The Social Contract*. He said that far from being a fundamental right, private property was the source of inequality in the world. To reach an equitable society, all private property had to be abolished, and with it, the idea that the individual had a right to determine her or his interests. Instead, everyone without exception had to submit the final determination of their interests to the general will so that true equality and freedom could be established. Those who refused were to be "forced to be free" by compelling their submission to the general will.

Rousseau's definition of freedom was almost the complete opposite of how most people use the word. But his strategy was similar to a tactic used by advertisers and other propagandists, namely, to take a word that has good associations, redefine it, and then as you use it, you count on people to accept what you say because of their positive feelings about the word.

Robespierre chose to implement Rousseau's ideas. He said the people demanded inexpensive bread, so he instituted price controls. He also made hoarding grain a capital offense, along with currency speculation. And since the people were angry, he decided to institute a program of "revolutionary justice," where terror became "the order of the day."[6] Anyone who was insufficiently enthusiastic about the Revolution was tried before a kangaroo court and executed — 1,961 people were guillotined in what would later be called the Place de la Concorde in Paris, only one of several sites in the city where people were executed.

DE-CHRISTIANIZATION

Robespierre also continued the attack on the Catholic Church. Rousseau had believed that a civil religion that promised eternal blessings to the obedient and eternal punishment to the disobedient was an essential prop for the state. So Robespierre decided to enforce civil religion — the Cult of the Supreme Being — and to rechristen the cathedral of Notre Dame "the Temple of Reason." He began to de-Christianize France systematically from top to bottom. For example, rather than counting years from the birth of Christ, he reset the calendar to I to date it from the Revolution. He renamed all of the months to negate traditional associations with Christian feast days and holidays. And since the seven-day week was a reflection of the Genesis creation story, he made each week ten days long.

THE FINAL MODERATE PHASE: THE DIRECTORY

Eventually, Robespierre overreached. He was himself condemned of treason and guillotined, bringing to an end the Terror. The subsequent government, known as the Directory, was much more moderate. Its only real goal was to try to steer itself between a return of mob rule and the radicals on the one hand and a royalist resurgence on the other. Ultimately, these leaders would be replaced by Napoleon, a man who would in many ways act like an "enlightened despot" but always by means of the trappings of republicanism.

COMPARATIVE REVOLUTIONS

What are we to make of the different courses of each of these revolutions? England and France had to contend with their own histories and cultures. England preserved the basic structure of the country while strengthening the parliament and definitively ending any possibility of absolutism. In France, once a constitutional monarchy proved impossible, the revolutionaries reacted against virtually all aspects of the state, eliminating the king, abolishing the social hierarchy, reorganizing the political units in the kingdom, replacing the religion, even changing the country's calendar. In other words, both revolutions were controlled in many ways by the past, either through embracing precedent with modifications or rejecting it completely. America, unburdened by the past, was free to take what it wanted from its history and introduce new institutions as well as to set up a system that suited its assumptions about the proper role and structure of government.

Then there were the conditions on the ground. Although a war was fought in the American colonies, neither England nor America faced the kinds of stresses that caused France to explode. With the economy in a shambles and people facing starvation, the violence of the radical phase of the French revolution was no surprise.

But beyond the circumstances of the revolutions were the ideas that motivated them. All were influenced by elements of Enlightenment thought, but with significant differences based on their ideas about human nature. John Locke rejected original sin and believed that right experiences would produce right behavior; he concluded, then, that if the government had the proper structure and provided the right laws, the best society would result, since even corrupt individuals would be controlled by the system.

The French took this conclusion even further, especially in the radical phase of the Revolution, advocating a utopian system where personal rights were subordinated to the general will to produce the perfect society. As in any utopia, nonconformists could not be allowed to pollute the system, since they would prevent the country from entering the Promised Land. In other words, utopian visions always end in totalitarianism, with nonconformists either forced to conform or be eliminated. As with those who head up Communist revolutions, the Jacobins declared all men to be brothers, except those they hung from the lampposts — or in this case beheaded.

How could this reign of terror happen in a revolution supposedly dedicated to liberty, equality, and brotherhood? The critical factor was the rejection of even the sort of formal Christianity found in England. As we have seen, from their earliest days, Christians had argued for the fundamental equality of all people based on their creation in the image of God and Jesus' sacrificial death for all. Thus early Christians worked to abolish slavery and over time developed the idea of civil equality to accompany spiritual and moral equality. No other civilization anywhere in history ever moved in this direction — only the West, under the influence of Christian principles. Along with equality came the idea of inalienable, God-given rights, which led to the Enlightenment emphasis on life, liberty, property, and virtue.

But once Enlightenment ideas were cut off from their Christian foundation, they no longer had a solid base to preserve them. They were free-floating ideas that sounded good but lacked any underlying rationale to preserve them when social, political, and economic stress combined to make them less popular or expedient. The net result? In the name of freedom and equality, nonconformists, the wealthy, and other victims of the mob's envy were executed.

In the American Revolution, most of the founders were orthodox Christians; only a small number were deists or rationalists. They thus lived with a tension in their minds between two paradoxical principles. On the one hand, human beings were seen as being created in the image of God. This meant in principle that each individual has equal value and inalienable rights and thus should be given equal opportunities with everyone else. On the other hand, we are fallen creatures who suffer the effects of original sin and are thus prone to corruption. As a result, the government created by America's founders was set up with checks and balances to prevent any branch of government from becoming too powerful and corrupt, and the Bill of Rights was formulated to try to guarantee that the people's inalienable rights would not be abridged by the government.

But at the same time, the founders did not rely on institutional structures to keep the country headed in the right direction. Instead, they knew the institutions would only be as good as the people elected to fill them, and thus they emphasized the character of those who would be elected far more than the structure of government. Some of the founders worked to establish a public school system to educate people, not just on the basic subjects, but on morality and the Bible; after all, education was not just about reading and writing but also about character formation. Others set up Bible societies and other religious organizations to try to instill virtue in the people, because only then would the government be kept from becoming too corrupt.

In short, although the conditions of each revolution were different, so were the ideas that motivated them — and the ideas determined the outcome every bit as much as the historical circumstances. But things did not stand still. The 1800s saw the consolidation of a much more secular, "modern" worldview grown from the roots of Enlightenment thought but progressing well beyond them. The next chapter examines how that worldview emerged.

MODERNITY AND ITS DISCONTENTS

Although its roots go back well into the eighteenth-century Enlightenment, the modern worldview really developed in the nineteenth century. To understand why it emerged, we need to go back to our discussion about deism.

FROM DEISM TO MATERIALISM

Although the various Christian denominations maintained orthodox theological statements, many members of the clergy and denominational leaders were already moving toward a functional deism, as evidenced by their rejection of enthusiasm, emotion, and overinvolvement (as they saw it) in religious matters in favor of a cool, rational, undemanding formalism. Deist ideas were also being gradually adopted by many theologians, and the accelerating attacks on the authority and reliability of Scripture led to further deterioration in traditional Christianity's hold on the thinkers of the period.

Unfortunately, however, deism is an unstable worldview. Because the only role God has is to kick-start the universe, if another alternative can be found to explain how the universe got here, we can safely eliminate God from the system altogether. All that is needed is a plausible-sounding explanation for the universe, and we are left with a world consisting only of matter and energy — a metaphysical system known as naturalism or materialism.

As it turns out, such an idea was already proposed by the ancient Greeks — the idea that the universe is eternal. If the universe is eternal, it never came into being and so was never created; the God of deism is thus completely unnecessary. You are left with a system that is explicitly atheist, that argues that "the cosmos is all that is, or ever was, or ever will be," to quote Carl Sagan.[1] (Or if you prefer *The Berenstain Bears' Nature Guide* — "Nature is all that IS, or WAS, or EVER WILL BE."[2] It amounts to the same thing.)

SCIENCE AND WORLDVIEW

Remember, ideas in worldviews all interlock. When you have a metaphysical system in place, it leads you directly to an epistemology — a system of knowledge — and to some extent vice versa. One of the reasons materialism was so appealing was the evolution of epistemology from an emphasis on reason to a codification of the scientific method. In the scientific method, you make a hypothesis, make predictions on the basis of that hypothesis, design an experiment to test whether those predictions do in fact occur, and then either modify the hypothesis or develop further experiments as necessary, depending on whether the earlier experiments confirmed or refuted the hypothesis.

Note that knowledge in this system is always fluid, always changing, never certain, but rendered probable by the results of the experiments. In other words, even if the experimental results align with the prediction, it does not necessarily prove the hypothesis correct, since further experimentation may not work out so well, and in any event there could be another explanation besides the hypothesis that would yield the same results.

From a worldview perspective, two things are important about the development of the scientific method. The first has to do with the use of the word *science*. The Latin *scientia* simply meant "knowledge"; thus any field of study was a "science" since it involved knowledge about the subject. Reducing the meaning of the word *science* only to studies that followed this particular methodology reflects a fundamental shift in the understanding of what it meant to know things. Now only things that could be tested and confirmed through the scientific method qualified as real knowledge; everything else was dismissed as subjective or irrelevant.

Second, the scientific method works well primarily in the natural sciences — in studies of the material world. Thus the shift to materialistic metaphysics was encouraged by the development of the scientific method, which was then enshrined as the one way to get true knowledge because the worldview said that the only thing there was to know was matter and energy. In other words, materialism and scientism — the idea that the only way you can truly know anything is through science — go hand in hand.

The shift to the scientific method may seem on the surface to be similar to aspects of the Enlightenment, but there are important differences. The scientific method is far less philosophical than Enlightenment thought; it relies on empiricism (observation of concrete data) rather than reason. This assessment comes from Auguste Comte, the founder of sociology in the early nineteenth century. Comte believed that societies moved through three stages — theological, in which the world is explained through supernatural agencies; metaphysical, in which the world is explained through philosophical abstractions (he placed the Enlightenment here); and scientific. Nonetheless, as had happened in the Enlightenment, the tremendous success in the natural sciences encouraged the development of the social sciences and the attempt to apply scientific methods to solve social problems, including the development of the fields of psychology, sociology, and criminology, all in the nineteenth century.

DARWIN AND NATURAL SELECTION

While the idea of an eternal universe was appealing, the question of where human beings came from was also important. Christianity teaches that human beings are created in the image of God and thus have dignity and worth and occupy a special place in the creation. Where did we come from and how do we explain human distinctiveness if we accept a purely materialistic view of the universe? The answer, of course, is that we evolved from "lower" species. Ideas of evolution had been around for some time by the nineteenth century; what no one had was an explanation of how that evolution occurred. That was the unique contribution of Charles Darwin in his book *The Origin of Species.*

Darwin's ideas paralleled in some ways Thomas Robert Malthus's argument ("An Essay on the Principle of Population") that species tend to overreproduce for the available resources. Taking this one step further, Darwin argued that, given the variability of creatures within a species, some would be more successful in competing for resources than others. Those who were would be more likely to survive to have offspring and would pass those successful traits down to their offspring. He hypothesized that large numbers of microchanges of this sort would accumulate to produce new species. This, according to Darwin, was the origin of *all* species. By implication, then, human beings were nothing more than highly evolved animals.

This idea caused quite a bit of controversy, in part because it contradicted the teaching of the book of Genesis and removed the basis for the uniqueness of human beings in the world. But there were other problems as well. For example, Alfred Russel Wallace, the co-discoverer of natural selection, eventually concluded that the human mind was too complex to be produced by small changes of the sort the theory proposed, and so he argued for a form of spiritualism to explain the mind. Darwin, distressed by Wallace's rejection of the theory, wrote *The Descent of Man*, making explicit the argument that humans and apes were descended from a common ancestor by the sole mechanism of natural selection.

DARWINISM AND WORLDVIEW

For people who found naturalism appealing, Darwin's theory was a godsend. It was the missing link needed to round out a fully naturalistic worldview, and Darwin's teaching has since become foundational for naturalistic thinking and scientism. Interestingly enough, his theory does not fit the definition of science. For a theory to be scientific, it must be able to be validated through the scientific method:

A theory is proposed and predictions are made from it.

These predictions are then tested through experimentation.

- If the experiment fails, the theory must be discarded or modified.
- If the experiment succeeds, it does not prove the theory true, but it does make it more probable that the theory is correct.

Darwinism is not itself subject to the scientific method any more than anything in history is. The past is over; you cannot revisit it, observe it, test it, or experiment on it. All you can do is look at the surviving evidence and try to make sense of it.

Darwin knew, of course, that he had no access to the past, but he reasoned that if his theory were true, then natural selection would still be operating today, and thus it should be possible to make specific predictions and test them. For example, Darwin thought that evolution occurred relatively quickly, as his experience with the beaks of finches growing longer during dry years suggested. He tried to breed pigeons into a new species to demonstrate this, but he found that while there was a great deal of variability in pigeons, the variability stopped well short of creating a new species. In other words, his experiment failed. You can take a goldfish and give it eyes that protrude, change its color to black, and divide its tail, but you cannot turn a goldfish into a goldfinch.

Darwin further predicted that innumerable transitional fossils would be discovered, probably within decades, and noted that if a sudden emergence of new species were to occur, his theory would be falsified. What the fossil record shows is that species are remarkably stable, and the innumerable transitions that Darwin predicted have not been found. Further, during the Cambrian period (usually dated to about 530 million years ago), most major groups of complex animals emerged suddenly, not by gradual evolution, in an event known as the "Cambrian explosion." According to Darwin himself, this simultaneous emergence of species without gradual ascent from earlier organisms should have disproved his theory.

Yet instead of falsifying Darwin, the basic concept of evolution has been retained, with alternative explanations suggested for the absence of transitional species. One popular theory, known as punctuated equilibrium, suggests that species tend to remain stable until, for some as yet unexplained reason, a series of rapid mutations takes place that produces new species. This happened so rapidly in terms of geological time that fossils, which are relatively rare things, were not produced in any of these periods of transition. Unfortunately, as Darwin himself said, this rapid evolution cannot be accounted for via natural selection. Rapid emergence of species falsifies his theory. It also sounds like special pleading, a "Darwin of the gaps" explanation, to say that the fossilization of the transitional forms predicted by Darwin never had the opportunity to take place in the emergence of *any* species on the planet, past or present. Nor is it much better to say the fossils are there but haven't yet been found. This is a statement of faith, not fact.

But, of course, none of this matters because Darwinism is not a scientific theory but a worldview assumption, and as such, it is not falsifiable. Certainly, naturalists think they have good reasons to accept natural selection, but people always believe this about their articles of faith. Ultimately, the evidence for Darwinism is circular:

- Naturalists assume Darwinian evolution.
- They use it as the framework for interpreting any evidence they find.
- They proclaim that the evidence proves the theory.

But as people employ this method, it is literally impossible to recognize evidence that would contradict Darwin because every explanation of the data begins by assuming that evolution is true and proceeds from there. In other words, Darwinism interprets the evidence rather than the evidence testing Darwinism. As a result, no matter how many failed predictions come from Darwinism, it can never be proven false. Simply put, naturalistic evolution is an article of faith.

If you are surprised or offended by this argument, then I would simply put this question to you: What evidence *would* falsify Darwinism? If you cannot think of or imagine anything that would, it is an article of faith and not a scientific theory.

DARWINIAN ETHICS

Like any worldview, materialism and Darwinism have implications that extend well beyond science. Metaphysical systems lead to ethical systems. If materialism is true, there is no such thing as good or evil. (If matter and energy are all that exist, what is goodness? What about evil? Are they matter or energy? They are neither, and so they do not really exist.) We are left with relatively few choices as anchors for ethics.

DARWIN AND RACE

Very early on, Darwin's ideas contributed to a movement now called Social Darwinism that argued that survival of the fittest should not simply be used to explain the origin of species; the concept also applied to competition, success, and survival among individuals, groups, races, and nations. In other words, *human societies* evolve in the same way that species do, namely, by competition.

Although some of this thinking preceded *The Origin of Species*, Darwin himself suggested something along these lines in chapter 6 of *Descent of Man*, when he commented, "At some future period, not very distant as measured by centuries, the civilized races of man will almost certainly exterminate, and replace, the savage races throughout the world."[3] Although Darwin himself rejected racism on the grounds that we all come from common ancestry, he still saw a difference between races and predicted that competition among them would result in some races destroying others. In fact, the subtitle of *The Origin of Species* is *The Preservation of Favored Races in the Struggle for Life*.

This kind of thinking contributed directly to rising racism and neocolonialism in the Western world. The basic idea was that the white race was superior because it had evolved in a harsher climate that killed off the mentally and physically inferior. Whites were thus more fit to survive, as evidenced by their aggressive interest in expansion into the outside world, as well as by their achievements in science, technology, and industrialization. They thus had a right and a responsibility to dominate the nonwhite races, either to give them the benefits of Western civilization or to exploit them for profit. Whites also had the right to compete with each other for colonies, which in turn led to a sharp rise in militarism and an alliance system that would be a major factor in the outbreak of the First World War.

Not everyone who accepted racial superiority felt "the white man's burden" to spread Western civilization throughout the world, however. Some, such as Charles Lindberg, believed that the white races were in danger of being overrun by the greater numbers of the brown races, since the inferior always overreproduce and the superior do not (an idea that had its roots in Thomas Robert Malthus). As a result, whites should keep technologies, such as airplanes, to themselves so they would maintain an edge over the browns.

Both the triumphalism of the colonialists and the paranoia of those who feared being overwhelmed demographically hinged on a concept of race that was given a quasi-scientific foundation by Darwinism. Historically, race was essentially the same as nationality — earlier writers talked about the English race as distinct from the French race, for example — but by this point a new definition had begun to emerge that found ample support in Darwin's theories. In fact, the principal use of race since this period has almost always been implicitly racist — that is, it focuses on which race is superior and which is inferior.

The most extreme version can be seen in Nazism, which was based on the premise that Aryans were the most highly evolved race and therefore the only ones who were truly and fully human. Other "races" were inferior and for all practical purposes subhuman. Whatever they had that the Aryans needed could legitimately be taken; they could be enslaved to work for the master race with no more moral qualms than those raised by hitching a horse to a plow and making it work. And if a race posed a threat to the Aryans in any way, the Aryans had the right and responsibility to exterminate it. Darwin's thinking contributed directly to this and other forms of racist oppression, since the theory focused so much on competition and "fitness" for survival. If this is true of individuals, why wouldn't it be true of races?

EUGENICS

Another idea that fit closely with Darwin's theories was *eugenics*, that is, actively encouraging the "more fit" members of society to have children while discouraging the "less fit" to do so to keep society from being overrun with "inferiors." Francis Galton (Darwin's cousin) was an early advocate of eugenics. Darwin himself was interested in the subject and discussed Galton's ideas in his book *Descent of Man*. Eugenics would later inspire Margaret Sanger in her founding of Planned Parenthood and lead to laws to sterilize forcibly the mentally or physically handicapped, Native Americans, African-American women, and criminals.

Altogether, between 1907 and the end of World War II, nearly 36,000 Americans had been sterilized in state-sponsored compulsory sterilization campaigns.[4] American eugenicists, in turn, helped inspire the Nazis in their eugenics campaigns, both in their attempts to breed the Aryan master race and in instituting programs to sterilize "inferior" people (e.g., individuals with mental or physical disabilities) and to exterminate the "inferior" races who competed with the Aryans for resources.

ALTERNATIVE APPROACHES TO ETHICS

Not everyone who accepted Darwin was a racist, a colonialist, or a eugenicist, of course. But the worldview logically led in that direction, as Darwin himself recognized. Remember, he saw it as inevitable that the civilized races would exterminate and replace the savage races. If the doctrine of survival of the fittest is correct, it points to an ethical approach in which those who are superior get to survive and those who aren't don't get to survive. In a world devoid of meaning (What is meaning — matter or energy?), what better basis for ethics is there than to argue that only the strong survive and thus deserve what they can get?

Some people have suggested alternative materialist frameworks for ethics. For example, *utilitarianism* bases ethics on what produces the greatest good for the greatest number. This approach has the disadvantage that it does not integrate as directly with the other components of the worldview as the variants on Social Darwinism do. In other words, utilitarianism does not flow directly from the basic premises of materialism and scientism.

It also leaves unresolved the definition of *good*. Who, ultimately, determines what is good? By removing the connection between ethics and what is real and knowable, utilitarian ethics (along with many other modernist systems of ethics) is completely arbitrary, a situation that, as we have seen in the French Revolution, provides no foundation for preserving human rights. In fact, utilitarianism explicitly rejects the rights of the individual. For a contemporary example, medical ethicist Peter Singer of Princeton University openly advocates legalizing infanticide of disabled infants, the elderly, and others who are a burden to society. By eliminating such people, the overall level of happiness goes up, since the struggle, pain, and suffering they and those who care for them experience simply disappears.

Another alternative ethical system suggests that ethics are *situational and relative*, that is, that there are no firm ethical principles. Since right and wrong have no objective reality, ethics cannot have an absolute or objective foundation, and so what is right or wrong depends entirely on perspective, cultural background, and circumstances. There is therefore no basis for offering a moral judgment on anything, since to do so would imply that there is some objective basis for making this moral judgment. While this conclusion sounds fine in daily life, it raises problems for criticizing, for example, slavery, racism, or genocide. On what basis can these be condemned if they are "right" for their own particular cultures?

There are other alternative approaches that stem from a naturalistic perspective, but they either are arbitrary or end up resembling eugenics or another program from Social Darwinism. In ethical terms, modern human beings have their feet planted firmly in midair, in the memorable phrase often attributed to British political commentator Harold Laski. This is a far cry from the "inalienable" right of each individual to life, much less liberty, property, and the pursuit of the good life that we saw promoted in the eighteenth century and earlier.

MATERIALISM AND ECONOMICS

Darwinism also has economic implications. If survival of the fittest is the means by which species improve themselves, thrive, and evolve, it would be logical to assume this is also true in economics.

As we have seen, free market capitalism was already an important and growing movement in Europe and America in the eighteenth century, though residual ideas from medieval- and Reformation-era theologians tempered this with moral restraints such as charging a fair price, paying just wages, not cheating customers or employees, personal obligations for the rich to help the poor (often by providing employment), and so on. Businesses were seen as providing an essential service to society. They provided employment and offered goods to people at a price that allowed them to make a profit — and a price that people were willing to pay. The people bought products when their desire for the product was greater than their desire to hold on to their money. The idea was to look for a win-win proposition, with both sides giving up something they had in return for something they more deeply desired.

Survival of the fittest in business, however, removed many of these moral restraints from the equation. Cutthroat competition became the order of the day, including the exploitation of workers.

THE INDUSTRIAL REVOLUTION

The industrial revolution was influenced by this new attitude toward economics. As scientific methods were applied to production, new technologies developed to make products more efficiently. New energy sources such as coal and steam powered the machinery in the factories. Division of labor further increased the efficiency of production.

But all of this also led to alienation of factory workers. The loss of the idea of the image of God in the materialistic assumptions of the age led to a rejection of the goodness of work, which meant that labor returned to drudgery. Workers no longer had the satisfaction of the old guild craftsmen who made a product from start to finish. Further, their hours and pace were set by the machines, and in the early days of the industrial revolution the workers were actually chained to the machines. There were no safety devices on the machinery, which was frequently dangerous. In fact, women and children were often hired because they had smaller hands and so could reach into the gears of jammed machines to remove whatever had caused the jam. Unfortunately, if the worker wasn't quick enough, the machine would restart and mangle hands and arms, crippling or killing her or him.

For all its faults, the old manorial system of lord and peasant at least involved some form of personal relationship and an element of respect. In the new factories, an impersonal system of management and labor developed in which mutual respect was completely lacking. Labor saw management as uncaring and greedy, while management saw labor as lazy drunks.

But while the brutality of the factories is well known, there is another side to the industrial revolution. The fact is that once it was well established, industrial production raised the standard of living for most people in industrialized countries. Some people lost out — an inescapable fact of life when fundamental economic change occurs — but many more prospered. Of course, this was cold comfort for those trapped in the coal mines and the factories while earning barely subsistence wages, where maximizing profits for owners was all that mattered.

MARXISM

The problems of industrialization fueled one of the most important materialistic philosophies of the nineteenth century — an idea that originated with thinkers who tried to apply scientific methods to history, even though history itself is not subject to the kind of prediction and experimentation possible in the natural sciences. Oddly enough, this line began with Georg Wilhelm Friedrich Hegel, a philosopher who combined Enlightenment faith in reason with a denial of both scientism and materialism.

Hegel believed that behind the individual human mind was an Absolute Mind that was constantly evolving and revealing itself in history. History was moving through a series of eras toward a goal of perfect freedom. Each era was governed by a principle known as its "thesis," which determined who was free and who was not. But as the era advanced, since true freedom was not present, a counter-idea or "antithesis" would develop within the society until eventually there would be a revolution; the thesis and antithesis would merge together into a synthesis, which then became the new principle for the next era. He described this process as *historical dialectic* (or logic).

For example, according to Hegel, history started with an era in which there was a king and all other persons were slaves. But the king could not rule alone, so he surrounded himself with slaves who acted as his administrators and the leaders of the people. These leaders eventually revolted and gained power as nobles, so now there was the king and the nobles, plus slaves. Then some of the slaves rose up, becoming free peasants. And so on. Eventually, when everyone is truly free, the dynamic that moves history forward will stop, and history itself will come to an end.

Although Hegel rejected both materialism and scientism, some of his followers did not. In particular, Karl Marx took Hegel's basic ideas but transformed them into a materialistic philosophy. He argued that since the material world was all that existed, all of Hegel's talk about ideas underlying the eras of history and progress toward freedom was nonsense. All that really mattered was economics — who owned the means of production, who worked, and who benefited from it.

Society was divided into owners and workers; no other distinctions mattered. The workers were the key to the system. Labor was the means of transforming nature and was what separated humanity from animals. The problem is, the owners controlled the means of production and the distribution of products, while the workers did the labor that was the critical factor in production. Everything in society was built around preserving the owners' power and keeping the workers down. Ideologies, political systems, social structures, laws, religion, even the concept of freedom itself, all existed simply to protect the economic status quo.

To Marx, history's eras were not about freedom but raw economic power — who owned, and who worked. In other words, rather than a Hegelian dialectic, Marx proposed a system of *dialectical materialism*. The revolutions that moved history forward occurred when a group of workers accumulated enough power to seize control of the means of production, merge with the earlier economic elite, and set up a system that would protect their newfound economic interests against the remaining workers. The final revolution would pit the "bourgeoisie" (factory owners and other capitalists) against the "proletariat" (factory workers). In the end the proletariat would seize control of the means of production, and history would end, since the workers and owners would merge into a single group.

Marx, then, was a materialist with a utopian vision for a perfected society based on the "laws" of history, class conflict, and revolution. Knowledge came from science plus his own ideology—the certainty that the Communist revolution would come. Ethics were based on what promoted the interests of the proletariat and hastened the revolution. Meaning and purpose were derived from working to hasten the revolution. In other words, Marx was an economic determinist. Everything about human life was built around economic classes and the implications of the movement of history toward his utopia.

THE COST OF COMMUNISM

As always is true of utopian schemes, when people tried to implement it, it resulted in totalitarianism. *The Black Book of Communism*, edited by French historian Stéphane Courtois, estimates that 94 million people were killed in Communist states in the twentieth century, including 20 million in the Soviet Union, 65 million in China, 1 million in Vietnam, 2 million in North Korea, 2 million in Cambodia, 1 million in Communist Eastern Europe, 150,000 in Latin America, 1.7 million in Africa, 1.5 million in Afghanistan, and 10,000 due to "the international Communist movement and Communist parties not in power."[5]

Contrary to popular belief, this makes Communism—an explicitly atheistic system—a far greater killer than any force in history, including religion. And these numbers do not include additional millions put into the gulag or forced labor or reeducation camps. In Communism, as in any naturalistic system, human rights do not exist. (Are they matter or energy?) All that matters is the historical dialectic leading to the utopia, and anything or anyone that gets in the way of the evolution of human society must be ruthlessly eliminated.

What Marx did not anticipate is that the free market system could reform itself. William Wilberforce, the evangelical who led the charge against slavery in the British parliament, also campaigned for workers' rights, including limiting the work week, paying a living wage, setting restrictions on child labor, and a host of other issues. As the nineteenth century progressed, trade unions — many led by Christians — pushed for reforms, and governments responded, so that over time the abuses in the factories were overcome and the horrendous living conditions of the workers were improved through a combination of government action and internal reform within businesses. As a result, the revolution Marx predicted never actually arose in industrialized countries.

THE MEANING OF LIFE

Materialism provides a ready answer to the question of the meaning or purpose of life: there is none (except in utopian schemes like Marxism). At best, we exist to pass on our genes to the next generation — and that's about it. Meaning, morality, purpose, truth, knowledge — all are fictions we live with that have no basis in the hard facts of a naturalistic world. To quote Shakespeare's Macbeth:

> Life's but a walking shadow, a poor player
> That struts and frets his hour upon the stage
> And then is heard no more: it is a tale
> Told by an idiot, full of sound and fury,
> Signifying nothing.[6]

Or as the popular group Kansas sang it, "All we are is dust in the wind."[7]

NIHILISM

The philosophy of "no meaning" is known as nihilism, from the Latin *nihil*, meaning "nothing." It is an inescapable consequence of materialism. As Bertrand Russell once said, "Unless you assume a God, the question of life's purpose is meaningless."[8] The philosopher most associated with nihilism is Friedrich Nietzsche. Nietzsche argued that since God is dead — since transcendence, truth, purpose, morality, and meaning are gone from the world — we need to find an *übermensch*, a superman or "overman," to overcome the problems created by the meaninglessness of existence.

Through the will to power, the *übermensch* would first destroy all moral and social norms and conventions, particularly those associated with Christianity. He would then use the will to power positively — to create meaning, truth, etc., out of whole cloth — to overcome nihilism. Once he had created meaning, he would achieve self-mastery and live in complete and absolute independence as the "judge and avenger of one's own law."[9] Only such a person could save society from the trap it was in and from the inescapable implications of materialism.

It is no accident that Nietzsche died in an insane asylum.

Most people are not, and have not been, ready to go as far as Nietzsche did in his attempts to deal with the meaninglessness of the world. But the problem will not go away in a materialistic worldview. Some people even celebrate meaninglessness. James Watson, the co-discoverer of the double helix structure of DNA, said at a luncheon given in his honor, "I don't think we're here for anything, we're just products of evolution. You can say, 'Gee, your life must be pretty bleak if you don't think there's a purpose,' but I'm anticipating a good lunch."[10]

NIHILISM-LITE

Others of a more philosophical bent have not been so sanguine. One of the more important movements in the mid-twentieth century that tried to deal with questions of meaning was existentialism, championed by Jean-Paul Sartre, Albert Camus, and Woody Allen (at least in some of his films). Existentialism is essentially nihilism-lite. It gets its name from the axiom that "existence precedes essence,"[11] that is, that our existence is more fundamental to who we are than some concept of human nature.

This means that we are radically free to determine what we do and who we are. This freedom, and the knowledge of our eventual demise, leads to anxiety — a common theme in existentialist writings and ubiquitous in Woody Allen films — against which we try to raise a bulwark of reason in the face of an absurd universe (another ubiquitous Woody Allen theme). Ultimately, to live an authentic life, we need to recognize the absurdity and lack of objective meaning in the world and then to decide for ourselves what we will consider meaningful, knowing that our "meaning" is a sham — but following through with it anyway. This obviously echoes Nietzsche's *übermensch* but on a much less earth-shattering level.

Interestingly enough, on his deathbed, Sartre confessed that he believed his life did have purpose, that there had to be some reason he was in the world. His lover was shocked and felt betrayed by this confession, since it put the lie to everything he had said and written during his life. But in the end, Sartre himself could not live with the implications of his ideas. Most other people cannot either.

THE CALL OF THE IRRATIONAL

Both materialism and scientism raise troubling questions about life, let alone the big issue of life's purpose. How do you explain great art scientifically? How do you do a scientific analysis of love in such a way that does not make it meaningless (along with the rest of the world)? If the human brain is the product of random chance plus time working on the primordial soup, how can we imagine that the brain is capable of understanding the world, or even of giving us accurate information about it? Why do people behave irrationally or badly?

Nietzsche attempted to come to grips with these questions, as did a host of other nineteenth-century and early twentieth-century thinkers. For example, Russian writer Fyodor Dostoevsky's novels contain a rediscovery of the idea of original sin (not surprising, perhaps, coming from a Russian Orthodox Christian). French philosopher Henri-Louis Bergson emphasized intuition as a source for knowledge over science, since science can only tell us about appearances and cannot uncover ultimate reality. French anarcho-communist Georges Sorel rejected the idea that science is truth and saw violence in the name of the liberation of the worker and of heroic action as an end in itself. French sociologist Émile Durkheim emphasized heredity and social forces over reason as motivations for human behavior and identified the decline of religion as a source of purpose and meaning for people. Italian economist Vilfredo Pareto argued that society was motivated by nonrational forces, and thus the elites should use the irrationality, passions, and feelings of the masses to their advantage, even using violence if necessary, so they could take power and rule—an important basis for much of Benito Mussolini's program.

German political economist and sociologist Max Weber argued that religious beliefs shape values and thus determine the structure of society; the modern world's application of science to all areas of life may have given us knowledge, but it killed our soul. The world has thus become "disenchanted"—the magic is gone out of life. As a result, he said people will attempt to "reenchant" the world through irrationality or following charismatic leaders in an attempt to find meaning for themselves. This is precisely what happened with Adolf Hitler, who was able to take advantage of economic hardships to spin a myth that won over enough of the German people that he could take over the country.

The most important of these thinkers was Sigmund Freud. Freud believed that human life was governed by dark, nonrational forces operating in our subconscious mind. In particular, the dominant motive for human behavior is the drive for sex, an idea very congenial to Darwinism in general and evolutionary biology in particular, since sex is the means by which we reproduce and thus through which evolution occurs. Since free sexual expression is disruptive to society, cultures repress the sex drive, allowing it to be expressed only in officially sanctioned ways (notably marriage), and typically associate sex with shame. This repression of our sexuality is the source of both human achievements—great art is produced, for example, by channeling the sex drive into creative activity—and human misery, as the origin of most of the neuroses and psychoses that plague our lives.

For Freud, then, the solution to human misery is to free ourselves from the constraints society places on our sexual behavior and to pursue our sexual desires as the means for personal fulfillment and emotional well-being. This idea became mainstream in American culture in the wake of the sexual revolution and has since become a central tenet of the worldview of many people today. More on that in the next chapter.

What all of these thinkers have in common is an uneasiness about modernity, a recognition that its description of the world and its explanation for life are incomplete and unsatisfying, and a recognition that society needs to move beyond bare rationalism if it is to survive. This has its corollary in the decline of representational art — from impressionism (with its desire to paint an impression of the day, as Claude Monet said) to expressionism (which aims to express emotions directly, as seen in the works of Vincent van Gogh or Edvard Munch) to Pablo Picasso's and Georges Braque's cubism (with its showing of multiple planes simultaneously and reduction of forms to simple geometric shapes) to abstract expressionism (which breaks ties with representational reality completely and expresses the randomness of a materialistic universe governed by chance, as observed in Jackson Pollack's work). The progression shows the artistic world's gradual absorption of philosophical ideas about the nature of reality and meaning, as well as a growing uneasiness with the bare, scientific way of observing and representing the world. This same trend appears in literature, theatre, and music.

The experience of two world wars, the Korean conflict, the Vietnam War, the Cold War, and all of the other problems and struggles of the twentieth century helped mainstream the ideas of critics of modernity. In essence, they prompted a reevaluation of the assumptions of the modern West and helped motivate the emergence of a number of new, interlocking worldviews in the closing decade of the twentieth century and the beginning of the twenty-first. The next chapter looks at some of these.

CHAPTER 10

THE DECAY OF MODERNITY

The twentieth century had a schizophrenic reaction to modernity. On the one hand, for most of the century, Western culture generally believed that secular humanism, technological progress, and scientific advances could usher in an era of peace and prosperity, despite threats from the Communist barbarians at the gates. On the other hand, the horrendous events of the century raised serious doubts about the viability and even the survival of the modern world.

ANTI-OCCIDENTS

Earlier anarchist and anti-industrial movements aside, the first broad threats to the dominance of the modern worldview in the Western world came in the wake of World War I. This era saw a rise in spiritualism in Britain as people sought to get in touch with the "lost generation" of men who died in the war. The period also saw a systematic assault in the more avant-garde sections of society on sexual mores and even on marriage itself.

In America, the Great Depression led to the Roosevelt administration, which began massive government programs that greatly expanded the powers of the federal government over the states and over business. The other Western powers moved even further in this direction than the United States did, especially in the years following the Second World War, effectively undermining the free market foundation of the classical liberal democracies. In its place, many of these Western countries shifted toward an interventionist economic vision, one that gave government a growing role in directing the economy rather than allowing the free market to do so.

In the United States, this shift came with the adoption of Keynesian economics (named after economist John Maynard Keynes), which has arguably been the basis of economic policy under every president since Franklin Roosevelt with the sole exception of Ronald Reagan. Since economics and politics are built on common worldview ideas about the natural relationship between people, this shift away from free markets toward government intervention signaled the beginning of a change from the notion of liberty and personal responsibility toward a statist mentality that believes the government's role is to take care of people rather than to protect freedom and provide a climate where people have the opportunity to take care of themselves — a shift that can be seen in the growth of social welfare programs in Europe, Canada, and the United States.

In Germany, the Nazis rejected much of the foundation of Western civilization, especially free market capitalism, representative democracy, and personal freedom, and replaced these with a totalitarian ideology that controlled people's lives from birth to death, with the myth of the superiority of the Aryan race and a virulent anti-Semitism, and with a hatred of Communism and all things Slavic. World War II followed, bringing with it even greater carnage than World War I.

Decolonization after World War II, the United States' civil rights movement, the feminist movement, and the Vietnam War all challenged the idea that Western civilization was the pinnacle of human culture. And when these historical circumstances collided with the nihilistic dead end of a materialistic worldview, the

West was ripe for the emergence of a new worldview in the second half of the twentieth century.

DECONSTRUCTING TRUTH

Some of the seeds for the destruction of the modern worldview came from within the West itself. Philosophers of language, such as Ludwig Wittgenstein, questioned whether it was possible for language to convey objective truth, or indeed to communicate at all. Words are arbitrary sounds or symbols that have no direct connection to their meaning. So, for example, there is no particular reason why the color green is called "green" rather than *vert* (French for "green"); "green" no more reflects the nature of the color than *vert* does. The sounds we use to describe the words are arbitrary and communicate only through the conventions accepted by people who speak the language.

So far so good. However, even within a language, words can vary in meaning. For example, is green a color, or is it a term to describe someone who is envious, a fruit that is not ripe (as in "blackberries are red when they're green"), a part of a golf course, something that is "environmentally friendly," or any number of other possibilities? The only way to tell is *context*. So words not only do not connect directly to the things they represent; they do not have a fixed meaning either. The question then becomes whether words have any connection to reality at all, or whether they simply point to other words, with none of them linking to the real world. If this is the case, words can neither convey truth nor have meaning outside of themselves.

Add to this the most basic problem of communication, namely, that it always involves more than one person. When you write something, the reader may not understand what you are saying in the way you mean it. Electronic communication is notorious for this, but it applies to anything written or even spoken. If this is the case, who "owns" the meaning of a text? Is it the person who wrote it, or the person who reads it? Can we even find the intent of the author, since all we have to go on are her or his words that pass through the filters of our minds, our cultures, our assumptions, our understanding? In fact, the intended meaning of a writer is impossible to determine, according to these theorists, and as a result no single interpretation can claim to be correct or definitive; *any* interpretation is equally legitimate. (Of course, writers who advocate these ideas tend to expect you to understand *their* meaning when they write rather than inventing your own, but that is another issue altogether.) To go one step further from what was said in the previous paragraph, the very idea that the text *has* a meaning is a problem. The only meaning that counts is the one the reader puts into the text — the one that derives from her or his social, cultural, linguistic, and personal experience.

This set of ideas is a branch of postmodern thought known as "deconstructionism," from the idea that texts can be deconstructed and reconstructed as suits the reader. Although this may seem pretty abstract, it has a number of important and immediate implications. The first, and hopefully most obvious, is that it eliminates the possibility of saying anything that is objectively true. All truth claims are equally true and equally false. And even if a speaker makes a subjective statement ("I am hot"), there is no guarantee that the listener will understand the statement in the way the speaker intends it or that it will be true in the listener's personal context.

This idea extends well beyond simple statements in normal language. In this system, virtually anything can be treated as a text and thus subject to deconstruction, including even such things as mathematics, scientific equations, theories of physics, and so on. Rather than being a guide to truth, science is just another cultural construct that cannot tell us anything about objective reality; it is simply a subjective exercise within its own cultural and linguistic system.

The implication is that a modern Western physician, for example, is no more or less accurate in understanding disease than a voodoo priestess or a Siberian shaman. None of them understand reality, and all that matters is what works within their own culture. Of course, since deconstructionists are products of Western culture, they naturally are most comfortable with their Western physicians. So they can have all the advantages of modern medical technology while rejecting the intellectual baggage that goes along with it, such as the troublesome idea that it works better than other cultures' health systems because it corresponds more closely to reality. By definition, this must be false because medical theory has nothing to do with reality. But it is still convenient for deconstructionists that they can take advantage of Western medicine. In practice, of course, no one really makes this kind of argument except in classrooms, but if deconstructionism is correct, the logic would seem to be inescapable and the conclusions not only unlivable but disastrous for fighting disease in the developing world.

Objective truth to a deconstructionist is thus inherently incommunicable and by implication unknowable. It is a small step from there to the idea that truth itself simply does not exist. All that is left is a radical cultural relativity in which no culture can claim superiority in any meaningful sense to any other. Under these conditions, ideas of good and evil, right and wrong, are also of necessity culturally relative. It is thus cultural imperialism to attempt to judge another culture by the standards of your own — which, oddly enough, is seen as a bad thing, despite there being no overarching standards by which to judge cultural imperialism as "wrong."

Of course, once again in this system it is impossible to criticize Pol Pot, Mao Tse-tung, Stalin, Hitler, Mussolini; racism or sexism; slavery; or any other individual or institution operating within its own cultural framework, since all are equally right. You cannot even claim that harming another person in pursuit of your interests is wrong, since to make this argument is to impose your views on another — and besides, there is no such thing as wrong. In short, we have arrived at nihilism from a different direction, not from the lack of meaning in a naturalistic world, but from the impossibility of knowing anything or judging anything to be right or wrong.

POSTMODERNISM

Most people are profoundly uncomfortable with this kind of thinking, so much so that even though they may accept some ideas from deconstructionism, they try to avoid its epistemological and moral nihilism. In the same way that existentialism is essentially nihilism-lite, most popular postmodernism is deconstructionism-lite. It tends to accept many of the premises of deconstructionism — a rejection of objective truth, insistence on cultural and moral relativity, and so on — without following through on all of the implications of these ideas or on the theory of language that supports them.

Typical postmodernists reject the idea of absolute truth in favor of the idea that truth is relative and personal. In other words, what is true for one person is not necessarily true for another, though in practice this belief is largely limited to areas of morality. Everyone agrees that gravity works, for example, but they do not agree on whether it is OK to cheat on an exam or on a girlfriend.

POSTMODERN VALUES

Here, then, is the single epistemological and moral principle in postmodernism, namely, the freedom, autonomy, and sovereignty of the individual. You alone decide what is true and false, right and wrong, for yourself. The only limitation is that you can do nothing that infringes on someone else's freedom. So, for example, the usual postmodern moral standard is that people have the freedom to do whatever they want *as long as it does not hurt anyone else*, which is another way of saying you can't do things to them that they do not freely choose to do as well.

The idea of radical freedom and autonomy also leads directly to the great postmodern virtue — tolerance. Not only can you not do anything that limits another's freedom or usurps their rights; you cannot suggest that there is anything wrong with what they decide to do with their freedom. To do so is to commit the unforgivable sin of being intolerant, judgmental, or bigoted (which all mean essentially the same thing to a postmodern).

This is a major shift in the idea of tolerance. In the past, tolerance applied to people. You could strongly disagree with certain ideas, while tolerating the people who held them. Increasingly, however, toleration applies to ideas and moral decisions, such that not only are they not subject to criticism but must be positively affirmed and celebrated.

THE POLITICIZATION OF LANGUAGE

This, at least, is the theory. It turns out that many postmoderns will take these basic ideas and develop alternate or extended forms of moral absolutes from them. One of the earliest and most pervasive emerged in the feminist movement. In feminist theory, everything is ultimately about politics, that is, the exercise of power. In patriarchal systems, power is competitive. It establishes winners and losers, hierarchies, and pecking orders. Because of this, patriarchal societies are prone to violence, war, pollution, and a host of other ills caused by the type of power they wield. Language is part of this mix as well. Since languages have meaning only in the context of a linguistic community, men use language as a means of social control, and specifically to exert power over other races, lower classes, and women. And since the widely accepted Sapir-Whorf Hypothesis states that "language shapes thought" rather than the other way around, control of language means control of thought and therefore of culture.[1]

In contrast, matriarchal societies are seen as cooperative, not competitive, and thus do not go to war, do not oppress, do not pollute Mother Earth, and are intrinsically egalitarian. This type of society is much more congenial to the postmodern worldview, since the radical freedom of the individual is not limited in an egalitarian society the way it is in the oppressive patriarchal system. So postmodernism and this form of feminism are natural allies. (The anticompetitive nature of the matriarchal vision also explains why many feminists are anticapitalist. Free markets are by nature competitive, making them intrinsically patriarchal.)

This worldview, whether described as postcolonial discourse, feminist theory, or any of a number of other terms, has some important implications for society. First, it argues that oppression, hate crimes, and so on can only be perpetrated by those in power (meaning whites and males), and thus members of the empowered classes cannot be victims of such crimes. As a result, white-on-black violence is treated as a hate crime, but black-on-white is not (even where there is evidence that race was a factor). Second, those seen as victims of those in power are accorded moral authority to speak on issues, whether or not their background would otherwise qualify them for this role. Presumably, as victims of oppression, their direct personal experience lends additional weight to their words, especially when speaking about the system that abused them. The effect is to create a situation where people promote the idea of victimization to heighten their moral authority and stature.

Beyond these kinds of immediate issues, however, this worldview also produces a specific agenda to wrest control of society by controlling language. So, for example, in the 1980s and 1990s, speech codes were instituted on college campuses that limited what kinds of things could be said in the name of eliminating hate speech and creating a "nonhostile" environment. While well-intentioned, these speech codes were written so broadly that if you were in a protected class, virtually anything that you found offensive could be considered a violation of the speech code.

At the University of Michigan, a student was cited for saying that "he had heard that minorities had a difficult time in [a specific] course and ... were not treated fairly."[2] At the same time, at the University of Wisconsin, for example, virtually anything could be said about white males since they had access to institutional power and thus by definition could not be offended or discriminated against, as I myself was told in a diversity training workshop. While these speech codes were struck down in the courts as violations of free speech, the attempts to control thought by controlling speech continue.

With the new definition of tolerance as the primary postmodern value comes the idea that we have the right not to be offended by what others say about us, our decisions, or our lifestyle. This right increasingly trumps free speech, as simply expressing views that differ from someone in a protected class is considered creating a hostile environment. For example, in Oakland, California, Regina Rederford and Robin Christy, two employees of the city, tried to advertise an informal group promoting "the natural family, marriage, and family values" on an employee bulletin board that included political and sexually oriented causes.[3] The announcement was removed because the supervisors decided it created a hostile environment for homosexuals, despite the fact that the announcement did not mention homosexuality. The employees sued on free speech grounds and lost. So in Oakland, it is perfectly fine to advocate on behalf of homosexual marriage in a public workplace, however offensive that may be to some employees, but it is not OK to advocate for traditional marriage because to do so is offensive to others, who have the right not to be offended.

The irony, of course, is that in the name of preserving individual autonomy and freedom, freedom of speech is limited only to approved messages. In this version of politicized postmodernism, the primary value of personal autonomy and freedom is actually secondary to a larger political and cultural agenda with its own set of values and ethics.

POSTMODERNISM AND THE SEXUAL REVOLUTION

This example leads to another implication of postmodernism. Since truth is personal, our identity (which in practice invariably means our sexual preferences and self-image) is determined by ourselves and only by ourselves. Thus biology does not determine gender; choice does. If someone is biologically male but feels like he is female, he becomes she — and the person can redefine himself as a woman. To suggest otherwise is to violate the individual's freedom and autonomy through a patriarchal assertion of power over another's life and thus to trample on the person's freedom to define her or his own existence.

Sexual preference is also an absolute right, though oddly enough the rhetoric on this is not that of choice but of biological determinism: homosexuals are born that way and cannot change, as is equally true of heterosexuals and bisexuals. So your sexual preference is biological, but not your gender.

At this point Sigmund Freud's ideas come to full fruition. Freud argued that the basic cause of human unhappiness is society's repression of our sex drives. If we were to allow our sexuality its full and free expression, our psychological problems would disappear, and we would live fulfilled and satisfied lives. Any constraint on our sex drives, whether imposed externally or through internalizing society's values and morality, is simply wrong. This fits in nicely with the emphasis on personal freedom and autonomy in postmodern ethics.

Since the sexual revolution, our society has been moving steadily in the direction advocated by Freud. The effect is that we now live in a sex-saturated culture, with fewer and fewer limits on what is considered acceptable behavior. "Hooking up" — casual sex and one-night stands — is part of the lifestyle on many college campuses, with some dorms even providing the rooms. Pornography is rampant, so much so that a BDSM website made enough money to purchase the Armory, a major historic landmark in San Francisco, to convert into its studio.[4] Television is full of sexual content day and night. Suggestive billboards and advertising are inescapable in many places, some of which are directly targeted at teens and tweens.

The sexualization of children is also proceeding apace, in everything from clothing styles to "age-appropriate" sex education as early as kindergarten. Psychiatrist and gynecologist Lena Levine, an associate of Margaret Sanger, put it this way:

> [Our goal] is to be ready as educators and parents to help young people obtain sex satisfaction before marriage. By sanctioning sex before marriage, we will prevent fear and guilt.... We must be ready to provide young boys and girls with the best contraception measures available so they will have the necessary means to achieve sexual satisfaction without having to risk possible pregnancy.[5]

These curricula typically also include material that normalizes homosexual lifestyles, even over parental objections. Judge Stephen Reinhardt of the Ninth U.S. Circuit Court said in a 2005 case involving exposure to sexual topics in a California public elementary school, "There is no fundamental right of parents to be the *exclusive* provider of information regarding sexual matters to their children." He added that "no such specific right can be found in the deep roots of the nation's history and tradition or implied in the concept of ordered liberty."[6] And in 2007, the Maryland Board of Education agreed. In a statement upholding a local school board's effort to insert curriculum material legitimizing homosexuality, it declared that "it is, of course, the fundamental rights [sic] of a parent to control the upbringing of his/her child ... but that right is not absolute. It must bend to the State's duty to educate its citizens."[7] In other words, the state rather than the family is to determine the values taught to children.

THE RESULTS OF THE SEXUAL REVOLUTION

Given the vast increase in sexual education and, it seems, sexual activity, what have been the results thus far? Unfortunately,

Freud's idea that sexual freedom would produce happiness does not seem to be working. Despite the sexual revolution, people are not happier or better adjusted. Instead, the quest for personal satisfaction through sex has brought with it skyrocketing rates of STDs and an epidemic of depression among sexually active young women, teenage pregnancies, and out-of-wedlock births and the accompanying single-parent households (which is the single biggest predictor of poverty in the United States).

And despite all this, birthrates are dropping across the board in Western culture. No major European state has ethnic Europeans reproducing at the replacement rate; the number of ethnic Europeans is decreasing. The same is true for Japan, and the United States is barely at the replacement rate. Economics are one factor, but the hypersexed society, combined with the antinatal tendencies, is a troubling sign for the future. Along with this, the changing conception of marriage has led to a divorce rate of about 48 percent in the United States[8] — which is hardly conducive to a couple's happiness either, not to mention the well-documented but little-discussed impact divorce has on children (and, according to researchers from Michigan State University, on the environment).[9]

FAMILY STRUCTURE

The high divorce rate reveals that in the new sexual environment, traditional family structures are being redefined or eliminated. Throughout history, in every society without exception, marriage in one form or another has had a privileged place as a means to regulate sexuality, so that children would be brought into the world and raised in a stable environment. The notion of homosexual marriage was thus absurd; it violated the very purpose of marriage. Some societies had provisions for temporary same-sex relationships, usually between an adult and an adolescent male, but nothing that allowed for permanency or gave the status of marriage.

Today, with contraception and in vitro fertilization, we have separated sex from childbirth. With out-of-wedlock births we have separated marriage from sex and childbearing, and with our divorce rate we have eliminated stability from marriage. The traditional concept of marriage thus seems increasingly irrelevant to society. What is left is the idea that marriage is built exclusively for personal satisfaction — again, it is all about freedom and autonomy — and companionship. So why not reconfigure marriage to suit whatever arrangements meet my desires?

This is the argument for homosexual marriage, as well as for polygamy, polyandry, and polyamory. The same logic applies in all of these cases. As Jack Nichols put it in *The Gay Agenda*, "The time has come to reject nostalgia for traditional family groupings and to seek new ways to realize the satisfaction they once brought ... [we must create] fresh new kinds of relationships, bearing no resemblance to past rituals, but opening doors to greater measures of individual happiness."[10]

This brings us back to some of the radical feminist thinkers, who see traditional marriage structures as inherently oppressive to women and as products of a patriarchal society. Only in a society without marriage can women be truly free. In feminist leader Sheila Cronan's words, "Since marriage constitutes slavery for women, it is clear that the women's movement must concentrate on attacking this institution. Freedom for women cannot be won without the abolition of marriage."[11]

Modernist concepts of the world and of society are thus being attacked from inside Western civilization through deconstructionism and postmodernism. But for some people, the problems raised by modernity are best answered by going outside of the entire Western paradigm altogether to new forms of spirituality. Along with postmodernism, this is the second major stream of the emerging worldview.

THE NEW SPIRITUALITY: EASTERN RELIGIONS, PSYCHOTECHNOLOGIES, AND PAGANISM

The appeal of mysticism to those wanting to escape from modernism is based on a simple idea: Since materialism leads logically to nihilism, the solution is to reject materialism. In fact, why not go in precisely the opposite direction and argue that the matter and energy of the physicists are not the prime reality — that instead there is a universal energy of which we are all a part and to which we can connect via meditation or other kinds of psychotechnologies?

The principal inspiration for this approach is Eastern thought, whether the Zen of the beatniks, the Indian religions of the Beatles, or the Taiji, Qigong, Reiki, or Yoga of the holistic health community. Eastern thought is based on a metaphysical system that believes that the fundamental reality of the universe is nonphysical, that the physical world and the distinctions between things are illusions, and that all is one and all is god. In Western terms, the ground of reality is a kind of subtle energy that runs through everything in the universe, sometimes identified with the Chinese concept of *qi* or the Hindu *prana* that are part of traditional Asian health practices such as Qigong or Yoga.

The problems we face in life come from seeing only the illusion that we are different beings, and not the reality that all is one. Science is thus something of a problem. It tells us about the illusion, not reality — which is why science did not develop in the East despite their remarkable technological achievements. The best minds were devoted not to studying the world but to seeing through the illusion via meditation, trying to perceive ultimate reality through direct personal experience. Through meditation — whether in stillness as in Zen, or in motion as in the martial arts or Yoga — we can shift away from our rational minds, our reliance on sense perception and reason, and pierce the illusions that surround us.

By doing so, we can experience oneness with the universe, known as achieving enlightenment or reaching Nirvana, which enables us to transcend the physical world. Otherwise, we are trapped in a cycle of reincarnation based on our *karma*, the positive or negative energy balance we earned by our actions. If we live according to the *dharma* — essentially the moral and spiritual law — we earn a positive balance and a higher state in our next life, and thus a better chance at enlightenment. Otherwise, we are reincarnated lower down in the hierarchy of being and have further to go to achieve enlightenment.

Eastern religions bring with them a complete worldview wildly at odds with Western thinking as it has emerged in the past two thousand years. Given how far off it is from Western worldviews, the whole system of thought is rarely presented directly. Instead, it is introduced through some form of experience, frequently based on meditation, martial arts, or holistic health practices. Once the experience occurs, elements of the worldview are introduced as a way of making sense of the experience. The whole system may not be introduced immediately — often only *qi* or *prana*, *chakra*, or other specific concepts — but this opens the door to bringing in more parts of the worldview later.

THE NEW AGE MOVEMENT

Another common approach defends Eastern mystical ideas by appealing to quantum physics, a subject few people actually understand (including those who make the appeal). Since there is still a great deal of faith in science in the culture, presenting cutting-edge, advanced physics as the means of confirming and rediscovering the wisdom of the ancients is a useful technique to help make monism (the idea that all is one) palatable. Evolutionary theory also can be used to support both the idea that we are all interconnected, having descended from the same earlier life-forms in the primordial soup, and the idea that we are now in the process of evolving into a higher, more spiritualized version of humanity, which will usher in a New Age.

This blending of science and mysticism is typical of the New Age movement, which is also characterized by its eclectic approach to "spirituality" (a popular but vague term that seems to mean an interest in mystical ideas and activities). New Age thought revolves around a variety of what have sometimes been called "psycho-technologies," methods of expanding consciousness and growing in awareness of the fundamental interconnectedness of all things.

This quest is typically seen as a personal one. Though you may have your guru whom you follow, overall there are many paths you can take, and they all lead to the same goal. In effect, every route, every religion, has at its root the same ideas and the same destination if properly understood, and thus you are free to follow whatever path or paths work for you.

The New Age philosophy provides another example of the postmodern thinking that concludes there is no right or wrong, only personal freedom and autonomy. All that matters is the experience of growing enlightenment, however you get there. The experience (as interpreted by your guru) is authoritative, and there is no real room for discussion about alternative explanations. In other words, *only you* have the right to determine the meaning (or truth) of your experience.

NEO-PAGANISM

The eclectic approach taken by the New Age movement means that Asian ideas and practices are only one set of choices among many that are available to seekers in the new spirituality. Native American religions, spiritualism, shamanism, UFOs, and a number of other sources have also contributed to the movement.

One particularly significant branch is Neo-Paganism, an updated revival of ancient pagan religions from the Celtic, Germanic, Baltic, and Slavic traditions (among others), minus the human sacrifice, as well as a more eclectic paganism drawn from a variety of sources. There is some tension in the Neo-Pagan movement between more traditional ethnic paganism and eclectic approaches, with the ethnic pagans viewing the eclectics as ungrounded in the authentic traditions and following a made-up spirituality, and the eclectics evaluating the ethnics as at best ethnocentric and at worst racist.

The largest branch of Neo-Paganism is Wicca and its variants. Although some Wiccans (also known as witches) claim that theirs was the first religion of humanity, dating back to the Stone Age, or that it is the descendent of a witch cult that was persecuted during the witch hunts of the fifteenth through seventeenth centuries, the actual roots are much more recent. Wicca was begun in the 1950s by Edward Gardner, who claimed to have learned its fundamentals from an earlier oral tradition of witchcraft. Yet Gardner's work was largely a combination of late Victorian occult practices (probably including elements drawn from famous British occultist Aleister Crowley), popular 1950s-era concepts of ancient matriarchal paganism, and Buddhist and Hindu influences. He seems to have drawn inspiration from some pagan revival groups dating to the early 1920s as well, but there is no evidence of a connection to any religious groups or magical traditions older than that.

Wicca is a diverse movement with no overarching structure, hierarchy, or doctrine, so it is difficult to summarize its ideas.

In many ways, it is an almost perfect postmodern religion. Each group can set itself up as it wants, following the ideas and rituals it finds most congenial to its interests. Most Wiccans worship a goddess who is typically seen as the supreme deity. In feminist versions, the goddess is the only deity, though some Wiccans add a god as a son and consort who is sometimes an equal to the goddess, sometimes a subordinate.

The deities are seen as sometimes impersonal and sometimes personal, sometimes immanent (tied to the natural world) and sometimes transcendent (a separate being from nature). Sometimes the religion is connected to animism, the idea that there are spirits in the natural world. Frequently, it includes nature worship. Rituals are secret, accessible only to initiates as in the ancient mystery religions, but typically involve the practice of magic and often divine possession of the chief priestess. The religion thus emphasizes connection and unity with the divine, substituting rite and ritual for the meditation of Eastern religions.

―

Ultimately, all of these new forms of spirituality follow variations of a common worldview focused on the idea that all things are interconnected, whether by subtle energies or by a fundamental unity masked by the illusion that we are different entities from the things around us. Though not precisely the same in its details as the ancient Platonic hierarchy of being, this outlook similarly emphasizes the idea that all things are essentially the same, and that there is continuity between, for example, animals and people — an idea reinforced by Darwinian evolution. And just as the hierarchy of being led people away from empirical studies of the natural world, there is much more interest among devotees of the new spirituality to explore their inner world, to develop their consciousness of their connection to the sources of spiritual power, and to find their significance through achieving personal power through magic, ritual, or developing their *qi*.

ECO-SPIRITUALITY

Ultimately, trends in postmodern thinking and politics have merged with elements of the new spirituality, particularly in uniting feminism and ecological concerns into a comprehensive critique of Western civilization.

One place where this is obvious is in the various forms of goddess spirituality, where more radical versions of feminism merge with new spirituality ideas. The underlying idea is that in the ancient past, goddess worship was the religion of humanity, and people lived in peace and harmony in egalitarian, matrilineal societies. (These were originally described as matriarchal, but the term implies that women were superior to men, which describes a hierarchical system that only came with patriarchy. So the description of the prehistoric state was rewritten as egalitarian but matrilineal, that is, based on tracing family lines through women.)

When patriarchal societies arose, they quite naturally used violence to overthrow the peaceful matrilineal societies, suppressed goddess worship, and began humanity's long history of war and oppression. Only by restoring goddess worship and egalitarianism can peace and harmony return to the world by eliminating the evil of patriarchy, competition, and oppression.

Taking this a step further, ecofeminism argues that the dominator patriarchal culture (and with it, capitalism) leads to a triple domination of women, the Earth, and the people of the global South (i.e., the developing world, most of which is south of the equator).[12] Ecofeminists sometimes see a mystical connection between women and the Earth, which is an immanent form of the divine — "Mother Nature," identified with the goddess — so that oppression of one leads directly to oppression of the other.

Ecofeminism frequently sees speciesism (the idea that humans are superior to animals) as part of the abuse of nature in patriarchy, arguing that animals are no different from humans and should not be viewed as economic resources. Some go so far as to argue that other species have the same rights as humans. Ingrid Newkirk of PETA observed, "There is no rational basis for saying that a human being has special rights. A rat is a pig is a dog is a boy. They're all mammals."[13] The secular form of this argument bases the connection on evolution; a spiritual version would tie it to the idea that all is one, and thus there is no essential difference between the rat, pig, dog, and boy. In reincarnational systems, in fact, the connection is even more direct. If you kill an animal, you simply don't know if you are also killing one of your ancestors.

THE GAIA HYPOTHESIS

Consider, too, the Gaia hypothesis, which states that the Earth (or Gaia) is a complex organism, with built-in feedback loops to keep it in balance. If pushed too far in one direction by human action, the whole system can overload with disastrous consequences. In other words, the observed feedback loops that collectively keep the earth relatively stable are turned in this hypothesis into a means by which an out-of-balance system feeds back on itself to produce more imbalance rather than stability, thus producing ecological disaster. This is precisely the opposite of how the feedback mechanisms in the world work. Gaia (from the Greek $g\bar{e}$, "earth," "land") is sometimes connected to the goddess of the Earth — though, just as in ecofeminism, there is a secular version of the Gaia hypothesis that is more common in the ecological community.

GLOBAL WARMING AS RELIGION

The obvious place where this hypothesis has become mainstream is in the agitation over human-caused global warming. Whatever the merits of the scientific arguments on this subject, the idea that the Earth has reached or soon will reach a tipping point in its climate is based on the Gaia hypothesis, which is now becoming an important factor in political, economic, and cultural decisions throughout the Western world.

It's critical to realize that because there is no cultural consensus on meaning or values, global warming is being presented by some political and environmental leaders as a cause that everyone can and should embrace. Cutting the emissions of carbon dioxide is increasingly being described as a universal moral obligation, with harming the environment seen as the one true evil in the world. This is not because the human causes of global warming are beyond question, as even its advocates sometimes admit.[14] For example, Timothy Wirth, former United States senator (D-Colo.), commented, "We've got to ride the global warming issue. Even if the theory of global warming is wrong, we will be doing the right thing, in terms of economic policy and environmental policy."[15]

Or as environmentalist Stephen Schneider argued, "We have to offer up scary scenarios, make simplified, dramatic statements, and make little mention of any doubts we might have.... Each of us has to decide what the right balance is between being effective and being honest."[16]

Most climate scientists would not go this far, of course. But for at least one segment of the environmental movement, the ends justify the means. Truth and honesty are irrelevant, because in a postmodern world, they are relative anyway. All that matters is the cause, the right policy, and the effectiveness. The goal is an increase in government control of the economy and restraints on business, free markets, and capitalism, since, as ecofeminism argues, these are the source of environmental problems, rooted ultimately in patriarchy — or in the West's concept of inalienable rights. In essence, environmentalism has now become the one moral imperative in the postmodern world that goes beyond personal freedom and autonomy.

In some circles, environmentalism not only has drawn in elements of the new spirituality but has also turned into a religion. Consider, for example, the following account, written by Samantha Smith, author of *Goddess Earth*, of a 1995 Earth Day celebration in Kansas City:

> The gathering held at the Westin Crown Center Hotel included a North American Native Indian praying to God, then praying to the Grandfather Spirit and to spirits of the Four Directions to bless the earth and oversee the conference. California Senator Tom Hayden, offered an Earth Day prayer, claiming the earth was speaking through him: "On this Earth Day let us say an earth prayer and make an earth pledge.
>
> "In the Bible 'ruah' means both wind and spirit, so let us take time to breathe with the universe, connect with the earth and remember what we need to know and do. Celebrate that ancient spirits are born again in us, spirits of eagle vision, of coyote craft, of bear stewardship, of buffalo wisdom, of ancient goddesses, of druids, of native people, of Thoreau and Sitting Bull — born again and over

again in John Muir and Rachel Carson and David Brower and Alice Walker." Hayden then asked us to "commit ourselves to carry the written word of Al Gore into official deeds." Thomas Berry offered a prayer for the healing of the earth.[17]

This is a perfect example of the union of ecological concerns with animism, New Age spirituality and eclecticism, and religion.

In many ways, the new spiritualities are counterparts to postmodernism:

- Both reject the fundamental premises of modernity.
- Both are based on personal autonomy and freedom of choice.
- Both are built around cultural and moral relativism and pluralism.
- Both see tolerance as the highest value and reject as bigotry any moral or intellectual absolutes.
- Both see continuity between humans and nature, whether through evolution or through the idea that all is one.

In short, in the union of postmodernism with the new spirituality, we have come full circle and returned to the worldview of ancient Rome.

TRAJECTORIES

Western civilization was the product of the interaction of Roman civilization with Christianity. As Christianity's influence on the Western worldview has declined, it is no accident that our thinking has become more like that of Rome. And since ideas have consequences, since worldviews inevitably shape culture and even their most extreme implications are eventually put into practice, it is also no accident that people in our culture are acting more and more like the Romans.

CONTEMPORARY VALUES

Consider our contemporary values, for example. In postmodernism, tolerance — the affirming and celebrating of virtually any exercise of personal autonomy — is the prime value. The unforgivable sin is being judgmental, that is, believing that an activity or lifestyle choice that does not hurt another person is wrong, immoral, or sinful. A second related unforgivable sin is claiming that what you believe is objectively true and thus binding on another person. A person who holds these beliefs is considered to be bigoted, narrow-minded, and arrogant, just as was true in ancient Rome.

You were welcome to believe whatever you wanted to in the Roman Empire, as long as you were inclusive and participated in emperor worship as well. Exclusive truth claims were ruthlessly suppressed, both because they offended Roman sensibilities and because in the religiously pluralistic Empire tolerance had to be enforced for the sake of political stability. Both of these arguments are used today, the latter particularly in Europe after the experience of the Wars of Religion that ended nearly four centuries ago.

As in Rome, recent experience shows that challenging the status quo worldview can lead to trouble with the law. Rome persecuted Christians for refusing to support the government policy of burning incense to the emperor and also for making exclusive claims to truth and critiquing Roman concepts of morality and religion. Today, "hate crimes" legislation, which effectively outlaws certain kinds of thought, has been used in Canada to prosecute pastors and to ban the reading of certain biblical passages that deal with homosexuality (and there are parallel cases in the United Kingdom and elsewhere in Europe). Personal freedom no longer extends to freedom of speech or religion in these cases. The government feels justified in silencing speech and curtailing religious ideas or texts it considers dangerous, antisocial, or intolerant.

ANTINATALISM AND DEMOGRAPHY

Speaking of sexuality, as was true for Roman citizens, we too live in a sex-saturated society — one that has a decidedly antinatal outlook. Contraception is seen as the solution to all sexual problems, from unwanted pregnancies to STDs.

Nonreproductive sexual activity has become normalized, and family sizes are shrinking. In Europe, the native ethnic populations in every major country are reproducing at below the replacement rate. The United States is barely keeping up with the replacement rate — and we are doing better than the Europeans largely because of immigrants, who have more children than people born and raised in America.

At the same time, the increasing reliance on the state to provide social services means that the tax base has to be maintained or increased, which in turn discourages having children (especially in Europe) because people simply cannot afford them. Further, to support the tax base, the Western countries must rely on immigration to shore up the social safety net.

While Eastern Europe is a major source for new workers in Western Europe, many more come from the Middle East and North Africa, bringing their culture, religion, and values with them. And they are the ones who are having larger families. The net result is that by 2050, Europe will be at least 20 percent Muslim, and probably more. If Turkey joins the European Union, Muslims may be the majority within Europe by that date. Either way, the increasing Muslim population will produce major changes in European society. As Muslim scholar Bassam Tibi put it, the only real question is whether "Islam gets Europeanized or Europe gets Islamized."[1]

In the United States, the workers are coming from Latin America and especially Mexico. While the cultural difference is less pronounced, this influx is still likely to lead to a transformation of American society. With all the debates on immigration in America, the most obvious explanation for the porous borders is being overlooked. Social Security is set up exactly like a Ponzi scheme, an illegal con game that relies on a constantly expanding base on the bottom to pay off the people on the top. If Social Security were run by anyone other than the government, its practice would be illegal. But birthrates have declined sharply — Generation X is less than half the size of the Baby Boomers. Social Security will need to be either eliminated or totally transformed to avoid driving the federal government into bankruptcy. And Medicare is in even worse shape.

The government is well aware of the coming train wreck. So where will the workers come from to shore up Social Security and Medicare? From immigration, illegal or not. If the immigration status of these workers can be normalized so they begin paying into the system, they may end up saving it from bankruptcy.

This situation of low birthrates and immigration is a direct parallel to the demographic situation of the Roman Empire. And just as Rome was gradually transformed (and then collapsed) with the influx of immigrants, most of whom simply wanted to get the benefits of Roman society and had no intention of destroying it, so too we can expect the transformation of European and American societies through the same process.

Why has the birthrate fallen in industrialized countries? Taxes are a problem in Europe, but a more important factor seems to be that attitudes toward marriage and family have changed. Since the postmodern moral imperative is personal freedom and autonomy, people have increasingly seen personal satisfaction as the primary goal in marriage, with children coming much farther down the list of priorities — or even seen as a hindrance to personal fulfillment. Children are not viewed as important for having a successful marriage or family, and thus families increasingly are trying to avoid pregnancy through contraception — following the pattern of Rome yet again.

ABORTION

And when unwanted pregnancies occur, abortion is always an option. If sex is about personal satisfaction, then what else should you do with unwanted pregnancies? To suggest that the baby should be carried to term, even if only to put him or her up for adoption, violates the personal freedom and autonomy of the woman — though statistics indicate that a very high percentage of abortions are done at the insistence of men, and very few in cases of rape, incest, or the health of the mother. (In fact, the National Organization for Women originally opposed legalized abortion because they thought it would give men the ability to take advantage of women and not have to deal with the consequences, a fear supported by experience.) Tens of millions of abortions have been performed in the United States since they were legalized, eliminating enough of the population to have made up for much of the projected shortfall in Social Security taxes over the next decades. Approximately one-third of the current generation of college students were aborted.

While even the most ardent pro-choice supporters reject the term *pro-abortion*, saying that abortion is always a tragedy, they make no real effort to slow the number except by encouraging "safe sex" to avoid unwanted pregnancies. In its annual report for 2004/2005, Planned Parenthood reported exactly zero referrals for adoption.[2] And any effort to regulate or restrict abortion is met with stiff resistance from women's groups, Congress, and the courts.

In practice, sexual freedom and abortion are the two most absolute rights in postmodern politics, because both reinforce personal freedom, personal autonomy, and an idea about human identity and happiness that sees unfettered sexual expression as the highest human good.

Abortion rates have dropped in the United States, down 9 percent between 2000 and 2005, with the total number of abortions per year down 25 percent from 1990 to 2005.[3] The reasons for the decline are less clear. Contraception seems to be playing a role, particularly among teens, but at the same time more women are deciding to keep their babies, whether because of counseling, ultrasound pictures, or for personal reasons. Nonetheless, 20 percent or more of all pregnancies in the United States still end in abortion.

INFANTICIDE

Abortion was also commonplace in Rome, particularly, it seems, when the pregnancy was the result of an extramarital affair. Far more common, however, was infanticide, mostly for girls or for disabled boys. The killing of infants is making a comeback today. As we saw in chapter 9, Margaret Sanger, founder of Planned Parenthood, advocated infanticide as part of her eugenics program, and Peter Singer, medical ethicist at Princeton University, also supports it.

They are just the tip of the iceberg, however. Francis Crick, who along with James Watson won a Nobel Prize for their discovery of the structure of DNA, commented to the Pacific News Service in January 1978, "No newborn infant should be declared human until it passed certain tests regarding its genetic endowment, and that if it fails these tests, it forfeits the right to live."[4] More recently, bioethicist John Harris of Manchester University pointed out the inconsistency of supporting abortion but not infanticide: "We can terminate for serious fetal abnormality up to term but cannot kill a newborn. What do people think has happened in the passage down the birth canal to make it okay to kill the fetus at one end of the birth canal but not at the other?"[5] Or consider the words of a spokesman for the Royal College of Obstetricians and Gynecologists (one of Britain's royal medical colleges):

A very disabled child can mean a disabled family. If life-shortening and deliberate interventions to kill infants were available, they might have an impact on obstetric decision-making, even preventing some late abortions, as some parents would be more confident about continuing a pregnancy and taking a risk on outcome.[6]

In other words, we can cut the number of abortions by legalizing the killing of disabled infants. Just as in Rome, the practice of infanticide is increasingly being advocated as a moral duty for eliminating children whose quality of life (or whose family's quality of life) is deemed low enough. This is explicit in the Netherlands in The Groningen Protocol for Euthanasia in Newborns and has been discussed as a serious option in the United States in the pages of *Pediatric Nursing* (May-June 2008). This article describes infanticide as a gray area that needs more study, particularly because keeping disabled babies alive diverts medical resources from others and raises social justice issues.[7]

This line of argument suggests we will be pushed to legalize the practice in the name of social justice and of not imposing values on others. In practice, a serial killer on death row has more advocates than a newborn baby with a serious, debilitating illness. We are approaching the point where smoking in public is greeted with more social condemnation than killing crippled children.

In a worldview that sees continuity between humans and animals, whether through a hierarchy of being, monism, or Darwinian evolution, human life is inevitably devalued. Infanticide was only ended in the Roman Empire by the concerted efforts of Christians, who believed that each individual was created in the image of God and therefore had infinite value, whether male or female, healthy or unhealthy, rich or poor.

HUMAN RIGHTS

As society has moved progressively away from this fundamental idea, it has steadily and inevitably devalued human life and human dignity. Many atheists will, of course, dispute this. The British school of atheism, followed by Richard Dawkins, Christopher Hitchens, and Sam Harris, insists that though science has made God irrelevant, we can still be moral anyway — by which they mean holding on to morals that are rooted in the Christian tradition. This is intellectually inconsistent at best, since the very foundations that make the morality work are removed.

Continental atheists, such as the French philosopher Michel Onfray, are far more honest. From Baron d'Holbach and Friedrich Nietzsche on, these atheists have insisted that the moral trappings of Christianity must be eliminated along with its God. To the continental atheist, the Anglo-Saxon variety of atheists are "Christian atheists" (just as Jefferson was a Christian deist) who retain residual Christianity in their social, moral, and ethical theory because they lack the courage to see their convictions through to their logical conclusions.

Consider Onfray's *Atheist Manifesto*, which decries "Christian atheists" who reject God while embracing a Christian ethic. He argues that ideas such as "charity, temperance, compassion, mercy, and humility, but also love of one's neighbor and the forgiveness of offenses, the injunction to turn the other cheek, indifference to the goods of this world, the ethical asceticism that rejects power, honors, and wealth"[8] — ideas that are shared by Christians and Christian atheists alike — must be jettisoned in favor of a postmodern atheism based on "philosophy, reason, utility, pragmatism, [and] individual and social hedonism."[9] Drawing from Jeremy Bentham and John Stuart Mill, Onfray argues that the good is found in producing "the greatest possible happiness of the greatest number," and, by implication, evil is anything that works against this.[10]

Utilitarianism, which is what this approach to ethics is called, may sound good on the surface, but it denies the concept of individual rights. For example, if a person is a burden to society, if he has mental or physical disabilities or is senile, if he does not contribute to the greatest happiness of the greatest number but uses resources that could be "better" spent improving other people's quality of life, then allowing him to stand in the way of the greatest amount of happiness of the greatest number is evil. Why not euthanize him? Or if an infant is disabled, why not let her die? It will certainly be a burden to the parents to allow her to live, unless perhaps they decide they want to keep her alive for their own happiness — but even then, this decision raises questions about the impact the child with disabilities has on the community and about the resources used to keep her alive.

What happens to the right to dissent or the right of conscience or the idea of inalienable rights? If any of these get in the way of social happiness, why should we keep them? This is the logic of utilitarianism, which is a far more consistent ethical position for an atheist than anything that involves altruism or "charity, temperance, compassion, mercy, and humility." The fact is, the further removed we are from the Christian foundation of human rights, the more we can expect to see human rights and dignity erode.

SLAVERY

We can see this in the ongoing problem of slavery and human trafficking. The numbers are unclear, but they are staggering by any reckoning. The International Labour Organization of the United Nations says that over 12 million people are trapped in forced labor; Andrew Cockburn, writing in *National Geographic*'s September 2003 issue, puts the number of those who live in slavery at 27 million. According to Kevin Bales, president of Free the Slaves, more slaves were taken from Africa in 2004 than during the entire period of the transatlantic slave trade.[11] UNICEF reports that more than a million children are enslaved *each year*. Many, even the children, are forced to work in brothels. Others make rugs, cigarettes, or bricks or are agricultural workers.

Slavery is illegal almost everywhere, but it is a significant part of the underground economy in virtually every country, in some cases with the collusion of government officials. In fact, human trafficking is a bigger industry than the trade in illegal drugs.

Governments have known about the problem for years. It only recently became a larger public issue because of pressure from the American Christian community on the Bush White House to do something about it. The White House then brought it before the United Nations, which passed resolutions against human trafficking.

While secularists decry slavery, they did little (or nothing) to bring the issue to the fore. It took the actions of people committed at the core of their beliefs to the principle of the dignity and worth of each individual before anything was done to try to address the problem — just as had happened in Rome. And just as in Rome, that movement was begun by Christians.

CHRISTIANITY OR PAGAN ROME?

The examples can be multiplied in many areas of life. What is the key point? All of the greatest achievements of Western civilization, from the abolition of slavery to the idea of inalienable rights and the dignity and worth of each individual, from the rise of science and technology to the development of universities, from the emergence of economic theories that maximized production and raised standards of living to the idea of representative democracies and limited government — all were the products of ideas that have roots in the Bible and a Christian worldview. Other ideas from outside of Christianity certainly had their own impact on these developments, but the deciding factor was Christianity. This influence is what has made Western civilization truly distinctive, and it is also the reason why none of these developments occurred in any other civilization.

As we leave behind our Christian roots, Western civilization is eroding the foundation that led to its unique features, its most important contributions, and its highest ideals and values. And in the process, we are, in many ways, returning to the cultured practices of Rome. History does not repeat itself; our civilization is certainly not identical to ancient Rome's. For example, we do not accept torturing or killing people for entertainment (except in films), and we continue to decry oppression on the basis of the residual Christian morality we inherited from previous generations.

Nonetheless, as our worldview becomes progressively more and more like that of the ancient Romans, we are beginning to follow them in practices that would have been unthinkable just a few decades ago. Remember, a society's underlying worldview and its implications will inevitably be expressed in the culture. We need to decide if returning to Rome — and all that this returning entails — is the direction we want to go, and if not, we must shore up the foundations of the one worldview that will preserve the value and dignity of human life and the best elements of Western civilization.

THE BIBLICAL WORLDVIEW IN THE TWENTY-FIRST CENTURY

Western civilization is at a crossroads. While far from perfect, Western civilization has brought more economic prosperity, more scientific and technological advancement, more political freedom, and more concern for human rights and equality than any other civilization in history. And all of this was based on a biblical worldview which believed that human beings are made in the image of God and thus have both the potential to understand the physical universe and an inherent dignity and worth that cannot be taken away.

We have already largely lost the idea of the image of God in Western culture, leaving us with a free-floating conception of human rights devoid of any overarching framework to support these rights. We have so internalized cultural relativism that we are on the verge of losing many of our culture's distinctive features in the name of a pluralism stripped of core values. We have already largely given up the idea that life is an inalienable right, as shown by the culture's acceptance of abortion, infanticide, and euthanasia. We are losing the right to property, the right to keep what we legitimately earn. And we have turned liberty — the freedom to pursue virtue — into license, into freedom from restraint.

THE IMAGE OF GOD

If we are to recover the promise of the West, we must recover the core ideas and values of the culture, beginning with the critical elements of the biblical worldview that we have lost. It is perhaps appropriate to end this book with a few thoughts about what this worldview has to say to the twenty-first-century world. A complete discussion would require several more books, of course, but some fundamental principles can be summarized briefly. Once again, the key idea is the recovery of a fully formed appreciation of the image of God shared by all people. When Western civilization embraced a robust vision of the image of God, we had our greatest successes; when we ignored it, we had our greatest failures.

In terms of human rights, the image of God is the source of human worth. Any time we value anything else — race, sex, social class, education, ethnicity, ability or disability, or any other element of our identity — ahead of the image of God that we share, we are guilty of idolatry and quite literally insult God to his face. Christians should thus be at the forefront of the fight for human rights, and we should adamantly oppose racism, sexism, or any other affront to the common humanity we share. This commitment includes taking a pro-life stance on abortion, because the child in utero carries the image of God as well.

At the same time, we must resist calls to consider other creatures on a par with humanity. Quite simply, humans are more important than plants or animals, regardless of whether Switzerland grants rights to plants, or Spain to great apes. One may not conclude, however, that we are to abuse animals or other parts of the creation. As noted in chapter 3, our creation in the image of God means that we are to act as God's regents and stewards on the earth. Scripture is clear that the earth is the Lord's, not ours (Psalm 24:1). Christians should be at the forefront of environmental concerns and creation care. Ethical and humane treatment of animals is one aspect of this, though again, not at the expense of humanity. We should also work for the best utilization of resources, with a minimum of pollution and harm to any part of the environment — land, water, air, plants, or animals.

In science and technology, we need to be as concerned about the ethical dimensions of our research as we are about the results — particularly with regard to biotechnologies. The first question we should ask about research is, *Should* we do this? not, *Can* we do this? Again, maintaining the dignity of the image of God is primary. Many people get more upset with those who use animals for testing than with those who do experimentation with human embryos. If we believe that human beings are made in the image of God, then we need to work to protect life at all stages, including the prenatal stage.

God worked in creating the world, and so should we. God gave humanity both intellectual and physical work to do in the garden of Eden, and thus we should view work as a positive good, not a necessary evil. God created all things and is interested in all things. All truth, then, is God's truth, and all areas of learning and all ethical jobs are legitimate areas of service to him and are part of what goes into building his kingdom.

We must develop a kingdom perspective on our work in every sector of the economy, whether manufacturing, service industries, business, finance, education, health care, arts, or media. On a social level, we need to provide meaningful work for others and seek to eliminate drudgery as much as possible, and so to affirm the dignity of the people around us. We also have the right to enjoy the fruits of our labor. Government has its legitimate functions and can collect taxes for those purposes, but we should be permitted to keep the bulk of what we earn.

At the same time, we must provide for the needs of others, honoring them as individuals and serving them rather than subcontracting our responsibilities to care for our neighbors to the government or to any other entity. Christians differ on just what role government agencies should play in providing for people's needs, but if we believe that our neighbors bear the image of God equally with ourselves, we will work to help those in need as well. Those whom Jesus welcomes into the kingdom are those who go out and help the needy (see Matthew 25:34–40). We *are* our brothers' keepers. Our responsibility goes well beyond charity, however. Our goal is not simply to give people "bread and circuses," as the Roman emperors did, but to supply their immediate needs while seeking to give them the opportunity to earn their own living and to provide for themselves and others — and by so doing to affirm their own dignity and worth.

We must work for social justice as well, to help to dismantle the legal and institutional structures that keep people in poverty, and instead to put in place policies that promote human flourishing. Among other things, this involves supporting a pro-family agenda that emphasizes the biological family of mother, father, and children established by God in the garden of Eden as the essential foundation for economic, cultural, and social stability.

In political life, we must keep the importance of the image of God shared by people of all nationalities front and center in our thinking. But we must be careful. Christ's kingdom is not of this world, and it will never be ushered in through political power. Instead, we must live lives consistent with our faith, and thus by our concern and our action on behalf of others we will earn the right to be heard. From there, we can persuade others of the truths and values of the kingdom and build the kind of grassroots movement that alone can bring long-term change to a society. Politics is downstream from culture, and while Christians can and should be involved in the political process, we must never forget that in this world the kingdom can only be built from the bottom up, never imposed from the top down.

We also need to insist on the right to dissent. Everyone has the right to freedom of conscience and the right to express themselves without fear of repercussion, whether or not they agree with us. The kingdom is not built on coercion, and since all truth is God's truth, the biblical worldview will always prevail in a free marketplace of ideas and a level playing field. But beyond those who adopt a different worldview altogether, those who hold to a biblical worldview may come to strikingly different conclusions concerning policies and the best means to promote the well-being of society. We need to give each other permission to disagree on both peripheral issues and on practical applications of principles.

Mostly, we need to follow the model of the early church. Living a biblically faithful life will not make us popular. It is no accident that the Beatitudes end with "Blessed are those who are persecuted because of righteousness, for theirs is the kingdom of heaven" (Matthew 5:10). In the face of a culture far more corrupt and decadent than our own, the early Christians lived lives of extravagant faithfulness, even to the point of torture and death. And they won. It took over three hundred years, but they transformed Roman society.

We tend to get discouraged over a single election cycle. If we are going to have the kind of impact on our society that the early Christians had on Rome, we need their courage, their perseverance, and their faithfulness. If we have those qualities, we can and will have an impact on our society far beyond our numbers and will produce cultural renewal and a better life for those who come after us, Christian and non-Christian alike.

NOTES

CHAPTER 2: THE WORLDVIEW OF ANCIENT ROME

1. The word *cult* is used in this book in its anthropological sense as "the group of religious practices that define membership in a religion." It is not used in the sense of a fringe, possibly dangerous, religious group. Every religion is (or has) a cult in the former sense of the word.

2. George Smoot, "Aristotle's Physics," *http://aether.lbl.gov/www/classes/p10/aristotle-physics.html*.

CHAPTER 3: CHRISTIANITY AND THE TRANSFORMATION OF THE PAGAN WORLD

1. Tacitus, *Histories* 5.5; quoted in Rodney Stark, *The Rise of Christianity* (Princeton, N.J.: Princeton Univ. Press, 1996), 118.

2. Quoted in Stark, *Rise of Christianity*, 84.

3. Eusebius Pamphilius, *Ecclesiastical History* 7.22 (Nicene and Post-Nicene Fathers, second series, vol. 1, Grand Rapids: Eerdmans, n.d.), 650. The great Roman physician Galen, who admitted fleeing when serious epidemics struck, commented as well on Christians' contempt of death (*http://www.earlychristianwritings.com/galen.html*), as did Marcus Aurelius, the Roman emperor and stoic philosopher (*http://www.earlychristianwritings.com/aurelius.html*).

4. Tertullian, "Apology," *Ante – Nicene Fathers*, vol. 3, 55; quoted in Gregory A. Boyd, *The Myth of a Christian Nation* (Grand Rapids: Zondervan, 2005), 181.

5. Karen L. King, *The Gospel of Mary of Magdala: Jesus and the First Woman Apostle* (Santa Rosa, Calif.: Polebridge, 2003), 213.

6. Quoted in King, *Gospel of Mary*, 61.

7. John 1:4; 8:12; 12:46; Isaiah 9:2; Malachi 4:2; Luke 1:78.

8. See Rodney Stark, *The Victory of Reason: How Christianity Led to Freedom, Capitalism, and Western Success* (New York: Random House, 2005), 5 – 9.

9. See Charles Colson, *Loving God* (Grand Rapids: Zondervan, 1987, 1996), 242 – 43.

CHAPTER 4: THE EMERGENCE OF THE MEDIEVAL WORLDVIEW

1. Quoted in *The Oxford Dictionary of Quotations* (New York: Oxford Univ. Press, 1999), 68 – 69.

CHAPTER 6: THE BREAKDOWN OF THE MEDIEVAL MODEL

1. For a handy summary of the Reformation, see my book *The Reformation for Armchair Theologians* (Louisville: Westminster, 2005).

2. Denis Crouzet, *Les guerriers de Dieu* (Seyssel: Champ Vallon, 1990), 1:103.

CHAPTER 7: A NEW PARADIGM OF KNOWLEDGE

1. John Maynard Keynes, "Newton, the Man," in *The World of Mathematics*, vol. 1, James Newman, ed. (Mineola, N.Y.: Dover, 2000), 277.

CHAPTER 8: ENLIGHTENMENT AND REVOLUTIONS

1. Alexander Pope, "Essay on Man," quoted in Paul Baines, *The Complete Critical Guide to Alexander Pope* (New York: Routledge, 2000), 87.

2. Alexander Pope, "Epitaph: Intended for Sir Isaac Newton," in *The Poems of Alexander Pope*, Alexander Pope and John Butt (New York: Routledge, 1966), 808.

3. See George Marsden, *Jonathan Edwards* (New Haven: Conn.: Yale Univ. Press, 2004), 65.

4. See Marsden, *Jonathan Edwards*, 64.

5. See Donald Lutz, *The Origins of American Constitutionalism* (Baton Rouge: Louisiana State Univ. Press, 1988), 136–49.

6. See David P. Jordan, *The Revolutionary Career of Maximilien Robespierre* (Chicago: Univ. of Chicago Press, 1989), 174, 181.

CHAPTER 9: MODERNITY AND ITS DISCONTENTS

1. Carl Sagan, *Cosmos* (New York: Random House, 1980), 4.

2. Quoted in Nancy Pearcey, *Total Truth* (Wheaton, Ill.: Crossway, 2004), 157.

3. Charles Darwin, *Descent of Man and Selection in Relation to Sex* (New York: Barnes and Noble Books, 2004), 134.

4. Daniel Kevles, *In the Name of Eugenics: Genetics and the Uses of Human Heredity* (1985; repr., Cambridge, Mass.: Harvard Univ. Press, 1995), 116. Kevles's book gives a thorough overview of eugenic policies in the United States.

5. Stéphane Courtois, *The Black Book of Communism* (Cambridge, Mass.: Harvard Univ. Press, 1999), 4.

6. William Shakespeare, *Macbeth*, act 5, scene 5; quoted in *Masterpieces of Religious Verse*, James Dalton Morrison, ed. (Grand Rapids: Baker, 1977), 309.

7. Kansas, "Dust in the Wind," lyrics by Kerry Livgren (1997).

8. Quoted in Rick Warren, *The Purpose Driven Life* (Grand Rapids: Zondervan, 2002), 17.

9. Friedrich Nietzsche, *Thus Spake Zarathustra* (New York: Macmillan, 1896), 84.

10. Quoted in The Center for Changing Worldviews with Sharon Hughes, "Quotes on Religion," *http://www.changingworldviews.com/quotes/show/41.* (Accessed January 26, 2009.)

11. Jean-Paul Sartre, "Existentialism and Humanism," quoted in Lawrence Cunningham and John Reich, *Culture and Values* (Belmont, Calif.: Thomson Wadsworth, 2005), 494.

CHAPTER IO: THE DECAY OF MODERNITY

1. See Deborah Tannen, *That's Not What I Meant!* (New York: Random House, 1992), 194.

2. First Amendment Center, "Hate Speech and Campus Speech Codes: Overview," *http://www.firstamendmentcenter.org/speech/pubcollege/topic.aspx?topic=campus_speech_codes.*

3. See Art Moore, "City Ties 'Family Values' to 'Homophobia,'" WorldNetDaily, July 31, 2003, *http://www.worldnetdaily.com/news/article.asp?ARTICLE_ID=33845.* (Accessed January 26, 2009.)

4. BDSM is an acronym derived from the terms *bondage* and *discipline, domination* and *submission*, and *sadism* and *masochism.*

5. Lena Levine, "Psychosexual Development," *Planned Parenthood News* (Summer 1953), 10. Quoted in Samuel Blumenfeld, "Sex Ed and the Destruction of American Morality," WorldNetDaily, January 18, 2003, *http://www.worldnetdaily.com/index.php?pageId=16801.* (Accessed January 26, 2009.)

6. Quoted in Hilary White, "Activist Judge Rules Palmdale Parents Have No Say in Sex Ed in Schools," LifeSiteNews, November 3, 2005, *http://www.lifesitenews.com/ldn/2005/nov/05110305.html.* (Accessed January 26, 2009.)

7. Quoted in Education Reporter, "Controversial Maryland Sex Ed Curriculum Is Adopted," September 2007, *http://www.eagleforum.org/educate/2007/sept07/sex-ed.html.* (Accessed January 26, 2009.)

8. The National Center for Health Statistics ("http://www.cdc.gov/nchs/data/nvsr/nvsr52/nvsr52_22.pdfBirths, Marriages, Divorces, and Deaths: Provisional Data for 2005, Table A") reports 7.5 marriages per 1,000 people in the U.S, and 3.6 divorces per 1,000 people, http://www.cdc.gov/nchs/fastats/divorce.htm. (Accessed January 26, 2009.)

9. See National Science Foundation, "Broken Homes Damage the Environment," December 4, 2007, *http://www.nsf.gov/news/news_summ.jsp?cntn_id=110798.* (Accessed January 26, 2009.)

10. Jack Nichols, *The Gay Agenda: Talking Back to the Fundamentalists* (New York: Prometheus, 1996), 112.

11. Sheila Cronan, "Marriage," in *Notes from the Third Year*, Anne Koedt, Ellen Levine, and Anita Rapone, eds. (New York: Quadrangle, 1971), 65.

12. See Maria Mies and Vandana Shiva, *Ecofeminism* (Atlantic Highlands, N.J.: Zed, 1993), 1–21.

13. Quoted in Katie McCabe, "Who Will Live, Who Will Die?" *Washingtonian* 21 (August 1986): 115.

14. For example, John Coleman, founder of the Weather Channel, called global warming "the greatest scam in history" (see Joe D'Aleo, "Weather Channel Founder: Global Warming 'Greatest Scam in History,' *Icecap*, November 11, 2007, *http://icecap.us/index.php/go/joes-blog/comments _about_global_warming/* [accessed January 27, 2009]), and the Oregon Institute of Sciences has collected signatures of over 31,000 people with degrees in relevant sciences (including over 9,000 with PhDs) who are calling into question human-caused global warming (see Global Warming Petition Project, *http://www.petitionproject.org/* [accessed January 27, 2009]). And climate scientists in Denmark and Australia are warning about global *cooling*. The degree of scientific consensus on the subject is frequently exaggerated.

15. Quoted in Julian Lincoln Simon, *The Ultimate Resource 2* (Princeton, N.J.: Princeton Univ. Press, 1998), 573.

16. Ibid., 574.

17. Samantha Smith, "The Pagan Howl-le-lu-ia Chorus," *The Eagle Forum* 15 (Winter 1995): 1.

CHAPTER II: TRAJECTORIES

1. Quoted in Christopher Caldwell, "Islamic Europe? When Bernard Lewis Speaks ...," *The Weekly Standard* 10 (October 4, 2004), *http://www.weeklystandard.com/Content/Public/ Articles/000%5C000%5C004%5C685ozxcq.asp?pg=2.* (Accessed January 27, 2009.)

2. "Planned Parenthood Reports Zero Adoption Referrals," June 13, 2007, *http://www.citizenlink.org/content/A000004840.cfm.* (Accessed January 27, 2009.)

3. Wm. Robert Johnston, "Historical Abortion Statistics, United States," *http://www.johnstonsarchive.net/policy/abortion/ab-unitedstates.html.* (Accessed February 10, 2009.)

4. Quoted in Francis A. Schaeffer and C. Everett Koop, *Whatever Happened to the Human Race?* (Old Tappan, N.J.: Revell, 1979), 73.

5. Quoted in Sarah-Kate Templeton, "Doctors: Let Us Kill Disabled Babies," *TimesOnline*, November 5, 2006, *http://www.timesonline.co.uk/tol/news/uk/article625477.ece.* (Accessed January 27, 2009.)

6. Ibid.

7. See Anita Catlin and Renee Novakovich, "The Groningen Protocol: What Is It, How Do the Dutch Use It, and Do We Use It Here?" *Pediatric Nursing* 34 (May/June 2008): 247 – 51.

8. Michel Onfray, *Atheist Manifesto: The Case Against Christianity, Judaism, and Islam* (New York: Arcade, 2007), 57.

9. Ibid., 58.

10. Ibid.

11. Kevin Bales, *Disposable People* (Berkeley: Univ. of California Press, 2004), 4.

NAME INDEX

Abel, 84
Adam, 75, 83 – 84
Alcuin, 59
Al-Ghazali, Abu Hamid, 70 – 71
Ali Pasha, 76 – 77
Allen, Woody, 178
Aquinas, Thomas, 44, 76, 100
Aristotle, 25, 26, 31, 34, 43, 65,
    67, 68, 69, 72, 88 – 89, 95,
    108, 118, 125, 133, 154
Arius, 49
Athanasius, 49
Augustine, Saint, 83 – 84, 86,
    87, 93, 126, 148

Bales, Kevin, 210
Barnabas, 42
Bathilde, 43
Bayle, Pierre, 125 – 126, 127, 138
Bentham, Jeremy, 209
Bergson, Henri-Louis, 179
Bernard of Chartres, 66
Berry, Thomas, 202
Blackstone, William, 152
Brahe, Tycho, 119 – 120
Braque, Georges, 181
Brower, David, 202

Burke, Edmund, 142

Caesar, Augustus, 33
Cain, 84
Caligula, 32
Calvin, John, 112, 131
Camus, Albert, 178
Carson, Rachel, 202
Cassiodorus, 53
Charlemagne, 59 – 60, 64, 87
Charles I, 106
Charles II, 107
Charles V, 104
Christy, Robin, 190
Cicero, 34, 98
Clement VI, Pope, 72
Cockburn, Andrew, 210
Columbus, Christopher, 108
Comte, Auguste, 165
Constantine, 48 – 52, 54
Copernicus, Nicolaus, 117 – 119,
    124, 131
Courtois, Stéphane, 176
Crick, Francis, 207
Cromwell, Oliver, 107
Cronan, Sheila, 194
Crouzet, Denis, 105

Crowley, Aleister, 197

Darwin, Charles, 166 – 171
Dawkins, Richard, 208
De Montaigne, Michel, 111
Descartes, René, 126 – 128, 129,
    130, 131
D'Holbach, Baron, 143, 209
Diocletian, 35
Dionysius of Alexandria, 44
Dostoevsky, Fyodor, 179
Durkheim, Émile, 179

Edwards, Jonathan, 146 – 147
Elizabeth I, 104
Erigena, John Scotus, 59 – 60
Estienne, Henri, 111
Eve, 83 – 84

Ficino, Marsiglio, 99, 100
Francis of Assisi, Saint, 82 – 83,
    88
Franklin, Benjamin, 151
Frederick the Great, 143
Freud, Sigmund, 180, 191, 193

Galileo Galilei, 121 – 122,
    123 – 125, 130, 131
Galton, Francis, 171
Gardner, Edward, 197
Gassendi, Pierre, 128, 129
Gelasius I, Pope, 86
Godric of Finchale, Saint, 82
Gore, Al, 202

Harris, John, 207
Harris, Sam, 208
Hayden, Tom, 201

Hegel, Georg Wilhelm
    Friedrich, 174 – 175
Henry of Navarre, 105
Henry VIII, 104
Hippocrates, 72
Hitchens, Christopher, 208
Hitler, Adolf, 73, 180, 187
Hooke, Robert, 131
Hume, David, 143 – 144

Ibn al-Khatib, 71
Ibn Khatimah, 71
Irving, Washington, 109

James II, 107, 149
Jefferson, Thomas, 150, 151, 209
Jesus Christ, 41, 43, 44, 46, 47,
    49 – 50, 82, 98, 110, 137, 214
Jethro, 152
John, apostle, 46
Julian the Apostate, 44
Justin Martyr, 46

Kepler, Johannes, 120 – 121,
    124, 130, 131
Keynes, John Maynard, 132,
    184
King, Karen L., 47

Laud, William, 106 – 107
Levine, Lena, 192
Lindberg, Charles, 170
Locke, John, 107, 138, 149, 150,
    152 – 153, 159
Louis the Pious, 59
Louis XIII, 105
Louis XIV, 107, 149
Louis XVI, 155 – 156

Luther, Martin, 104, 112

Malthus, Thomas Robert,
    141 – 142, 166, 170
Mao Tse-tung, 187
Marsden, George, 147
Marx, Karl, 175 – 176
Mary, Queen, 107, 149
Mary Magdalene, 48
Mary (Virgin), 52
Mill, John Stuart, 209
Monet, Claude, 181
Montesqueiu, Charles de
    Secondat, 152
Moses, 152
Muir, John, 202
Munch, Edward, 181
Mussolini, Benito, 180, 187

Napoleon, 159
Newkirk, Ingrid, 199
Newton, Isaac, 125, 130 – 133,
    139
Nicholas of Cusa, 69, 119
Nichols, Jack, 194
Nietzsche, Friedrich, 177 – 178,
    179, 209
Noah, 109 – 110

Onfray, Michel, 209
Oresme, Nicholas, 69, 119
Origen, 52
Osiander, Andreas, 118
Otto I, 60
Otto II, 60
Otto III, 60
Ovid, 28

Pareto, Vilfredo, 179
Pascal, Blaise, 128 – 129, 145
Patrick, Saint, 57 – 58
Paul, apostle, 42
Philip II of Spain, 104
Philo of Alexandria, 36
Picasso, Pablo, 181
Pico della Mirandola, Giovanni,
    99 – 100
Plato, 24, 25, 27, 28, 31, 34
Pollack, Jackson, 181
Pol Pot, 187
Pope, Alexander, 138, 139
Protagoras, 100
Pseudo-Dionysius, 46
Ptolemy, 116 – 117, 118
Pyrrho, 110 – 111, 113, 129, 132
Pythagoras, 117

Reagan, Ronald, 184
Rederford, Regina, 190
Reinhardt, Stephen, 192
Richelieu, Cardinal, 145
Robespierre, Maximilien,
    157 – 158
Roosevelt, Franklin, 184
Rousseau, Jean Jacques, 144,
    157 – 158
Russell, Bertrand, 177

Sagan, Carl, 164
Sanger, Margaret, 171, 192, 207
Sartre, Jean-Paul, 178, 179
Schaeffer, Francis, 172
Schneider, Stephen, 201
Sextus Empiricus, 110, 111
Shakespeare, William, 177
Simon Peter, apostle, 48

Simon Styletes, 53
Singer, Peter, 172, 207
Sitting Bull, 201
Smith, Adam, 140 – 143
Smith, Samantha, 201
Smoot, George, 26
Sorel, Georges, 179
Southern, R. W., 64
Spener, Jacob, 145
Stalin, Josef, 187
Stark, Rodney, 53

Tacitus, 37
Tertullian, 45
Thomas, apostle, 48
Thoreau, Henry David, 201
Tibi, Bassam, 205
Tolland, John, 139
Toscanelli, Paolo, 109

Van Gogh, Vincent, 181

Voltaire, 143, 144

Walker, Alice, 202
Wallace, Alfred Russel, 166
Washington, George, 151
Watson, James, 178, 207
Weber, Max, 180
Wesley, Charles, 147
Wesley, John, 147
Whitefield, George, 146, 147
Wilberforce, William, 147,
    176 – 177
William and Mary, 107, 149
William of Ockham, 76
William of Orange, 107, 149
Wirth, Timothy, 200
Wittgenstein, Ludwig, 185

Zinzendorf, Nikolaus Ludwig
    von, 147
Zwingli, Ulrich, 112

SUBJECT INDEX

abolitionism, 147
abortion, 33 – 34, 54, 206 – 207
Absolute Mind, 174
absolutism, 106 – 108
adoption, 206
Age of Reason, 140 – 144
agriculture
feudalism and, 57, 60
medieval, 61, 79
property rights and, 77
American Revolution of 1776,
150 – 155, 160 – 161
ancestor worship, 22
animals, 213
discovery of New World,
109 – 110
eco-spirituality and, 199 – 200
antinatalism, 33 – 34, 54,
204 – 206
apologists, 45 – 48
Arians, 50
aristocracy
oligarchy and, 89
Roman, 31
armadillos, 109
arts, the, 72 – 73, 181
asceticism, 52 – 53

astronomy and the Bible,
122 – 123
atheism, 164, 209

baptism, 41, 50 – 51
Battle of Lepanto, 76 – 77
Battle of the Milvian Bridge, 48
*Berenstain Bears' Nature
Guide, The*, 164
Bible, the
astronomy and, 122 – 123
deism and, 137 – 138
on helping the needy, 214
on living a biblically faithful
life, 215
on Noah and the animals,
109 – 110
Bill of Rights, United States,
150 – 152, 151, 161
bill of exchange, 81
*Black Book of Communism,
The*, 176
Black Death, 71 – 72, 97
Book of Thomas the Contender,
47
Buddhism, 28, 197

Calvinism, 105, 106, 136

Candide, 143

capitalism
  classical economics and,
    140 – 142
  materialism and, 172 – 173
  personal morality and
    American, 153 – 154
  roots of, 75 – 77

Cartesianism, 126 – 128

Catholic Church, the, 43 – 44
  conflicts with Protestantism,
    104 – 105
  conflicts with science,
    124 – 125
  during the French Revolu-
    tion, 156 – 157
  during the Glorious Revolu-
    tion, 107, 149
  involvement in politics,
    86 – 87, 103
  limited government in,
    90 – 91
  Protestant Reformation and,
    102 – 108
  wealth of, 87 – 88

Celts, 29 – 30

checks and balances, government, 152

children
  abortion of, 33 – 34, 54,
    206 – 207
  changes in marriage and
    divorce effects on,
    193 – 194, 206
  disabled, 207 – 208, 209 – 210
  infanticide of, 33 – 34, 42, 54,
    207 – 208

  in the Roman Empire,
    33 – 34
  sexualization of, 192, 193

Christianity. *See also* Religion
  adoption of pagan elements
    into, 52 – 53, 65
  American Revolution and,
    150 – 155
  apologists and, 45 – 48
  baptism in, 41, 50 – 51
  City of God and, 84 – 87
  conversions to, 48 – 49,
    50 – 51, 57
  deism and, 136 – 140
  early worldview and lifestyle,
    42 – 45
  Enlightenment, 145 – 148
  evangelicalism, 147
  Glorious Revolution of 1688
    and, 107, 149
  Gnosticism and, 47 – 48
  Great Awakening, 146 – 147
  helping the poor and sick,
    44 – 45, 214
  introduced to Ireland, 57 – 58
  legalization in the Roman
    Empire, 48 – 54
  on lending money at inter-
    est, 80
  in the modern worldview,
    211 – 215
  Neoplatonism and, 46 – 47
  original sin and, 89 – 90,
    100, 152 – 153
  origins of, 39 – 41
  persecution of, 35, 45, 50, 204
  prayer in, 53 – 54

in the Roman World, 20, 34 – 35

slavery and, 43 – 44

social justice and, 214

spiritual equality in, 42 – 43

spread of, 39 – 40

study of, 53 – 54

women and, 42 – 43

Christianity not Mysterious, 139

Ciceronians, 98

circumcision, 39

City of God, The, 83 – 87

civil religion, 158

civil rights movement, 184

Clapham Sect, 147

classical conservatism, 142

classical economics, 140 – 142

classical liberalism, 142

climate change, 56, 61, 200 – 202, 221n14

clockmakers and God, 137

Cloisters, The, 78

communication and context, 185 – 186

Communism, 176 – 177

Condemnations of 1277, 67 – 69, 71

confessionalization, 136

Constitution, U. S., 150 – 153, 154 – 155

Constitutional Convention, 151

contemporary values, 203 – 204

conversions to Christianity, 48 – 49, 50 – 51, 57

Copernican revolution, the

Galileo and, 121 – 122

heliocentrism and, 117 – 119

Tychonic system and, 119 – 121

Cosmographic Mystery, The, 120

cosmology, 69

Galileo and, 121 – 122

heliocentrism and, 117 – 119, 120 – 121, 123 – 124

Ptolemaic system and, 116 – 117

Tychonic system and, 119 – 120

Council of Nicea, 87

Council of Trent, 123

Cult of the Supreme Being, 158

culture and worldview, 15 – 16

Darwinism, 165 – 171

de-Christianization, 158

Declaration of Independence, 91, 150, 151, 154

"Declaration of the Rights of Man and Citizen," 156

deconstructionism, 185 – 187

deductivism, 127 – 128

deism, 136 – 140, 150 – 151, 163 – 164

Descent of Man, The, 166, 169, 171

dialectical materialism, 175 – 176

Dialogue Concerning the Two Chief World Systems, 123, 124

Directory, the (France), 158 – 159

disabled persons, 207 – 208, 209 – 210

divine right of kings, 106

divorce and marriage, 193 – 194
Donatists, 49 – 50, 83
Druids, 57
dualism, 47
Dutch Reformed churches, 146

Eastern religions, 195 – 196
ecofeminism, 199
economics
    American government and,
        153 – 154
    capitalism and, 75 – 77,
        140 – 142
    classical, 140 – 142
    Communist, 176 – 177
    Enlightenment, 140 – 143
    guild system, 77 – 78
    image of God in, 213 – 214
    lending industry and, 80 – 81
    Marxist, 174 – 176
    materialism and, 172 – 173
    medieval, 75 – 83
    medieval trade and, 79 – 80
    personal morality and,
        153 – 154
    property rights and, 76 – 77
    Roman Empire, 31 – 33
    technology and, 78 – 79
    utopian, 176
    wealth of the church and,
        87 – 88
eco-spirituality, 198 – 202,
    221n14
Edict of Milan, 48
Edict of Nantes, 149
education
    Condemnations of 1277 and,
        67 – 69, 71

Ireland and, 57 – 60
in medieval Europe, 64 – 69
natural philosophy and, 69,
    70 – 73
Platonic humanism, 64 – 65,
    69
scholasticism, 65 – 67, 97 – 98
science, 69
Émile, 157
English Civil War, 106 – 107
Enlightenment, the
    as the age of reason, 140 – 144
    American Revolution and,
        150 – 155, 160 – 161
    Christianity in, 145 – 148
    classical economics and,
        140 – 142
    comparative revolutions and,
        159 – 161
    de-Christianization during,
        158
    deism and, 136 – 140
    French Revolution and,
        155 – 158, 159 – 160
    Glorious Revolution and, 107,
        149
    philosophes, 143 – 144
    society and religion, 148
    worldview, 142, 144 – 148
entomology, 146 – 147
environmentalism, 200 – 202
epistemology, 13, 26, 110 – 113,
    164
Essenes, the, 39
ethics
    Darwinian, 169 – 171
    situational and relative, 172

utilitarianism, 171 – 172, 209 – 210
ethnic cleansing, 63
Eucharist, 40, 41, 45
eugenics, 171
evangelicalism, 147
evil, 138
evolution. *See* Darwinism
evolution of worldviews, 16
exchange, bills of, 81

fall of the Roman Empire, 55 – 57
feminism, 184, 189, 194, 198, 199
feudalism, 57, 60
formalism, 163
freedom of speech, 191
French Revolution, 155 – 158, 159 – 160

Gaia hypothesis, 200
Gay Agenda, The, 194
gender. *See also* Women
    early Christian worldview on, 42
    in the Roman Empire, 30
Gentile Christians, 40 – 41
geocentrism, 123
geoheliocentrism, 119 – 120
global warming, 200 – 202, 221n14
Glorious Revolution of 1688, 107, 149
Gnosticism, 47 – 48, 83
God
    astronomy and, 122 – 123
    clockmakers and, 137
    deism and, 136 – 140, 163 – 164
    as eternal, 126 – 127
    evil and, 138
    geometry used by, 120 – 121
    image of, 212 – 215
    Italian Renaissance thinkers on love of, 99 – 100
    Jesus as, 137
    Jewish views of, 36 – 39
    nature of, 136 – 137
    physics and gravitation and, 131 – 132
Goddess Earth, 201
God-fearers, 39, 40
Golden Bough, The (Frazer), 28
grand synthesis, 99 – 102
gravitation, 131 – 133
Great Awakening, the, 146 – 147
Great Depression, the, 184
Greco-Roman gods, 21 – 23
Groningen Protocol for Euthanasia in Newborns, 208
guild system, 77 – 78, 173 – 174

hate crimes, 189, 204
heliocentrism, 117 – 119, 120 – 121, 123 – 124
hierarchy of being, 29 – 34, 99 – 100
Hinduism, 15, 197
historical dialectic, 175
Holy Roman Empire, 60
homosexuality, 190, 191, 192, 194, 204
honor killings, 15
humanism, platonic, 64 – 65, 69
humans

City of God and, 83 – 86
Greek and Roman mythol-
    ogy on, 29
hierarchy of being and,
    29 – 34, 99 – 100
natural law and inalienable
    rights of, 91 – 92
original sin, 89 – 90, 100
rights, 208 – 210
sacrifice of, 29 – 30, 57
value of human life to,
    29 – 30, 54
what it means to be, 14 – 15
Hundred Years War, 97

idealism, 25
image of God, 212 – 215
immigration, 34, 205
inalienable rights, 91 – 92, 149,
    150, 151
Incoherence of the Philosophers,
    The, 70
Indian religions, 195 – 196
Industrial Revolution, the,
    173 – 174
infanticide, 33 – 34, 42, 54,
    207 – 208
Inquisition, the, 63
interest payments, 80 – 81
Ireland, 57 – 60
irrationality, 179 – 181
Islam. See Muslims
Italian Renaissance, the
    absolutism and, 106 – 108
    common misconceptions
        about, 95 – 96
    discovery of the New World
        during, 108 – 110

fatal flaw in attempts to
    synthesize knowledge in,
    100 – 102
grand synthesis of thought
    in, 99 – 100
hierarchy of being and,
    99 – 100
Pyrrhonical skepticism in,
    110 – 113
rational explanations for
    physical phenomena in,
    135 – 136
religious wars during,
    104 – 108, 113
true nature of, 97 – 98

Jacobins, 157 – 158, 160
Jansenism, 145
Jesuits, 112 – 113
Jews, 20, 138
    Christianity spread among,
        40
    God-fearers and, 39
    in the Roman Empire,
        36 – 39
justice, social, 214

karma, 195
kings, divine right of, 106

language
    context and, 185 – 186
    politicization of, 188 – 191
La Nouvelle Héloïse, 157
Latifundia, 32
law, natural, 91 – 92
legalization of Christianity in
    the Roman Empire, 48 – 54

legal systems. *See also* Politics
medieval Europe, 62 – 63
natural law and inalien-
able rights protected by,
91 – 92
Roman Empire, 61 – 62, 63
life
meaning of, 177 – 179
value of human, 29 – 30, 54
lifestyle, early Christian,
42 – 45
limited government, 89 – 91,
106, 151 – 152
Lord's Supper, 40
love, Italian Renaissance
thinkers on, 99 – 100

Magna Carta, 91
Manichaeism, 83
manorialism, 57, 60
marriage and divorce,
193 – 194, 206
martyrdom, 52 – 53
Marxism, 174 – 176
materialism, 144, 163 – 164,
172 – 173
dialectical, 175 – 176
nihilism and, 177 – 178
meaning of life, 177 – 179
mechanical philosophy, 136
Medicare, 205
Medieval Europe
Aristotelian ideas on politics in, 88 – 90
art in, 72 – 73
capitalism in, 75 – 77
church involvement in politics in, 86 – 87

condemnations of 1277 and,
67 – 69
economy of, 75 – 83
education in, 64 – 69
fall of the Roman Empire
and, 55 – 57
growth of trade in, 79 – 80
guild system, 77 – 78
industrial revolution in,
78 – 79
the Inquisition in, 63
Ireland and, 57 – 60
legal developments in, 62 – 63
lending industry in, 80 – 81
limited government in the
church in, 89 – 91
the plague in, 71 – 72
Platonic humanism in,
64 – 65
political theories, 83 – 90
poverty in, 81 – 83
property rights in, 76 – 77
scholasticism in, 65 – 67
science in, 69
St. Augustine and *The City
of God* in, 83 – 86
urban life in, 61 – 62
wealth of the church in,
87 – 88
worldview and natural
philosophy, 69, 70 – 73,
92 – 93
Metamorphoses (Ovid), 28
metaphysics, 13, 24 – 26, 27,
113
Middle Ages. *See* Medieval
Europe
modern worldview, the

abortion in, 206 – 207
antinatalism in, 204 – 206
anti-occidents and, 183 – 185
Darwin and natural selection in, 165 – 171
deconstructionism in, 185 – 187
from deism to materialism, 163 – 164
eco-spirituality in, 198 – 202, 221n14
ethics and, 171 – 172
human rights in, 209 – 210
image of God in, 212 – 215
Industrial Revolution and, 173 – 177
infanticide in, 207 – 208
irrationality in, 179 – 181
maintaining Christianity in, 211 – 215
materialism and economics in, 172 – 173
meaning of life and, 177 – 179
new forms of spirituality in, 194 – 198
nihilism in, 177 – 179, 187
postmodernism and, 187 – 188
scientific method and, 164 – 165
sexual revolution and, 191 – 194
slavery and, 210 – 211
monarchy and tyranny, 88 – 89
monasteries, Irish, 57 – 59
moneylenders, 80 – 81

morality and economics, 153 – 154
Moravian Brethren, 147
Mormons, 15
Muslims, 15
    Platonic humanism and, 65
    population growth in Europe, 205
    science, 70 – 72
mystery religions, 23 – 24
mysticism, 194 – 197
mythology, 28 – 29
Mythology (Bullfinch), 28

National Assembly, French, 156 – 157
National Organization for Women, 206
naturalism, philosophical, 144, 164
natural law, 91 – 92
natural philosophy, 69, 70 – 73, 121
    physics and, 124 – 125, 131 – 133
natural selection, 165 – 171
natural theology, 69
Nazism, 170, 171, 184
Neo-Paganism, 197 – 198
Neoplatonism, 24 – 28, 36, 45 – 47
New Age movement, 196 – 197
News of the Republic of Letters, The, 125, 138
New World, the, 108 – 110, 113
nihilism, 177 – 179, 187
nymphs, 29

oligarchy and aristocracy, 89

On the Divisions of Nature, 59

original sin, 89 – 90, 100,
    152 – 153

Origin of Species, The, 166, 169

paganism, 20 – 21, 45
    elements adopted into
        the Christian church,
        52 – 53, 65
    Greco-Roman gods and,
        21 – 23, 49 – 50
    mystery religions and, 23 – 24
    neo-, 197 – 198

Paris consilium, 72

Pediatric Nursing, 208

Pelagianism, 83

persecution of Christians, 35,
    45, 50, 204

PETA, 199

Pharisees, 39

philosophes, 143 – 144

philosophical naturalism, 144,
    164

philosophy
    Bible blended with, 121
    mechanical, 136
    natural, 69, 70 – 73, 121,
        124 – 125
    naturalism, 144, 164
    personal, 13 – 14
    in the Roman Empire,
        28 – 29

physics, 124 – 125, 130 – 133

pietism, 146

plague, the, 71 – 72, 97

planetary science. *See* Cosmol-
    ogy; Science

Planned Parenthood, 171, 206,
    207

Platonic humanism, 64 – 65, 69

Platonism, 24, 26, 59

pluralism, religious, 15, 212

politics and government.
    See also Legal systems;
        Revolutions
    absolutism and, 106 – 108
    American structure,
        154 – 155
    Aristotle on, 88 – 90
    checks and balances, 152
    church involvement in,
        51 – 52, 86 – 87, 103
    classical economics and, 142
    Communist, 176 – 177
    conflicts between Protes-
        tantism and Catholi-
        cism affecting, 104 – 105
    deism in, 150 – 151
    divine right of kings and,
        106
    feminism in, 184, 189, 194
    forms of, 88 – 89
    image of God in, 214 – 215
    inalienable rights and,
        91 – 92, 149, 150, 151
    limited, 89 – 91, 106,
        151 – 152
    Marxist, 174 – 176
    medieval, 83 – 90
    natural law and, 91 – 92
    original sin and, 89 – 90
    politicization of language
        and, 188 – 191
    resistance theory, 105 – 106
    in the Roman Empire, 51 – 52

St. Augustine on, 83 – 86
totalitarianism, 176 – 177
utopianism in, 157 – 158,
   159 – 160
Wars of Religion and,
   104 – 108
polygamy, 15
population, 141 – 142, 166
antinatalism and, 33 – 34,
   54, 204 – 206
populism, 153 – 154
pornography, 192
postmodernism, 187 – 188
politicization of language
   in, 188 – 191
sexual revolution and,
   191 – 194, 206 – 207
spirituality, 194 – 202
poverty
Christian servanthood and,
   44 – 45, 214
medieval, 81 – 83
Thomas Malthus on, 142
prayer, 53 – 54, 151
*Preservation of Favored Races
in the Struggle for Life,
The*, 169
probabilism, 128 – 130, 145
property rights, 76 – 77
Protestant Reformation, the
Catholicism revitalized in
   response to, 103 – 104
conflicts between Catholicism and, 104 – 105
worldview and, 102 – 103
Ptolemaic system, 116 – 117
Pyrrhonism, 110 – 113
refutations of, 125 – 133

Qigong, 195

racism, 169 – 170, 170, 171, 184
realism, 25
reason, age of, 140 – 144
Reformation, the. *See* Protestant
   Reformation, the
reign of terror (France),
   157 – 158, 160
Reiki, 195
reincarnation, 195
relative and situational ethics,
   172
religion. *See also* Christianity
civil, 158
conflicts with science,
   124 – 125
deist, 136 – 140, 163 – 164
Eastern, 195 – 196
eco-spirituality, 198 – 202,
   221n14
feminism and, 198, 199
global warming as,
   200 – 202, 221n14
Great Awakening and,
   146 – 147
medieval education and,
   64 – 69
mystery, 23 – 24
Neoplatonism, 24 – 28, 36,
   45 – 47
New Age, 196 – 197
philosophy and mythology
   as, 28 – 29
pluralism, 15, 212
politics and, 51 – 52, 103
prayer and, 53 – 54, 151

Pyrrhonical skepticism and,
110 – 113, 125 – 130
in the Roman Empire,
20 – 29, 34 – 35
traditional Roman, 21 – 23
universals and particulars
considered in, 24 – 27
wars of, 104 – 108, 113, 136,
148
Renaissance, the. *See* Italian
Renaissance, the
republic and democracy, 89
resistance theory, 105 – 106
revolutions. *See also* Politics
and government
American, 150 – 155,
160 – 161
comparative, 159 – 161
French, 155 – 158, 159 – 160
Glorious, 107, 149
sexual, 191 – 194
worldview and, 148,
159 – 161
rights, inalienable, 91 – 92
Roman Empire, the
abortion in, 33 – 34, 54, 207
antinatalism in, 33 – 34, 54,
205
Apologists and Gnostics in,
45 – 48
average life span in, 17
under Constantine, 48 – 54
crucifixion of Jesus and,
39 – 40
early Christian worldview
and lifestyle in, 42 – 45
fall of, 55 – 57
greatness of, 19

hierarchy of being in,
29 – 34
human sacrifice in, 30
immigration into, 34
infanticide in, 33 – 34, 42, 54
Jews in, 36 – 39
legalization of Christianity
in, 48 – 54
legal systems, 61 – 62, 63
mystery religions in, 23 – 24
Neoplatonism in, 24 – 28
origins of Christianity and,
39 – 41
paganism in, 21 – 24, 49 – 50,
52 – 53
paradox of, 19 – 20
persecution of Christians in,
35, 45, 204
philosophy and mythology
in, 28 – 29
politics in, 51 – 52
religion in, 20 – 29, 34 – 35
sexuality in, 32, 33
slavery in, 19 – 20, 31, 32,
43 – 44, 54
St. Augustine on, 83 – 86
traditional Roman religion
in, 21 – 23
work and wealth in, 31 – 33
Royal Society for the Prevention of Cruelty to Animals,
147 – 148

sacrifice, human, 29 – 30, 57
Sadducees, 39
Saint Bartholomew's Day Mas-
sacre, 105, 107, 149
Sapir-Whorf Hypothesis, 189

scholasticism, 65 – 67, 97 – 98
science
    Cartesianism and, 126 – 128
    the Copernican Revolution
        and, 117 – 125
    Darwinism and, 165 – 171
    discovery of the New World
        and, 108 – 109
    Galileo and, 121 – 122,
        124 – 125
    heliocentrism and, 117 – 119,
        120 – 121, 123 – 124
    heresy and, 123 – 124
    image of God in, 213
    laws of physics in, 124 – 125
    medieval, 69, 70 – 72
    Muslim, 70 – 72
    natural philosophy and, 69,
        70 – 73, 121, 124 – 125
    natural selection and,
        165 – 171
    physics and gravitation,
        124 – 125, 130 – 133
    planetary, 116 – 117
    probabilism, 128 – 130
    Ptolemaic system, 116 – 117
    Pyrrhonism and, 110 – 113,
        125 – 133
    scientific method and,
        164 – 165
    traditional model of the
        universe in, 115 – 117
    Tychonic system, 119 – 120
scientific method, 164 – 165
sculptures, medieval, 72 – 73
selection, natural, 165 – 171
serfs, 56, 61
sexuality
    abortion and, 33 – 34, 54,
        206 – 207
    antinatalism and, 33 – 34, 54,
        204 – 206
    in the early Christian
        worldview and lifestyle,
        42 – 43
    Greek views of, 45 – 46
    irrationality and, 180
    marriage and divorce and,
        193 – 194
    postmodern, 190
    in the Roman Empire, 32,
        33
    sexual revolution and,
        191 – 194, 206 – 207
sexual revolution, the,
    191 – 194, 206 – 207
sin, original, 89 – 90, 100,
    152 – 153
situational and relative ethics,
    172
skepticism, Pyrrhonical,
    110 – 113
slavery
    Declaration of Indepen-
        dence signers and, 154
    early Christian worldview
        on, 43 – 44
    modern, 210 – 211
    in the Roman Empire,
        19 – 20, 31, 32, 54
Social Contract, The, 157
social Darwinism, 169 – 171
social justice, 214
Social Security, 205
speech, hate, 190
spiritual equality, 42 – 43

sterilization, 171
suicide, 15
Summa Theologica, 100

Taiji, 195
technology, medieval, 78 – 79
Thirty Years' War, 107 – 108
Toleration Act, 149
totalitarianism, 176 – 177
trade, medieval, 79 – 80
traditional Roman religion,
    21 – 23
treason, 63
truth and deconstructionism,
    185 – 187
Tychonic system, 119 – 120
tyranny and monarchy, 88 – 89

UNICEF, 210
Unicorn Tapestries, the, 78
United Nations, 210
United States, the
    after World War II,
        184 – 185
    American Revolution of
        1776 and, 150 – 155,
        160 – 161
    Bill of Rights, 150 – 152, 151,
        161
    birthrates in, 204
    Constitution, 150 – 153,
        154 – 155
    Declaration of Indepen-
        dence, 91, 150, 151, 154
    economics and personal
        morality in, 153 – 154
    Enlightenment ideas and,
        150 – 152

European reaction to the
    founding, 154 – 155
Great Depression in, 184
immigration into, 205
original sin and the Consti-
    tution of, 152 – 153
slavery in, 154
Social Security in, 205
universals and particulars,
    24 – 27
universe, traditional model
    of the, 115 – 117. *See also*
    Science
University of Paris, 68, 72
urban life, in medieval Europe,
    61 – 62
usury, 80 – 81
utilitarianism, 171 – 172,
    209 – 210
utopianism, 157 – 158,
    159 – 160, 176

value of human life, 29 – 30, 54
values
    contemporary, 203 – 204
    postmodern, 188
Vietnam War, 184
Vikings, 61

Wars of Religion, 104 – 108,
    113, 136, 148
wealth and work. *See*
    Economics
Wealth of Nations, The, 140
Wicca, 197 – 198
witchcraft, 63
women. *See also* Gender

early Christian worldview
     on, 42 – 43
feminism and, 184, 189, 194,
     198, 199
Gnosticism and, 48
Greek views of, 45 – 46
marriage and, 193 – 194, 206
in the Roman Empire, 30
sexual revolution and,
     191 – 194, 206 – 207
work and wealth. *See*
     Economics
worldviews
absolutism in, 106 – 108
American Revolution and
     Christian, 150 – 155,
     160 – 161
Christianity in modern,
     211 – 215
classical economics and, 142
Communist, 176 – 177
culture and, 15 – 16
Darwinism and, 166 – 171
defined, 13 – 14
deist, 139 – 140, 163 – 164
early Christian, 42 – 45

Enlightenment, 142,
     144 – 148
evolution of, 16
Industrial Revolution and,
     173 – 177
irrationality, 179 – 181
Italian Renaissance, 99 – 100
Marxist, 174 – 176
materialism and, 144,
     163 – 164, 172 – 173,
     175 – 176
medieval, 69, 70 – 73, 92 – 93
modern ethics and,
     171 – 172
as philosophy, 13 – 14
postmodern, 187 – 194
Protestant, 102 – 103
revolutions and, 148,
     159 – 161
scientific method and,
     164 – 165
on what it means to be
     human, 14 – 15
World War I, 183, 184
World War II, 184 – 185

Yoga, 195